PHALAENOPSIS CULTURE:

A WORLDWIDE SURVEY OF GROWERS

Edited by Bob Gordon

Published by
Laid-Back Publications
Rialto, California, USA

ISBN 0-9615714-4-6

Cover:
Phalaenopsis Bonnie Vasquez 'Zuma Creek'
FCC/AOS

Typesetting by
Archetype — Riverside, CA USA
Artwork by
Laura Landrum — Moreno Valley, CA USA
Photo by
Wesley Higgins

PHALAENOPSIS CULTURE:
A SURVEY

TABLE OF CONTENTS

UP FRONT

THE GOOD STUFF STARTS RIGHT HERE.

It is unlikely a truly scientific study will ever be done to develop sophisticated cultural techniques for all conditions under which Phalaenopsis orchids are grown.

Recognizing that gloomy prospect, we present here the next best thing: an accumulation of empirical data from accomplished, astute growers worldwide. In a more scientific setting these data would be bases from which conclusions might be drawn; the major flaw here being the undisciplined method by which it was collected. IF THE BOOK DOES NOTHING ELSE, IT WILL NARROW THE RANGE OF ACCEPTED PRACTICES AND VALUES IN PHALAENOPSIS CULTURE. IT'S FAR FROM PERFECT...BUT IT'S A START.

PERFECT GROWING CONDITIONS: For Phalaenopsis, a perfect set of cultural conditions is held in a delicate balance of light, temperature, water, air movement and rooting medium porosity. The cultural equation of each grower is likely to be unique...requiring that each solve his or her own rather than accepting someone else's calculations. This book will offer some direction for those calculations.

VISITING WITH THE EXPERTS: Reading the book is like visiting with 130 of the world's best Phalaenopsis growers and asking them the fundamental questions of how to grow the plants well. It also answers the question "How does the best grower in this region grow them?" IT IS 130 INTERVIEWS REDUCED TO WRITING. It's probably even better than that, because the responses are unhurried and thought out without distraction.

I've heard from some of the respondents that answering the questions made them search through their memories and experiences for the best ways of doing things...and being startled to find they weren't doing all the things that they knew from experience were best for their plants.

I'm sure you will recognize it is a very human thing to do. We <u>know</u> better, but...

BALANCE   If there was any single truth that emerged from the mass of information that came in, it had to be the need for a balance in conditions given to the plants. Too many of us arbitrarily change one of the major controls, increase the light for example, and give no thought to how that affects the rest of the cultural balance...and a delicate balance it is.

An increase in light from a stable condition carries with it the need to increase air movement to keep leaf temperatures down, for example. And the increase in light is going to convert more food to plant tissue, so an increase in nitrogen fertilizer is needed. This message comes through over and over again, and if the reader gets no other gain from this book, let it be this:

WHEN YOU CHANGE A PART OF THE PLANT'S ENVIRONMENT, LOOK AROUND TO FIND WHAT ELSE NEEDS TO BE CHANGED TO KEEP THE PLANT COMFORTABLE AND HAPPY.

The ancient Chinese saw life as a constant struggle to maintain a balance between negative and positive, earth and sky, cold and heat, wetness and dryness, gloom and happiness, woman and man. They called the two forces Yin and Yang and an important part of their lives was spent in bringing the two together in productive harmony and balance.

Try it on your phals. It has worked on rice for thousands of years. See the chart in Comments and Opinion in Section 1.1.

One of the things which has astonished me during the assembly of the book is the diversity of ways of doing some things, **all of which seem to work.** And, on the other hand, there is an equally astonishing agreement of opinion on other things; for example, the need to keep potting medium moist. Fully half of the growers I know allow their media to dry out...probably a carryover from their earlier days as cattleya growers. It may be good for catts, but is <u>not</u> good for phals.

I want to thank editors Chris Bailes of the <u>Orchid Review</u> and Dr. Jack Fowlie of the <u>Orchid Digest</u> for their upfront support of this project from its inception. Their vision in recognizing this effort to popularize Phalaenopsis culture bodes well for the future of the orchid-growing arts and sciences.

THE OBJECT OF THIS BOOK IS TO LIST CULTURAL PROCEDURES THAT WORK WELL FOR DIFFERENT GROWERS UNDER DIFFERENT GROWING CONDITIONS...AND THAT GO BEYOND THE CONVENTIONAL WISDOM. (WHICH IS USUALLY CONVENTIONAL, BUT OFTEN IS NOT WISDOM)

The book is for those growers who want more than just to keep their plants alive and blooming. It's for those who want to approach perfection in their culture and, in turn, perfection in their flowers.

HEREIN YOU WILL FIND TECHNIQUES OF PHALAENOPSIS CULTURE THAT WORK FOR SOME OF THE BEST PHAL GROWERS IN THE WORLD TODAY...a menu of proven techniques to choose from. Find what suits you; mix it with the procedures you know to be good; use the new method and evaluate its use to you; grow a better phal...and approach communion with the Master Grower.

In the case of some responses I've taken the liberty of paraphrasing the language for the sake of continuity of the book...and save the reader from having to shift literal gears with each menu item read.

HOW TO USE THIS BOOK:

• Scan it cover to cover to survey the contents.

• Refer to it as a specific problem arises, noting how growers with conditions similar to yours cope with problems. If they match yours, go for it. It worked for someone who has the same conditions you do...and who may know something about the subject that you don't.

If worst comes to the worst, you can always write to them (addresses in the back of the book); they may not answer but, what the hell, all it costs is a stamp. (Don't tell them I said it was OK. I didn't ask for permission, but I doubt many will refuse.)

• Refer periodically to sections that cover cultural steps even on matters in which you are satisfied with your own.

• Note that in answering some specific questions, some respondents lapped over and answered other questions...and did not repeat the opinion under the other question's listing. For clarity of meaning, I did not separate the elements. **BOTTOM LINE: FOR A COMPLETE PICTURE, READ THE ENTIRE SECTION ON THE SUBJECT IN WHICH YOU ARE INTERESTED**...and reread it periodically. It is astounding how ideas that you skipped over on the first reading sometimes become the answer to your current problem.

• One last bit of legal protocol: Neither the editor nor the respondents cited in this book represent that the techniques listed herein are the only ways to properly grow Phalaenopsis orchids. The methods and materials cited, especially the pesticides, are ones used by them and in no way may this recitation be construed as a recommendation carrying legal liability.

ARTIFICIAL LIGHT GROWERS TAKE NOTE: Responses from those who grow under lights are marked with an asterisk (*) before the growers locality.

A PUZZLE: Something that has puzzled me in this book-project...is the phenomena of the hobbygrower who plods along, enjoying his or her flowers, and seeming to have few of the sophisticated answers to some of the questions posed in this book. And yet, these very people will consistently produce the best-grown, cleanest, prettiest-to-look-at phals you can imagine. Better than the experts who know all the answers, have all the hottest breeding stock around and have all the technology to do the job well. I'd wager you know a few of them, too.

They don't have the best stock and seldom get quality awards from the American Orchid Society, but they seem to get more out of their plants than the rest of us do. Why? What is their secret? How do they do it? I had hoped to capture some of that magic in this project, but I fear I've failed. Their answers are bland and uninformative for the most part...and give no clue to how they account for their success. They don't seem to know, either.

Maybe it is in the pace at which they work...leisurely and having only the purpose of amusing themselves and filling their days with work, pride and satisfaction. No hurry; no distractions; no one to please but themselves; no plants or blooms to sell; no awards to be gained; only idyllic days to be filled with wonder and love; yes, love.

Maybe these little beauties are their surrogate children...who show gratitude by being beautiful and reenacting the Scheme of Life each season. A reflective look at their own lives?

Maybe they are a means of communing with the Master Grower; of finding a language with which to talk to Him, now and later. Maybe we have to talk to <u>Him</u> to learn the secret of these gifted growers. He appears to have talked to them.

Maybe, too, they're planted among us to show and remind us that we don't have all the answers, or even very many of them. Maybe they are here to teach the rest of us some patience, reverence, and a sense of wonder at the beauty of it all.

Maybe.

— Bob Gordon
September 1988

SECTION ONE
LIGHT

(a) How much light do you give your mature Phalaenopsis plants?
(b) How do you measure it?   (c) How do you control it?
(d) Do you intentionally vary that amount at times?
If so, when and by how much?

SECTION 1.1 LIGHT CONSENSUS AND OPINION

Q 1(a) HOW MUCH LIGHT?

The majority of the respondents allowed their plants about 1,200 to 1,500 footcandles of sunlight with many using a higher light level in the autumn and winter seasons. The latter settings may have been prompted by prospect of free heat and a reduced heating load, but many indicated that the brighter light was involved in the flower induction process and would lead to heavier flower production. It was not a conclusion reached only by cutflower growers. For whatever reason, the consensus was for brighter light in the cool weather.

Removing shading in the autumn does not necessarily mean raising light levels. It may, but could also just compensate for the loss of total insolation from shorter days and lower sun angle.

It is my personal belief that the higher light levels also cause the plants to develop tougher hides and become, therefore, more resistant to diseases and insect damage. They may not be as pretty to look at, but they're more likely to survive and prosper.

The 130 or so responses have an unspoken, but implied, message to the effect that WE SHOULD BE WATCHING OUR PLANTS CLOSELY TO SEE WHAT THEY ARE TELLING US REGARDING THEIR LEVEL OF SATISFACTION WITH THEIR ENVIRONMENT. Whatever else we know or think to be true, the condition of the plant will tell you just how good your culture is.

BUT YOU MUST LOOK FOR THE CLUES.

To maintain some degree of discipline in how you go about making changes, keep a Journal of changes made...and results produced. The alternative, as we see so often, is chaos and frustration.

Some changes are cyclic. **Most top growers adjust light, heat, water, humidity, and air circulation to meet the needs of the changing seasons.** For example, they change light levels to match those in the natural situation with the changing seasons.

If you leave the same shade cloth on throughout the year, the plants will probably have the right amount of light only twice in a year's time; just like you'll have the right time twice each day when your watch has stopped.

PHALAENOPSIS CULTURAL NEEDS ARE NOT CONSTANT THROUGHOUT THE YEAR, nor should the conditions given them be...not if you want peak performance out of them. Winterize your plants like you winterize your car...or yourself. Fine tune for best performance and read the plant for ideas on what to do.

ULTRAVIOLET LIGHT: David Grove's commentary to the effect that (full spectrum) light intensity needs may not be the same as ultraviolet light needs...warrants closer examination. The significance of this statement is that light intensity as measured with a standard light meter may not be directly related to plant growth...

12

but the intensity of the UV component may. Read: in clear air, lower light levels are needed than are needed in less than clear air. I see that as meaning not just man-made smog, but also natural shading as well, such as clouds, humidity, and haze...which may be lessened at higher altitudes. This phenomena may account for the diverse reports of what is the 'best light level' for phals (800-3,000 footcandles reported here). I hope more work will be done in this area soon.

SURVIVAL: Regarding plant survival, many growers believe with good reason that plants in cultivation gradually lose their ability to survive. Older plants are more likely to be virused than the younger ones and, for reasons unexplained, don't seem to last in cultivation more than 20 years or so.

That should not happen because there is little, if any, reason why they should not survive given they have every need fulfilled...except stress, if that is a need. Maybe some stress is necessary for survival. Every grower seems to have a story of the heater quitting in cold weather and the following year they having better blooms than ever. Ever notice that never happens when the <u>cooler</u> goes out? A light stress load certainly seems to motivate animals, humans included, to achievement and health.

We may be killing our phals with kindness. Perhaps a little stress is good for the phals...and as long as we're going to stress them, why not make it a form that benefits the plant? Bottom line: go with the brighter light, but compensate with increased air circulation, increased cooling, increased water and humidity, and with heavier feeding; and reduce the light when they flower. (See Yin and Yang at the end of this section.)

Jim Mackinney's motivation in growing with higher light levels than necessary is interesting: it hardens the plants so his customers don't have trouble growing them under different (less ideal) conditions. Many, many new phal growers are frightened off when they lose their first plant...and don't come back. This is a serious problem to the industry and a persistent limiting factor to the growth of phal culture in the home.

What Jim is doing is providing a little post-purchase insurance. (A good beginner's phal culture book falls into the same category. See me after the meeting is over for a book discount schedule. ed.)

LIGHT CONTROL WITHOUT A COOLER: Phil Seaton's dilemma (in the South of England) of limiting light intensity to whatever comes with 90°F ambient in the greenhouse...is probably a familiar story with phal growers in the cooler climates. The alternative is to put in a cooler which may only be used a few weeks of the year, if that long. A thread running through many of the responses is the use of increased air circulation to cope with high temps associated with summertime light levels. That's the way it's done in nature. Add a little fan in the hot weather, one with a thermostat if you're adventurous. Stage several fans with progressively higher settings if your in-laws own a thermostat store.

Artificial light growers may want to consider solid-state ballasts on their fluorescent lamps...or the use of high-intensity discharge lighting which produces less heat per unit of light than fluorescents or incandescents; and a little fan. (Artificial light growers see the article by Joseph Van Acker at the end of Section One.)

I had more than one twinge of sympathy for the growers in the cooler latitudes where these desirable light levels are just not available in the winter. Supplementary light would seem to be in order. I've received a few mentions, but no detailed information on growing under high intensity discharge (HID) lighting with sodium, halide and mercury vapor. Most of the growers under lights used fluorescent fixtures. I don't know if there are any significant differences in culture, but the big advantage with the HID lighting systems seems to be in lower operating costs and less attendant heat to get rid of. The fixtures are more expensive than fluorescent lighting.

There were several responses from growers who supplement the short winter daylight with artificial light. Note Fritz Bieth and Louis Guida's comments.

TOTAL LIGHT NEEDS: IS A LOWER LIGHT LEVEL SPREAD OVER A LONGER TIME AS BENEFICIAL TO THE PLANTS AS HIGHER LEVELS OVER SHORTER TIMES? (other limits under control, of course) I haven't seen an answer to this question that is asked often.

Artificial light growers seem to do nicely with their phals by giving them 500 footcandles or so for 12-16 hours daily, a much longer day than natural light growers can get. If total **insolation** (light intensity x time) is the answer as appears to be the case here, we may have to re-think the methods we conventionally use for controlling light.

Hybrid systems of artificial and natural light have been used for a long time and may be the answer to adjusting total insolation to the phals at an ideal level. I know many growers, particularly in urban areas, who are hampered by trees and buildings that obstruct the light to their plants and they would be good candidates for the use of these hybrid systems. (I have shady corners in my greenhouses here in sunny southern California that could stand a little help, too.)

Perhaps some enterprising eyeglass maker will apply the 'Photo Sun' or 'Photo Gray' principle (used to make variable density sunglasses) to greenhouse (or skylight) glazing at an affordable price. Dream on.

Q 1(b) HOW DO YOU MEASURE IT?

From what the respondents said, the General Electric Company must be selling a lot of their Model #214's. (They sold me one recently when I got suspicious of my 35-year old meter, also a GE, and found what I thought was 1,200 footcandles in my greenhouse was actually only 800. It was still working fine; I just didn't know how to calibrate it.) They're easy to use, perfect for orchid culture, relatively inexpensive (US$50 here), are readily available and are durable...and essential for good phal culture unless you have calibrated eyeballs.

Some of the more experienced growers can get by nicely without them, but their 20 to 50 years of experience is hard to come by. (And just about the time you get all that experience, your eyesight, hearing, hair and memory go all to hell and you need glasses, a hearing aid, a toupee, a secretary...and maybe a light meter.) If you haven't got one, get one. Light level is important to good phal culture. (You don't go around estimating the time of day, do you?)

Arthur Harris' comment on using a meter only to establish initial, acceptable conditions reflected a fairly common response. But, my own experience leads me to be a little skeptical of my memory of what things ought to be, especially with a roof of reinforced fiberglass that becomes less transparent as the years roll by.

I think it is important to check periodically. I use my meter to place plants that need more light than the average or plants that I want to push a little. As with temperature, no hobbyist greenhouse (and few commercial greenhouses) have uniform lighting throughout...and that changes as the seasons progress. A plant placed for perfect lighting in July can get scorched in October as the sun angle changes.

Light conditions in a greenhouse also change when roofing gets dirty and when trees and shrubs grow up...and these things work at reducing the light that reaches the plants. Get a meter and check the light intensity on 3 consecutive days at the same hour...and continue to do that at 6-8 week intervals from now on. You will be astonished at how radically light levels will change. Take readings in a few key points in your growing area and note changes.

The hoary hand-over-hand shadow method is only accurate to about plus or minus 1,000 footcandles. Reason: the sharpness of the shadow is a function of clarity of the light making it, more so than a hoped-for measure of light intensity. If it works at all, it's when you have a single point source of light, but not when it is diffused. Atmospheric haze will diffuse light, giving a softer shadow and a lower apparent-reading. The hand shadow, 12" above the other hand, works fairly well only when light is sharp and clear. (In southern California, that is about 3 days each year.)

Unquestionably, the best followup in determining if your plants are getting enough light is the color of the leaves, but a season is a long time to wait to find if you guessed right. Also, as several respondents pointed out, different species are characterized by different shades of green in their leaves. (I think the giganteas and the violaceas like more light than average and the mariaes seem to like less, but I wish I had a reference listing of all the species and their likes in this regard.) This difference in the way leaves of the different species respond to light further complicates the job of gauging light accurately by this method.

• ARTIFICIAL LIGHT GROWERS take note of Arden Robert's conversion factors for light meters when measuring light from fluorescent lamps. Here's why your meter hasn't been reading correctly.

Phals are tolerant of a wide range of light intensities, but I think some growers take this tolerance to an extreme and let the plants do the measuring of light and then reacting to its appearance. That will work if you are close to the acceptable range. If it's over to any great degree, the plant will fry. The dead plant will then be nature's way of telling you it was getting too much light.

Q 1(c) HOW DO YOU CONTROL THE LIGHT?

Shade cloth of varying densities is the overwhelming favorite of hobbyists, while shading compound (sometimes mixed with inexpensive white latex paint) is the favorite of commercial growers...and where appearances are not a principal concern. Roller blinds are used in a few cases.

Some growers avoid the use of the convenient shade compound, which is essentially the old-fashioned whitewash, because it is difficult to apply. For some ideas on how to use it conveniently, see editor's remarks...in the G's.

David Grove's comments on allowing a higher light level and compensating for the peaks with an elevated humidity are useful in developing an environmental program for any growing area.

The artificial light growers have this problem wired...literally. They use timers and vary the length of the bench-day. With lamps of relatively constant output, they can control the total amount of light given the plants precisely. Beside changing tubes every few years, the only problem I've run into with fluorescent lamps in the greenhouse and on a light bench is the need to periodically clean the tubes and polish the electrical contacts. Both practices are needed in the moist environment of a greenhouse.

I used to think the tubes were bad, but found all it took was a little steel wool or sandpaper to the pins.

Q 1(d) DO YOU VARY THE LIGHT AT TIMES?

Comments from several of the respondents support the idea of shortening the time between spike induction and flowering by raising light levels during that time. As much as 30 days can be cut from development time by this method. See Mick Dennis' comments in this section and Woody Carlson's/Hugo Freed's in section 9 (a). Read Hugo's caution note.

This section and the counsel of these three experts (among others) was one of the most enlightening and enriching experiences of the whole project for me. In addition to shortening the flower development time, pinpointing flowering times can become a reality...if you are able to control light and temperature. These skills are of great value to hobbyists and commercial grower alike.

THE YIN AND YANG OF
PHALAENOPSIS CULTURE

(Adjustments needed to balance the culture equation when changes are made)

		Y	A	N	G
		LIGHT	TEMP	WATER	FOOD-N	AIR
	↑ LIGHT	N/A	↑ INCR	↑ INCR	↑ INCR	↑ INCR
Y	↑ TEMP	↑ INCR	N/A	↑ INCR	↑ INCR	↑ INCR
I	↑ WATER/ HUMIDITY	↑ INCR	↑ INCR	N/A	↑ INCR	↑ INCR
	↑ FOOD - NITRO	↑ INCR	↑ INCR	↑ INCR	N/A	↑ INCR
N	↑ AIR CIRCUL	↑ INCR	↑ INCR	↑ INCR	↑ INCR	N/A

N/A = Not applicable   ↑ INCR = Increase or raise

When a condition listed in the left-hand column is increased or raised, the condition shown in the top horizontal column should be raised...to balance conditions. An increase in Yin, must be combined with an increase in Yang to keep harmony. (How about a little Chinese cosmology on your phals...Why not? It's worked for them for 10,000 years.)

For example, if light is increased, increase also the temperature max, the watering schedule, the humidity, the nitrogen fertilizer and air circulation.

Heat is ordinarily the factor determining plant growth. Note, however, that for those not growing under artificial light, light is the pacing factor because although you can adjust other factors up and down, light can only be adjusted downward. In less than ideal light conditions, lower the temperature to adjust growth rate to the amount of light available. The alternative is fast, soft and weak growth.

THE REVERSE IS ALSO TRUE: WHEN A CONDITION IN THE LEFT-HAND COLUMN IS LOWERED, MAKE THE CHANGES OPPOSITE THOSE CALLED FOR ON THE CHART. On gloomy winter days when the light level is down, lower temps a little, cut down on the nitrogen, let up a little on the watering schedule, and slow the fans down a bit.

I read somewhere that when you try to pick out something by itself, you find it hitched to everything else in the universe. That certainly is true in Phalaenopsis culture.

The bottom line: when you raise one, raise the other and vice versa.

— Editor

General Electric Type 214 light meter. The meter most commonly used by respondents.

SECTION 1.2 LIGHT:
SELECTED RESPONSES

QUESTION 1(a) HOW MUCH LIGHT DO YOU GIVE YOUR MATURE PHAL PLANTS?

(Indian Coast South Africa) Phals are lovers of clear light in abundance, but I think it is important that each grower evaluate his growing area carefully throughout the first year of culture of Phalaenopsis to note the difference in light levels with each season. I did and now change shade cloth densities ranging from 30 to 50% with the changes in season.
— A. Adriaanse

(California US) 1250 footcandles of sunlight which is supplemented with high intensity discharge artificial lighting to maintain winter day length at 12 hours.
— F. Bieth

(East Texas US) 1,750 to 2,000 footcandles.
— T. Brown

(Southeastern Australia) I diffuse the sunlight with 50% shade cloth over translucent, cored plastic "Acriflute".
— M. Black

(California Coast US) 800 to 900 footcandles.
— E. Carlson

(Mid-Atlantic Coast US) Late February to November, 60% shade. December to late February, full sun...controlled year round with aluminum slat shades.
— L. Clouser

*[1] (Northeastern US) Under artificial lighting...My phal area has one 2-tube 40-watt fixture and one end of a 2-tube 80-watt (nominal) fixture. Fixtures are fairly low over the plants except during blooming season when the end of the long fixture is raised to accommodate inflorescences. Day-length is 19 hours most of the year. During the summer, when my cattleyas are outdoors, I put the biggest phals under a more intensely lighted 4-tube fixture (where the cattleyas spend the winter).
— I. Cohen

---

[1]. Asterisk indicates grower uses artificial lighting. Symbol throughout the book in Selected Responses.

(Indian Coast South Africa) We are very fortunate here for we have sunlight almost all the time apart from a total of, say, 30 days out of the year that one doesn't have continual sun. We use a 60% shade cloth over clear plastic roofs.
— C&I Coll

(Southern California US) Our air is especially clear and the sunlight very bright, so I use 63% shade cloth year round and an additional 63% layer during the summer months.
— W. Cousineau

(South of England) 50% green plastic shade netting from early March to late October. 10% shade the rest of the year.
— R. Dadd

(Florida Caribbean US) 1,200-1,800 footcandles.
— D. Davis

(Central California US) Because our summers are very hot and dry, I keep half of my phals on the bench and half under it. Those under the bench grow better than those on it.
— P. De Lucia

(South Australia) Summer, 80% shade. Winter, full sunlight.
— M. Dennis

(Florida Gulf Coast US) Winter, 1400-1500 footcandles. Summer, 1,000-1,250 footcandles.
— J. Eich

(Rome Italy) Brighter during the winter than the rest of the year. I adjust the light based on daily observations to keep (1) the leaves of the plant a grass-shade of green, and (2) a heavy level of flower production (3 racemes per plant).
— A. Fanfani

(Holland) 15,000 lux. (About 1,400 footcandles)
— A major commercial grower

(Maui Hawaii US) About 1,500 footcandles for mature plants; 800 fc for seedlings.
— R. Fukamura

(Atlantic US) We normally try to give the plants about 1,000 footcandles of light.
— K. Griffith and others

(Southcentral US) 1,200 to 1,300 footcandles, but that isn't easy because we have a lot of cloudy weather here.
— J. Grimes

(Northeastern US) 1,500 to 2,000 footcandles seems ideal for mature phal plants. Some, especially violaceas, seem to prefer the higher end of the range. Large plants with an abundance of healthy roots in a medium that is in good condition will take 3,000 footcandles easily and will produce more and better flowers provided humidity is kept high (at least 70%) and watering is frequent. In some locales where ultraviolet intensity is strong because of atmospheric conditions, 1,000 to 1,500 footcandles produces better results than the 1,500 to 2,000 footcandles range mentioned above. Optimum light intensity depends on atmospheric conditions, day length, and on cultural practices.

— D. Grove

(Southeastern US) Mature phals, 1,200 footcandles; higher to 1,500 in the winter. Seedlings, 900 to 1,000 footcandles.

— T. Harper

(Southwest US) A mature Phalaenopsis should get about 1,000 footcandles on the average.

— E. Hetherington

(Midlands of England) Around 1,200 to 1,500 footcandles is aimed for, but this can only be achieved between mid-March and early October.

— P. Hirst

(Arizona Desert US) April to September, 900 fc; October to March, 1,400.

— J&G Johnson

(East Central US) I grow on windowsills and give mature plants an hour and a half of direct morning light and bright shade the rest of the day, year round.

— K. Kehew

(Florida Caribbean US) Phals are grown under 52% saran covered with Monsanto plastic, in a Quonset hut-type construction. This is a bright condition, but lends to heavier flower production.

— W. Kelly

(Southeastern Australia) In our climate I like a basic cover of a sheet of 50% shade cloth, a layer of horticultural PVC (light inhibited) with a clear glass roof. In summer an extra sheet of 50% shade cloth is added to eradicate the heat radiation that I feel on my face during the middle-3 or -4 hours of the day.

— J. Kilgannon

(Southern California US) 800 to 1,200 footcandles.

— T. Koike

(East Java Indonesia) I give the plants as much light as they are able to take without burning the leaves.

— A. Kolopaking

(Holland) mid-September to mid-April, full sunlight. April first to May first...and mid-August to mid-September, 40% shade. First of May to mid-August, 64% shade.
— H. Kronenberg

(France) Earlier in this century, we used wooden blinds which could be rolled and unrolled to control light in the greenhouse. Those are too expensive to use now, so we use white paint (shade compound) sprayed on the glass in successive light coats to reach desired degree of shading. When some is washed off and the light gets too high, we re-spray.
— Marcel LeCoufle

(North of England) I AM VERY CONCERNED ABOUT HEATING COSTS. I can only afford to grow phals in this northerly climate if I can keep heating costs to a level that will not unduly affect the overall running costs of a home and family of four. In order to do this, I've had to insulate to a degree which may have proved difficult for the plants to grow. Although I am using artificial light on two areas in the phal house, the amount of available light reaching the remaining plants seems sufficient to sustain GROWTH OF 1-INCH PER WEEK, MAXIMUM, ON THE FASTEST GROWING PLANTS (emphasis mine. ed.)

From November to March, the external shading comes off. That is the only control and variation that takes place. Using your way of measuring light, I calculate that the plants receive 736 footcandles on a sunny day and 90 on a cloudy one. This really makes your light requirements a bit suspect, as we have had 4 weeks of almost perpetual rain and cloud, and my plants seem to be growing and flowering OK.
— P. Lindsay

(Mr Lindsay's accommodation certainly seems to challenge his phals to survive, but I've long since learned not to pooh-pooh success. Phals are survival experts and I would not be surprised to hear of them managing under even such trying conditions; but, it must be like living on a bubble. ed.)

(Central California US) I give what I feel is about 1,200 fc to mature plants.
— B. Livingston

(Florida Caribbean US) The mature phals are given bright light conditions, approximately 1,500 footcandles for growing, and this is reduced when the plants come into spike.
— L. Lodyga

(Northeastern US) Our plants are grown in a room with a row of windows that face southwest and a skylight overhead. All plants are well back from these windows. Only during the winter is the sun angle low enough for any direct sunlight to reach the plants. At that time, burning is not a problem.
— B&C Loechel

(Queensland Coast Australia) We do not actually measure the light our phals receive, but tend to let them tell us whether the light is too bright or too dull. The leaves should be firm and holding up at an angle of about 30⁰ off the horizontal, but should neither be hard or stunted nor too green and soft. There are natural colour variations to the leaves according to the species in their backgrounds; e.g. phal violacea leaves will always be much greener and softer than most of the others. We tend to grow under higher light levels than is necessary because we like to grow our plants fairly hard. That way, our customers do not have trouble when they take them to different conditions.

— J. Mackinney

(Texas Gulf Coast US) For early spring and summer I use 68% shade cloth. As soon as the average daytime high drops below 80⁰F, I remove the cloth and let the large trees on the south and west side take care of the afternoon sun.

— J. Margolis

(Luzon Philippines) About 3 to 4 hours of 60-70% of full morning sunlight and 55-60% of afternoon sunlight of similar duration. Light is controlled by plastic net blinds over the plants 10-12 feet from the ground. Plants are situated 3-4 feet above the ground.

— D. Mendoza

*(Mid-Atlantic Coast US) Under artificial lighting...10,000 to 15,000 footcandlehours per day at an average rate of 1,000 fc. Up to 20 hours @ 1,000fc will benefit the plants, but over 20 hours will cause stress. With extended light up to 20 hours, better flower color will result. I use a mixture of cool-white and wide-spectrum light tubes (fluorescent) at a ratio of 2:1, respectively. Cool white tubes produce an abundance of yellow, green, and blue wavelength light, but are deficient in red light which is necessary for good plant health. Wide-spectrum tubes provide an abundance of red light and thus aid the plants; however, they are much dimmer than the cool white type. A mix of the two types is used to get a wide range of beneficial light without compromising light intensity.

— E. Merkle

(Queensland Coast Australia) In winter, natural light through opaque plastic sheeting. In summer, a 50% sarlon fabric is hung under the plastic sheeting. An illuminometer at 9:00 AM gave a reading of 3,500 lux (325 footcandles); at 1:00 PM, the reading was 5,500 lux (510 footcandles.

— R. Merritt

(Southern California US) Having lived in the Philippines for many years, I like to think I grow intuitively and go more by what looks and feels right than by more rigid standards. Here in southern California, I do not find it necessary to vary light requirements during the course of a year.

— J. Miller

Phalaenopsis Culture

(Southern California US) I give my plants as much light as they'll take without damaging them. When I can see a faint shadow of my hand in the greenhouse, the light is just about right.

— H. Moye

(California Coast US) About 800 to 1,000 footcandles, depending on uncontrollable factors such as "...spring and summer late night and early morning clouds." (A California weather forecaster's jargon for 'cloudy all day'. ed.)

— N. Nash

(California Coast US) I use 85% shade cloth as my particular location is quite bright. A highly-reflective garage is located at one end of the greenhouse.

— M&J Nedderman

(Mid-Atlantic Coast US) 1,500 to 2,200 footcandles.

— M. Owen

(Mid-West US) 2,000 footcandles. The leaves of my phals are yellow-green, not a lush, dark green, but I find I do not have insect and fungus problems by growing my plants a little harder. With more light and higher humidity, I get the maximum growth in the summer growing season.

— R. Pallister

(Southeastern US) Between 1,200 and 2,500 footcandles in the summer and 325 to 2450 in the winter.

— S. Pridgen

(Western Australia 50% shade year round with an additional 50% (total 75%) during late spring to early autumn.

— K. Rex

*(Northcentral US) Under artificial lighting...1100 footcandles measured at leaf tips.

— A. Roberts

*(Northcentral US) Under artificial lighting...in a Wardian case, four fluorescent lamps: 2 Vitalight, 1 Gro-Lux and 1 cool white. I use 14 hours duration in the summer and 9 in the winter, changing gradually. Artificial light is supplemented with indirect sunlight each afternoon.

— Randy Robinson

(Queensland Coast Australia) Phals are grown in Northern Queensland under 80-90% shade cloth throughout the year.

— R. Robinson

24

(Mid-Atlantic Coast US) Seedlings and mature plants are grown together under the same conditions! Fifty percent of full sunlight in the summer and up to full sunlight in the winter until the end of February. The primary purpose of shading is to control temperature elevations. Small plants greatly benefit from high light levels, also.

— E. Rutkowski

(Southcentral US) 1,500 to 2,000 footcandles late fall through early spring. I lower light levels with lath shading to 800 to 1,000 footcandles as the flower spikes show first buds.

— P. Scholz

(South of England) It is a question of balancing light intensity with greenhouse temperature. I do not want my greenhouse to go above 90°F, even on the brightest day (not always achievable) or 80°F routinely. I see the problem as one of giving the plants enough light without exceeding these temperature maximums (No cooler is used). 60% shade cloth, raised on wires above the glass for air circulation, gives me best results.

— P. Seaton

(North of England) 800 to 900 footcandles.

— D. Shuker

(Pacific Northwest US) About 2,000 footcandles in the greenhouse and 1,000-1,500 under lights.

— S. Skoien

(British Columbia Pacific Canada) In a west-facing window getting full light except at peak sun hours in the afternoon. I use no special lighting...after all, it is MY livingroom, at least so far.

— L. Slade

*(Mid-Atlantic Coast US) Under artificial lighting...We grow our phals under fluorescent lights using 'Verilux' full-spectrum tubes. These tubes give an average of about 600 footcandles of light just below the tubes as measured by a Weston lightmeter. The top leaves of the plants vary from 8" to 20" from the lights and receive about 300-450 footcandles of light. These lights are controlled by timers. In the summer the phals get 16 hours of light; in the spring and fall they get 14.5 to 15 hours, while in the winter they get 13.5 to 14 hours.

— K&M Smeltz

(Midlands of England) Slight shading in winter. Full shade with lath blinds with 14" gaps. The blinds set 6" from the glass roof.

— F. Smith

*(Northeastern US) Under artificial lighting...four 40-watt tubes (2 cool white; 2 Gro-Lux) per 2- x 4-foot shelf.

— D&D Strack

(Oahu Hawaii US) 73% shade cloth over Filon panels.

— R. Takase

(Midlands of England) Heavy summer shading is removed in the autumn giving the plants extra light. If you try to regulate it in this country, you would be at it all day long with the vast variation in light intensity throughout the day.

— H. Taylor

*(Northeastern US) Under artificial lighting. . . About 1,500 to 2,000 footcandles during the spring, summer and part of autumn; 900 to 1,200 footcandles during the latter part of the autumn and winter season.

— J. Vella

(Central California Coast US) 400 to 1,200 footcandles, depending on whether I want fast growth, slow growth or flower quality.

— J. Watkins

(Southeastern US) I give my species and primary hybrids more light than my complex hybrids because they like and can take more. I move most phals, especially young plants, down to a lower level in the greenhouse during the summer. . . to their 'summer benches'. . . for less light and lower temperatures. As fall approaches, I move them back. (A sizeable chore since Linda Zeeman has a lot of plants. ed.)

— L. Zeeman

*(Northcentral US) Under artificial lighting. . . 12 inches away from a bank of Vita-lite power twist tubes. In cool weather, they get 12 hours of light per day; in warm weather, they get 16.

— M. Zimmer

QUESTION 1 (b) HOW DO YOU MEASURE THE LIGHT?

(Indian Coast South Africa) A light meter will measure the light at any given time, but if you observe carefully during the first year of growing, you should have a good idea of light levels.
— A. Adriaanse

(California Coast US) By light meter in June.
— L. Batchman

(Southeastern Australia) By pure guesswork, no reliable light meter being available at practical cost.
— M. Black

(Central California US) Have never meter-measured light. I still use the simple, but effective, method of holding my hand one foot above a white paper and checking for a shadow.
— R. Buchter

(Northeastern US) Under artificial lighting...A light meter would not be of any use as I use plant growth tubes, mostly Gro-Lux Wide Spectrum. Plants will tell you if they are getting the right amount of light.
— I. Cohen

(South Australia) With a camera-type light meter.
— M. Dennis

(Gulf Coast US) General Electric light meter #214.
— J. Eich and many others

(Holland) By computer.
— A major commercial grower

(Northeastern US) A General Electric light meter which measures footcandles with a range of 0 to 10,000. Readings taken during hours of peak light.
— D. Grove

(Southeastern US) Primarily by leaf color, but I intend to get a light meter soon.
— T. Harper

(Indian Coast South Africa) Initially used a light meter to establish acceptable conditions.
— A. Harris

(Southern California US) We measure it with a footcandle meter.
— E. Hetherington

(Southeastern Australia) I don't. Over the years I've made changes to what I had...to overcome difficulties. The plants told me that they had too much light, so I gave more shade until they were happy.

— J. Kilgannon

(France) The intensity of the light in our greenhouses varies according to the thickness of the shading compound. We have no precise verification of the light, but no matter, in the wild it is the same and underneath the trees some plants get much more or less light than others...

— Marcel LeCoufle

(Central California US) I measure the light by sight. After growing for all these years, I can come very close to the proper 1,200 footcandles.

— B. Livingston

(Florida Caribbean US) We don't measure the light with a light meter.

— L. Lodyga

*(Mid-Atlantic Coast US) Under artificial lighting...According to the fluorescent tube manufacturer's information, a bank of six new 40-watt lamps at a distance of 10 inches will provide 1,000 footcandles of light per hour on a 24-inch wide shelf. This amount diminishes gradually as the tubes age. I replace the tubes of the mature plants with new ones after 12 months. These older tubes are then used over the seedlings which do better with less light. After 2 years, the light tubes may have lost as much as 30% of the brilliance and I throw them away.

— E. Merkle

(Southern California US) When I see a faint shadow of my hand over a plant, I know the light level is about right.

— H. Moye and others

(California Coast US) Experience. We use a light meter if we're not sure. It should look right and feel right.

— N. Nash

(California Coast US) I watch the coloring of the leaves.

— M&J Nedderman and others

(Mid-Atlantic Coast US) Light meter held one foot from the glass on bright days.

— M. Owen

(Indian Coast South Africa) By 'nose'.

— G. Paris

(Southeastern US) By Gossen Paulux electronics II light meter.

— S. Pridgen and others

*(Northcentral US) Under artificial lighting...I use a footcandle meter:

- With white tubes, read it directly in footcandles from the scale of the meter, e.g. scale reading of 600 = 600 footcandles.

- With Gro-Lux wide spectrum tubes, multiply scale reading by 1.44 and read footcandles, e.g. scale reading of 600 x 1.44 = 864 footcandles.

- With standard Gro-Lux tubes, multiply scale reading by 2.19 and read footcandles, e.g. scale reading of 600 x 2.19 = 1314 footcandles.
— A. Roberts

(Southcentral US) With a light meter and a 10'' white square card.
— P. Scholz

(South of England) I haven't measured my light intensity; but if I were to do this, it would have to be done throughout the year and under a range of different climatic conditions if the answer were to be of much use.
— P. Seaton

*(Northeastern US) Under artificial lighting...With an old-fashioned 'Gilwin Light Meter', which measures available light in lux units.
— J. Vella

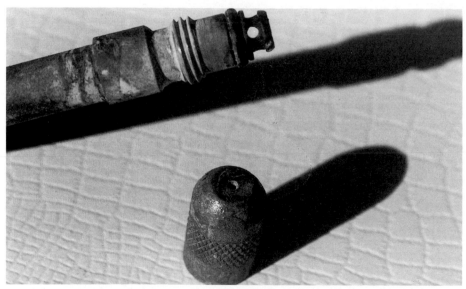

Garden sprayer modification: Ream sprayer wand crossed ports and nozzle slightly to accommodate shading compound slurry. Does not significantly affect the sprayer's use with pesticides.

Greenhouse shading kit: Garden sprayer, slightly modified; shading compound; kitchen whisk; strainer; and a bucket.

Shading compound strainer: a funnel; a laundry-line clothes peg; and a square of screening. Fold the screen into the funnel and secure with the peg.

QUESTION 1 (c) HOW DO YOU CONTROL THE LIGHT?

(Indian Coast South Africa) By interchanging light frames which are covered with different densities of shade cloth.
— A. Adriaanse

(Southern California US) Winter, 50% shade cloth; summer, 73% shade cloth.
— E. Campuzano

(California Coast US) With a shading compound (powder) mixed with latex paint.
— E. Carlson

(Indian Coast South Africa) We have a roller blind with 60% shade cloth which can be rolled up or down depending on the time of year. In Durban we roll up the shade cloth blinds about early April...and let them down in the spring, that is September or October.
— C&I Coll

(California Coast US) 1,500 footcandles year round. I use Sun-Lite HP lightweight, shatterproof panes with an ultraviolet filter for glazing.
— W. Eckberg

(Rome Italy) I add shading compound (powdered lime) progressively in the spring and summer to control light and temperature.
— A. Fanfani

(Holland) By computer.
— A major commercial grower

(Southern California US) I mix shade compound powder with three times the water...or one-third the consistency...called for on the package, add a tablespoon of dishwashing detergent per gallon of mix, then blend the whole mess thoroughly with a kitchen whisk. Allow the mix to stand half an hour, whack it again with the whisk and pour through a funnel, lined with a piece of window screening, into a standard garden hand-pump sprayer. Apply to the exterior of the greenhouse. (I've bored out some of the nozzle holes of one sprayer a little to permit the use of a shade compound solution-slurry.) Shake often to keep the white stuff in suspension.

Add additional coats to 'fine tune' the amount of light reaching the plants or replace compound washed away by rain. Put it on heavier on the areas of the roof that are closer to the plants, i.e., thinnest at the peak of the greenhouse roof. Contrary to conventional wisdom, I do not use any latex paint mixed in with the shading compound. The hot sun here fuses it to the plastic and it is just too damned hard to get off when I want more light in the winter...and it sticks harder to old plastic than it does to new. Which leads me to a point:

A lot of people, including me, figure that they had taken one light reading when they first put up a greenhouse and it wouldn't be necessary to do it again. Right? Wrong. If you are using any kind of plastic covering, the odds are that it will craze, oxidize and otherwise pass a lot less light through as it ages...and this is especially true in the southwest of the US and, I'm sure, in dry, bright areas elsewhere. What happens is that with the same amount of shading applied, you get progressively less light as the plastic ages.

I was stunned to find my noon light reading in the summer, instead of being about the 1,200 to 1,400 footcandles I expected, had dropped to 800. (John Miller had accused me of trying to grow my phals in the dark, and that's why I rechecked.) It happened slowly over the period of 5 years or so it took the fierce sunlight here in the southern California desert to damage the Filon. The point? Check your light level regularly.
— editor

(Southeastern US) I think it helpful to increase the light in the fall and winter up to 1,200 or even 1,500 footcandles. This seems to make them spike better. We control light by shade cloth and spraying the houses with cheap latex paint. We normally need at least four changes during the year to maintain the proper level of light.
— K. Griffith

(Northeastern US) Two ways: (1) control by shade screening and (2) by making compensatory changes in humidity levels by readjusting misting and watering schedules, together with adjustment of air movement.

In other words, within fairly wide limits, one can control maximum light or try to compensate for light that is excessive. Most growers don't do enough of the latter, a course that often is easier and gives better results than reducing light intensity in peak hours. There is a danger that, in reducing light intensity in peak hours, you will end up with too little light during certain other hours and on dull days, unless you have a (usually complicated or inconvenient) system for rolling shading material up and down frequently. I FIND IT EASIER TO REGULATE HUMIDITY AND LET LIGHT VARY CONSIDERABLY MORE THAN WOULD OTHERWISE BE TOLERABLE.
— D. Grove

(Florida Atlantic US) By moving plants to different sections of the greenhouse. Greenhouse runs from east to west; the farther west you go in the greenhouse, the denser the shade becomes due to the overhang and the shade provided from live oak trees overhead.
— C&L Hagan

(Southeastern US) I control light with white greenhouse shading. I go to K-Mart (a large, chain retailer in the US featuring low prices), buy the cheapest interior latex white paint, mix it 3 to 4 parts to one with water, put it in a pump sprayer and go to it. The application is heaviest during the summer months and lightest during the winter. I begin spraying it on with one

application in March, another in mid-May and a last one for the summer in July.
— T. Harper and others

(Southern California US) Slow wash-off shading compound.
— E. Hetherington and others

(Midlands of England) During the period March through October, I apply 'summer cloud' (shade compound) to the exterior glass surfaces. This has two advantages over the green woven nylon. It reflects some heat away from the greenhouse and it admits a better, brighter quality of light into the house.
— P. Hirst

(Arizona Desert US) Controlling greenhouse light here in Phoenix is not easy. We have enormous amounts of sunlight to contend with. We use two layers of 65% shade cloth in the summer. I remove one layer about the first of October and the second one about the end of November.
— J&G Johnson

(Florida Caribbean US) A light application of greenhouse paint is made in the spring-summer; light enough so that it will dissipate by September or October.
— W. Kelly

(Queensland Coast Australia) The roof of our glasshouse has a permanent covering of plastic paint, but at the start of summer, we spray on extra 'Parasaline' which is usually washed off by winter.
— J. Mackinney

(France) White paint.
— Marcel LeCoufle and others

(Queensland Coast Australia) The structure of our bush house is 50% sarlon on the roof and sides other than the fern/Phalaenopsis area where there is an opaque plastic sheeting on the roof. (With the single exception of watering, maidenhair ferns and Phalaenopsis receive the same treatment.) In the summer, I run 50% sarlon underneath the plastic. So far, there has been no burning.
— R. Merritt

(Southern California US) Shading compound mixed with a little linseed oil.
— H. Moye

(California Coast US) Supr-Stick Koolray Shade Compound.
— N. Nash

(California Coast US) I use only shade cloth as this makes a nicer appearance than white wash...and keeps my wife happy!
— M&J Nedderman

33

(Southeastern US) Saran; 35 mesh in the winter and 70 mesh in the summer.
— S. Pridgen

*(Northcentral US) Under artificial lighting...I use timer for a 13-hour day.
— A. Roberts

(California Coast US) Two layers of shade cloth, one of which is removed during the winter.
— F. Robinson

*(Northcentral US) Under artificial lighting...I move plants around; closer or farther away from the fixtures to adjust light.
— W. Schumann

(North of England) Using 'Coolglass' stippled plus Roller Blinds made of 30% and 60% Rokolene I have two sets of blinds.
— D. Shuker

(South of England) Shade cloth, spring through autumn...Oh sorry, Bob, 'fall' to Americans. (My source says the American use of the term 'fall' came to the New World in the 17th century... from the southwest of England. Devon. ed.)
— P. Seaton

*(Northeastern US) Under artificial lighting...timers. I also clean the tubes often and measure regularly to maintain light intensity.
— D&D Strack

*(Northeastern US) Under artificial lighting...Two ways; either by shading or by rheostats. I use mercury vapor and high pressure sodium lighting.
— J. Vella

(Mid-Atlantic Coast US) Roll blinds to maintain about 800 footcandles year round.
— J. Webster

(Texas Gulf Coast US) Shade cloth.
— C&J Wilson and others

QUESTION 1(d) DO YOU INTENTIONALLY VARY THAT AMOUNT OF LIGHT AT TIMES? IF SO, WHEN AND BY HOW MUCH?

[Many of the responses to this question are contained in the answers to parts (a), (b), and (c) above. ed.]

(Southern California US) I'm a windowsill grower and Nature varies the amount of light my plants get seasonally by changes in the sun angle.
— W. Adams

(Southeastern Australia) No, I don't, because there would be seasonal variations in the natural habitat. So I leave the same shading, winter and summer.
— M. Black

(MidAtlantic Coast US) Sometimes more in autumn to increase flowering. I give as much light as I can without burning or yellowing the leaves. I use a southeastern exposure.
— M. Bowell

(Central California US) I remove saran shading at the start of our customary rainy season (normally mid-October through the end of February.) However, I normally replace the saran (regardless of rainy days that may continue) as soon as spikes are advanced and buds are developing.
— R. Buchter

(California Coast US) I let winter rains and hail remove the shading until the footcandles reach about 1,600 to 1,700 and then I shade again. This is usually about March.
— E. Carlson

(Southern California US) From April to October, we move our phals from the Warm House to the Regular House.
— D&R Cowden

(Florida Atlantic US) More shade in summer helps to reduce greenhouse temperatures.
— D. Davis

(South Australia Using shade cloth of 80% for the summer months and none during the winter. This (higher light level) helps the flower spikes to mature in 90 days or so. If shading is used in the winter, flowers will take longer to develop. Spikes appearing in April (southern hemisphere) should bloom in July/August. If they bloom later, too much shade is the answer. Increase the light if you want to have flowers (sooner) for a particular time. You can vary your light conditions to accommodate show times.
— M. Dennis

(Southern California US) In southern California we are fortunate in that the first seasonal rains come in October (after being dry from April on) and they begin eroding the shade

compound. . . just as the plant's need for light increases. Couldn't work any better if it was on 'automatic.'
                              — editor

(Holland) At the end of summer and the beginning of autumn, we increase the light slowly to 17,000-18,000 lux (1,580-1,680 footcandles) to get higher production of flowers.
                              — A major commercial grower

(Northeastern US) Here in the Northeast, winter snows, leafless trees, and fairly long, bright days can produce enormous swings in light intensity and some very high peaks in light levels. Plants hung high in the greenhouse become very vulnerable and quickly can 'cook', so I keep plants at normal bench level, with rare exceptions. To 'control' light, one has to think in terms of 'compensating' as well as reducing light intensity that is higher than ideal, using whatever opportunities are available. (such as increasing humidity or air circulation. . .or both. ed.)
                              — D. Grove

(Southeastern US) The wearing away of the shading by weather. Plants do better with less shading in winter, the time when we receive the least amount of sun.
                              — T. Harper

(Southern California US) We do not vary the light as much as cattleyas, as Phalaenopsis are more tolerant of lower light temperatures.
                              — E. Hetherington

(California Coast US) I intentionally control the light. Starting in March, I start applying the first coats of shading. In the latter part of October, I start removing the shading to allow more light in.
                              — B. Livingston and others

(Luzon Philippines) The normal amount of light is maintained up to the time when the first floret opens; then the plant is moved to a lower light intensity.
                              — D. Mendoza

*(Mid-Atlantic Coast US) Under artificial lighting. . .Phalaenopsis respond to a number of environmental factors which encourage definite growing and blooming seasons. One of those factors is daylength. Many of the Phal species and hybrids normally bloom in early spring, after a short-day season which occurs during the winter months. Day length as well as chemical and temperature factors are involved to work together for proper blooming. By growing indoors under artificial lights, an orchid grower can convince his or her plants to bloom 'out of season' by creating a short-day period at other times of the year.

Several years ago I noticed that many of my Phals, which normally bloomed during the winter, began their blooming cycle in August when growing outdoors. This was actually just fine with me because our local orchid society's annual show is held in early fall and I ended up having lots of Phals in bloom. (More on the reason for this in my response to Q 2(c).) Taking the cue from the Phals, I have since encouraged this early fall blooming by giving the plants short days in June and July...10 hours of light. I have had a greater number of plants blooming with better quality flowers as a result. During the remainder of the year, the plants are given 16-18 hours of light to promote good plant growth.

— E. Merkle

(California Coast US) Nope. Rains wash the shade compound off in winter and we repaint as needed...usually about April-May as days lengthen.

— N. Nash

(California Coast US) Weak, newly repotted phals are placed in the shadier north end of the greenhouse until their root systems are established.

— M&J Nedderman

(MidAtlantic Coast US) Pay extra attention from February 15th on when snow is on the ground and the sun is out bright.

— M. Owen

*(Northcentral US) Under artificial lighting...I start reducing lighting time August 15th by one-half hour per day until I reach 8 hours of total lighting time. Hold this time for about one month and cool room to as low as 50°F.

— A. Roberts

(Puerto Rico US) During the winter months, I remove one layer of shade cloth.

— R. Rodriguez

*(Northcentral US) Under artificial lighting...It is my firm conviction that doritaenopsis types take much higher light intensities, perhaps as much as cattleyas. Certain phal species such as violacea and gigantea take much lower intensities and the rest of the phals are somewhere in between.

— W. Schumann

(Bill Schumann grows under lights and his theory probably applies to that situation. However, I grow my giganteas and violaceas up near the glass at about 1,800 fc and they thrive...doing much better than they did at bench level, about 1,000 to 1,200 fc. Temperature may well have something to do with the difference. ed.)

(South of England) There is a vexing problem in that the amount of light reaching the plants varies from time to time throughout the year. Automatic blinds would help. I put on and remove the cloth when the weather dictates. It is left on throughout the summer.

— P. Seaton

(North of England) In mid-October I raise the light level to 1,300 footcandles from a norm of 800-900.

— D. Shuker

*(Pacific Northwest US) Under artificial lighting...I vary the amount of light by daylength regulation...down to 12 hours immediately in fall (September) from 16 hours.

— S. Skoien

(Midlands of England) Yes; if I see the colour of the leaves changing, i.e., to a red tint or to a paler colour. Too little shade, or too much. I use judgment based on experience.

— F. Smith

*(Northeastern US) Under artificial lighting...Normal duration of the lighting day is 16 hours; October to November, 14 hours; December to January, 12 hours; and February to March is 14 hours.

— D&D Strack

*(Northeastern US) Under artificial lighting...Yes. During the period of reduced vegetative growth, the 20th of September through the 25th of February, I lower the high from 1,500 to 1,000 footcandles and the low from 1,250 to 750 footcandles.

— J. Vella and others

(MidAtlantic Coast US) No, I don't vary it. Although flower production is better, the plants look strained under the brighter light. I like growing plants that look happy the whole year.

— J. Webster

SECTION 1.3 ABOUT LIGHTS FOR ORCHID GROWING

GENERAL:

The oft-stated misrule that light levels diminish inversely according to the square of the ratio between the distances from the light source plane and the reference plane. . .is not correct in all instances.

The rule applies only to point light sources, not to line sources such as a single fluorescent lamp or area sources comprising several lamps. There are other areas of misinformation: Lamp life, spectral characteristics, and lumen output. I will try to correct these.

Incandescent lamps have no place in orchid growing. They generate too much heat and cost far too much to operate. Their spectral characteristic (color) is claimed to be beneficial, but the benefit can be far better obtained by use of a standard warm white fluorescent lamp.

Fluorescent lamps are the best choice for the growing of any plant. They give close to the most light for the dollar, and the spectral characteristics and life are the most favorable. All fluorescent lamps use a low-pressure, low-temperature mercury vapor arc which takes place between heated cathodes at the ends of the lamp. Lamp life is a function of the number of starts and the number of hours of use. If a fluorescent is lit continuously, its life will be between 18,000 to 20,000 hours (only one start). If on a 12-hour on/12-hour off duty cycle, life will be reduced to about 12,000, or 1,000 days, or about 3 years.

LAMP LIFE:

Reduction in light output is often stated as the reason for re-lamping annually. A new lamp is noticeably brighter than the one it is to replace. But, what is seldom known is that initial brightness deteriorates very rapidly and that the rated light output is much less than that initial brightness. Light output drops very rapidly during the first 100 hours. . .9 days in orchid service. . .and then stabilizes and decays very slowly for the rest of its life.

The rated lumen output of lamps is the average of the levels reached at 100 hours and at 80% of life. Lamps should be kept in service at least until a noticeable black ring is visible at one or both ends. The black ring will first become visible at 80-90% of lamp life. It is not realistic to re-lamp after only one year of service as some people advise.

SPECTRAL AND LUMEN CHARACTERISTICS:

Fluorescent lamps are very efficient converters of electrical energy into radiant energy. Much research has gone into materials testing and processing to make commercial lamps produce the most light for the dollar with a close approximation to natural sunlight.

The most efficient lamp is the 'cool white' fluorescent which in the 80-watt size produces 80 lumens per watt. The 40-watt size is slightly less efficient. The lamp is also very cheap, often available in the 40-watt size at little more (or less) than one dollar each.

However, its spectral characteristic (color) peaks in the yellow region with a noticeable drop in the orange-red area. (Plants use the yellow-orange-red portion of the solar spectrum to carry out photosynthesis. Red is the lowest on the spectrum level; blue highest.)

The "deluxe cool-white" fluorescent has a substantial increase in the orange-red output with only a very small drop in efficiency. The "warm-white" lamp peaks sharply in the yellow region, but has a much lower output in the blue-green.

THE "DELUXE WARM-WHITE" HAS A STILL MORE SUBSTANTIAL INCREASE IN THE ORANGE-RED REGION AND IS MY RECOMMENDATION AS THE MOST-BALANCED COLOR CHARACTERISTIC FOR PLANT GROWING. It is, however, less efficient in that only 60 lumens of light are generated per watt. This is still better than the 30-40 lumens per watt obtained from the so-called "grow lights".

I will confess to a prejudice against the "grow lights", but it has nothing to do with their ability to grow or not grow plants. The lamps have a low conversion efficiency and lower lamp lumen output than any other. The visible spectral output was bunched in three lines: one in the blue and two others in the red-orange.

A LITTLE ABOUT LIGHT

Plants appear green because they absorb the yellow to orange-red portion of the spectrum of natural sunlight. In other words, plants reject the green, and to some extent, the yellow and blue portions of sunlight. (The human eye sees a blend of yellow and blue light as green.) Plants use the yellow-orange-red portion of the solar spectrum to carry out photosynthesis. Plants do not convert ultraviolet or infrared light into useful chemical energy. Infrared light is not used in photosynthesis because it is not energetic enough to stimulate the photosynthesis process. At the other extreme, ultraviolet light carries higher energy levels and penetrates too deeply into plant cells and does no good for the plant.

PLANT'S RESPONSE TO LIGHT

Plants, being living things, have the ability to adjust their photosynthetic processes to best meet their needs. If light levels are lower than the plant needs, the plant will expand its sensitivity up the spectrum level (red being lowest, blue being the highest) and start making more use of yellow light. This becomes apparent to the human eye as a change in color of the plant.

Its green will become deeper, more blue, because there will be less yellow light reflected to combine with the reflected blue.

At the other extreme, if a plant has more than enough light for its photosynthetic needs, it will narrow its spectral absorbtion range and start rejecting (or reflecting) light at the edges of its useful range. This becomes apparent to the human eye by a color shift; it will be either more yellow or more red. When plants get more light than they need, they often develop a red pigmentation to shield their light receptors from the excess. They start rejecting red light; the red becomes visible to the human eye.

From that, it becomes apparent that the optimum spectral output of a lamp should be in the orange section, with some red and yellow for flexibility.

WHICH LAMP TO BUY?

The lamp known as the "Deluxe Warm White" is by far the best available in a fluorescent lamp. It also has a high lumen output; more light for the dollar.

The "Deluxe Cool White" lamp is a second best; it has still higher lumen output than the Warm White, but it is lacking in some red light (not a serious defect) and its higher lumen output almost compensates for its red deficiency.

The ordinary "Cool White" lamp is lowest in cost and has a higher lumen output than the Deluxe Warm White, lower than the Deluxe Cool White, but is also more deficient in the orange and red.

High pressure sodium lamps (Lucolox) come closest to being ideal artificial light sources for plants. However, while they have the most lumens per unit of electricity used (and are the cheapest to operate), have their own drawbacks.

They are a too-bright spot source, are slow starting (and re-starting after a fraction of a second power interruption), and the fixtures and lamps are expensive. They must be elevated high above the plants, or down low and aimed up to a reflective ceiling above the plants. The lamps are also position-sensitive, so you must purchase either base-down or base-up lamps depending on how you want to use them. If you have the space, the money and the number of plants to justify their minor problems, high-pressure sodium vapor lamps are the most economical in the long run and the most spectrally ideal for orchid growing. Lucolox lamps also emit almost no ultraviolet light and run coolest for their size.

— Joseph Van Acker

(This article appeared in the *Newsletter* of the Greater New York Orchid Society and was condensed from the original printed in the New Jersey Orchid Society *Newsletter.*)

SECTION TWO
HEAT

(a) How much heat do you give your mature phal plants? (b) How do you control it? (c) Do you intentionally vary that temperature at times? If so, when and by how much?

SECTION 2.1 CONSENSUS AND OPINION

Q 2(a) HOW MUCH HEAT?

No big surprises here. Most called for a normal minimum winter night temperature of about 60/62°F (16°C) and, in warm climates, 85°F (29/30°C) maximum day temperature. In cooler climates, growers sought a daytime <u>minimum</u> of 70/72°F (22°C). These were the values for times other than the flower induction period in mid-autumn.

While a major commercial grower in Holland said their normal night minimum was 68°F, in her book, <u>Orchidiana Philippiniana</u>, Dr. Helen Valmayor suggested a low of 60°F was needed to induce flowering in Phalaenopsis plants in the natural situation. I haven't the least doubt that both are correct, but if that is true, what are the other possible conditions that can bring on flowering beside a 60°F minimum?

Lower light intensities seem to be out, but how about brighter light? My own experience tells me this is a possibility and a look at the weather conditions in the Philippines during the month of November tends to support the idea. The monsoon clouds clear away and daytime light intensity is higher. The earth radiates more heat energy to deep space on the clear nights than on cloudy ones, so night temperatures are decidedly cooler. It seems very possible this is the combination of changes that stimulate the flowering of phal plants in the natural setting...and most of those in culture as well.

(It was curious to note that Dr. Valmayor's research showed while Phalaenopsis species in a natural situation in the Philippines tended to bloom at certain seasons of the year...as might be expected...those in culture tended to bloom over a much longer period of time, centered on the time of the wild species blooming.)

Many growers increase their light levels in the autumn through the act of removing shading and possibly overdose the plants with light in the first few weeks after ...and in doing so may, inadvertently, give them just what they would have gotten in the wild.

I've heard, and tend to agree, that a 25/35°F temperature differential between the night lows and the day highs will have the same effect as a cool soak at 55/60°. Notice the comments by several of the British growers who say they have a problem <u>keeping</u> their plants from blooming. Most allow a minimum night temp of 65/66°F. How come? Maybe the day-night differential? It certainly is not an excess of light.

Q 2(b) HOW DO YOU CONTROL IT?

It seems from the responses that there are no two phal greenhouses alike in the entire world. They range from the bare-bones setup to the elaborate. Phal growing facilities give the tinkerers among us an opportunity to build all manner of things and develop our own solutions. For some of us this is half the fun of growing orchids. This section should provide some new ideas and stimuli for the do-it-yourselfers.

Personally, I enjoy putting together control systems that cost little to make and operate and the measure of my enjoyment is in how well it works and how little it costs. A three-part system for protection of plants in the event of a power outage in either hot or cold weather is detailed in an earlier book, Culture of the Phalaenopsis Orchid. The three parts are a heat-motor vent, a solar chimney and an overhead (exterior) sprinkling system. Details for construction of the solar chimney are shown in Section 4.

Q 2(c) DO YOU VARY THE TEMPERATURE AT TIMES?

With few exceptions the respondents lower the greenhouse temps to the range of 55/60°F in the autumn to aid in flowering. The period of cooling ranges from 2 to 4 weeks, and the average is 3. A sizeable group makes no intentional effort, but allows natural cooling to take place, often by simply delaying the turn-on of the heating system...if any is used. The results are reported as being the same.

Carmen and Ivan Coll (and a few others) expressed some doubt that the chilling had any significant effect on flowering and it seems likely there is another stimulant at work for them.

The practice of the Dutch commercial grower is one of those naggingly obvious things we all should be doing: When the light level is low, it makes sense to lower the temperature to slow the growth rate and avoid soft tissue and lost buds. Match the rate of growth of the plant to the availability of light. If the rate of growth is too fast, the plant tissues will be soft and bud drop likely. Conversely, when the light level is high, allow the temperature to rise a little to permit faster growth; the alternative is smaller, harder flowers.

There was a consensus on the need to keep the temperature up after the emergence of the flower spikes, but 'up' ranged from 62 to 70°F. The figure has to be a compromise between what the plants would like and what is economically feasible. If you own stock in the utility company, go for 70. My own experience tells me that 60 is a little low. Now that my kids are educated and married off, I can go for 66°F on sunny days in the winter...after the spikes start up. After the reminder from the big Dutch firm, I'll lower the minimum temps during the few cloudy weeks we have in Southern California.

— editor

SECTION 2.2   HEAT: SELECTED RESPONSES

QUESTION 2(a) HOW MUCH HEAT DO YOU GIVE YOUR MATURE PHAL PLANTS?

(California Coast US) Minimum temperature of heated benches is thermostatically controlled to 65-68°F in the winter. Leaf temperature may drop below 65°F in winter as the air is not heated; only the bench surface is. Plants may go to 90°F in the summer. Bench temperature is not varied during the year.
> — L. Batchman

(Central California US) . . . 60 to 85°F night-day max range.
> — R. Buchter

(California Coast US) Night temps, 60-62°F; days, 75-85°F.
> — E. Carlson

(Mid-Atlantic Coast US) Using finned-radiation steam heat we maintain 70°F minimum all year except 60°F minimum September and October to help initiate spikes.
> — L. Clouser

*(Northeastern US) Under artificial lighting. . . Most of the year, the minimum night temp is 61°F; day max is 75-80°F.
> — I. Cohen

(Indian Coast South Africa) We maintain a high of 85°F and a low of 66°F throughout the year.
> — C. Coll

(Southern California US) I maintain a minimum temperature in the winter of 60°F, but turn the heaters off in May. After that we occasionally will have a nighttime low in the '40s for an hour or so, but I find no ill effects and growth is good.
> — W. Cousineau and others

(Southern California US) From April first through October first, the phals are in our 'Regular House' where temps range from 40 to 100°F. (Why is everyone sucking in his breath? ed.) From October first through April first, the plants are moved to the 'Warm House' when temps range from 60 to 85°F.
> — D&R Cowden

(South of England) 65°F minimum at night. 70 to 75°F daytime minimum.
— R. Dadd and others

(South Australia) 16°C (60°F) minimum in the winter. In the summer months I water heavily every day to cool down the plants, always watering early in the day. Our daytime temps exceed 40°C (104°F) daily during the summer and it rains very seldom. I keep the floor of the glasshouse wet constantly in summer.
— M. Dennis

(Mid-Atlantic Coast US) Winter temperature is 62°F at night. Summer temperature will go as high as 75°F in August. In September when evening temperatures start to fall to the low '50s and high '40s, I keep the heat back and this will initiate spiking in certain white phals depending on genetic background. Not all will spike with this treatment this early.
— R. Drejka

(Holland) Nighttime temperature minimum of 20°C (68°F) and daytime temperatures of 25/26°C (78°F) before we open the windows.
— a major commercial grower

(California Coast US) Between 70 and 80°F.
— H. Freed

(Maui Hawaii US) About 80°F.
— R. Fukamura

(Atlantic Coast US) During the winter we run the phal house at 65°F at night and we drop it down to 55°F for the last 3 weeks of December to help the plants that have not spiked.
— K. Griffith

(Northeastern US) 65°F. minimum at night. 60 will do, but results definitely are visible if the lower temperatures are maintained for a long period. I let the sun raise the daytime temperature to 80 degrees, or even 85. In the winter, or on gray days, raising the daytime temperature to 70 degrees is desirable. That is especially important if one has just watered or misted heavily.
— D. Grove

(Florida Atlantic Coast US) Between 60 and 90°F.
— C&L Hagan

(Southeastern US) 68°F minimum at night; 82/85°F by day.
— T. Harper

(Indian Coast South Africa) We use only our natural ambient conditions. I live in Durban, virtually at sea level and we are fortunate with our conditions and, in fact, don't really need

any special attention as regards temperature and humidity control. (I think I'm going to be sick...with envy. ed.)
— A. Harris and others

(Southern California US) Our mature Phalaenopsis are grown at 60-65°F minimum night temperature.
— E. Hetherington

(Midlands of England) I aim for a year-round minimum of 65°F, but this figure may vary by plus or minus 5°F according to the time of the year. A maximum of 90°F is tolerated during the summer although 85° is preferred. During the colder days of winter, 78°F is considered adequate. Financial constraints are a factor in arriving at this figure.
— P. Hirst

(Arizona Desert US) It's not a question of how much heat we give our phals in the summer here; it's how cool we can keep the greenhouse. With 115°F (46°C) a daily summer occurrence and 90°F nighttime minimums an average, (sometimes the night min temps stay up around 96°F! Hot water comes out of all the taps. ed.) we try to maintain 70°F as a nighttime low and 88°F max during the day. This means the coolers run almost 24 hours a day. We use evaporative coolers along with a high-pressure misting system and shade cloth.
— J&G Johnson

(Southeastern Australia) Maintain a basic minimum temp of 21 to 22°C (70°F) at night and a maximum of 32°C (90°F) daytime temperature. Night temps are controlled by thermostat, but day temps are controlled by gentle venting of the house with an eye on the wet and dry (bulb) temps.
— J. Kilgannon

(East Java Indonesia) Heat is the climate where they grow in nature where I grow them.
— A. Kolopaking

(Holland) During the growing season of March through November, minimum daytime temperature of 20°C (68°F); minimum nighttime temperature of 18°C (66°F). Daytime winter (November through March) minimum temperature of 18°C; minimum night temperature of 16°C (60°F).
— H. Kronenberg

(France) We keep a minimum temperature of 18°C (64°F) in the winter. Botrytis can occur below that temperature.
— Marcel LeCoufle

(North of England) My summer minimum night temperature is 64°F and 60°F in the winter with a 10° rise in daytime. This can rise to near 90°F in sunny weather. I don't vary from these temps.
— P. Lindsay

(Western US) We try to maintain a 62-65°F night temperature and an 80-85°F daytime temperature.
— B. Livingston

(Northeastern US) Heat fluctuates with the seasons, as does our humidity. Summer provides the plants with 75-85°F days and 65-70° nights with humidity holding at about 60-80%. Winter heat is provided by wood stove. We try for 70-75° in the daytime...and if the sun is out, we make it. Nights drop to 50°. For this reason, some of our plants are grown in hanging slat baskets. More heat higher up and less chance of roots staying too cold and wet. Humidity at this season stays around 40-50%. If it drops any lower, we mist the plants.
— B&C Loechel

(Queensland Coast Australia) Winter minimum is 14°C (57°F) and at the first sign of spike initiation, we raise the minimum to 15-16°C (60-61°F).
— J. Mackinney

(Texas Gulf Coast US) I try to keep the greenhouse at 58-60°F minimum during the winter.
— J. Margolis

(Puerto Rico US) Our greenhouses are open on all sides.
— R. Melendez

(Luzon Philippines) This question is probably not applicable to our tropical situation, but the 26-30°C (80-85°F) is very good for our phals.
— D. Mendoza

(Queensland Coast Australia) We're very lucky, I suppose. Phalaenopsis grow in the rain forest less than 40km from here and, as a result, we are lazy growers; no heating or artificial lighting. They just grow with just a little help from us. We do, however, hose the floor and walls down in the summer to cool things down. (Nobody said it was going to be easy...ed.)
— R. Merritt

(Southern California US) For economy reasons I use under-the-bench circulating hot water with a maximum temperature set for 90°F and a minimum temperature of 60°F. I believe the optimum settings would be 85 max and 65 min. Flasks of seedlings are kept at a minimum of 70°F.
— J. Miller

(California Coast US) Nighttime minimum of 65-68°F year round. No heat is added except for maintenance of night minimum.
— N. Nash

(California Coast US) I try to keep a minimum night temperature of 68°.
— M&J Nedderman

(Mid-Atlantic Coast US) 68-70°F night temp, 75-80°F day temp during winter. In summer, vents are set to open at 78°F. Don't control summer low temps.
> — M. Owen

*(Northcentral US) Under artificial lighting.....I maintain 65/85°F day temperature and 58/68°F night temperature.
> — A. Roberts

(Florida Gulf Coast US) Winter, 60-62°F to keep down Botrytis. Summer, the low 90's is the coolest we can get in the middle of the day.
> — J&M Roberts

*(Northcentral US) In a Wardian case...Under artificial lighting...heat from the ballasts provide enough warmth on all but the coldest winter nights...and then I keep the house thermostat set at 60-62°F.
> — Randy Robinson

(Queensland Coast Australia) We leave the heat to nature here in Townsville. (19° latitude south) We are well into the tropics. Phalaenopsis amabilis grows naturally 30 miles north of here.
> — R. Robinson

(Puerto Rico US) In Puerto Rico we have warm temperatures the year round. In the winter the difference between day and night temperatures is 15 to 20 degrees.
> — R. Rodriguez

(Mid-Atlantic Coast US) Minimum of 65°F in the winter, except for periods of extreme outside cold. Greenhouse temps in the summer usually run 10-15°F above outside temps. Temps have gone as high as 120°F with no ill effects.
> — E. Rutkowski

(Southcentral US) 50°F minimum in winter up to 95+° in the summer.
> — P. Scholz

*(Northcentral US) Under artificial lighting...70°+F during the day; 60-65°F nights, the lights going on and off.
> — W. Schumann

(South of England) Minimum 60°F with a 10° lift during the day. I try not to go above 80°F.
> — P. Seaton

*(Mid-Atlantic Coast US) Under artificial lighting...Normally nighttime minimum of 55°F, but I suspect the pots and moist medium keep the minimum temp the plant sees to a higher level...unlike in nature.
> — M. Steen

(Mid-West US) During cold weather, I provide bottom heat with Agritape, set at 70°F. (Agritape Systems: Ken-Bar Products for the Grower, 24 Gould St, Reading MA 01867 US)

Much better growth.

— W. Stern

*(Northeastern US) Under artificial lighting...My temps under lights have been running too high, because the environment is uncontrolled and the ballasts generate a lot of heat. Summer, 90° days and 78° nights. Winter, 80° days and 70° nights.

— D&D Strack

(North of England) 65°F minimum at night and 75°F during the day. When temp rises to 85°F, the second Bayliss Autovent Mk III comes into operation. The first Autovent starts to open at 78°F.

— D. Shuker

(British Columbia Coast Canada) The plants get the same heat as the rest of us who inhabit our living room; 70 during the day and 64-65°F at night.

— L. Slade

*(Mid-Atlantic Coast US) Under artificial lighting...we grow our phals in our basement approximately 10 feet from a gas-fired hot-air furnace and 14 feet from a gas-fired, hot-water heater and its uninsulated storage tank. In the immediate area there are also 20 ballasts that control 39 fluorescent tubes. All of these combine to provide daytime temps of 75-85°F and 57-70°F nighttime temperatures. In the fall and spring a transom-type basement window is opened at night. A fan near the window is used to draw in the cool/cold air to bring the basement temperatures down to 57-62°F. In this way a 15-20°F daytime/nighttime differential is achieved. During the summer the windows and inside basement door are open most of the time.

An incident related to this basement growing arrangement: when we had our present furnace/air-conditioning system installed some years back, we also had an electronic air cleaner put into the system. When this electronic air cleaner was operated, the odor of ozone was quite noticeable. Further, some phal and paphio buds turned black and died. I rewired the air cleaner to reduce ozone formation and changed the wiring system so the air cleaner would only operate when the fan of the furnace ran. As a final modification, I replaced the standard air filter with one whose filter element was made of carbon...and the problem disappeared.

— K&M Smeltz

(Gulf Coast US) Phals love our hot, humid summers in New Orleans.

— B. Steiner

(Oahu Hawaii US) Not applicable since we depend on Mother Nature.

— R. Takase

*(Northeastern US) Under artificial lighting...I usually try to keep the temperature between 62 and 85°F.

— J. Vella

QUESTION 2(b) HOW DO YOU CONTROL IT?

(Indian Coast South Africa) [Few controls are needed, but]...if low temperatures are expected I close the greenhouse completely so a temperature of 12-14°C (53-57°F) can be maintained.
— A. Adriaanse

(Southeastern Australia) Thermostatically-controlled gas heater and fans.
— M. Black and others

(Western US) Eight-foot 'Duotherm' electric heaters placed 15 inches below growing bench are controlled by individual 'Dayton' thermostats wall-mounted 12 inches above the bench.
— R. Buchter

(California Coast US) Gas heat for nights and vents open for days.
— E. Carlson

(Southern California US) Summertime we try to control it with a fan jet/Kool Cell setup and misting every hour for 5 minutes. Gas heat in the winter.
— D&R Cowden

(South of England) Thermostats in each house approximately 2 feet above the plants. Water circulation in fast response finned 15 mm pipes under the staging. External boiler house with 2 boilers and 2 pumps in parallel.
— R. Dadd

(California Coast US) I keep the heater on throughout the year and hold a 60°F minimum at night. Daytime max is 83. I have a solar-operated vent in the roof that will open at 85°F if needed.
— W. Eckberg

(Gulf Coast US) Liquid propane, vented heaters and wet-pad fan cooling.
— J. Eich

(Holland) Computer.
— A major commercial grower.

(Maui Hawaii US) My greenhouse is not enclosed, so I have no need for controls.
— R. Fukamura

(Gulf Coast US) No primary heaters needed, but I use two 1,500 watt electric space heaters. (I will be switching to gas soon.) Four- by six-foot Kool Cell (pad and fan system).
— J. Grimes

(Northeastern US) By thermostat and fans (including evaporative coolers), aiming for 65-80°F range, or even a bit higher.

— D. Grove

(Florida Atlantic US) I maintain a low of 60° with an oil furnace and try to hold to the low 90's with large fans.

— C&L Hagan

(Southeastern US) Thermostatically-controlled Modine propane gas heaters. Fan jet tube (large, plastic, holed, distribution sleeves) below the benches for distribution getting the heat where it belongs. Fan speed can be varied by speed controller. This method is providing us with excellent results in flower quality and plant health.

— T. Harper

(Southern California US) The heat is infrared radiant on the mature plants to heated air on seedlings. Seedlings get higher temperatures...up to 68°F minimum at night.

— E. Hetherington

(Midlands of England) Control of the coke-fired furnace is by manually-operated thermostat which adjusts the burn rate.

— P. Hirst

(Arizona Desert US) By the first of November the nighttime low temperatures start to drop to the low '50's. Winters are mild enough that heating the greenhouse is not a problem. After a couple of chilly weeks to get the plants to spike, the heating of the greenhouse is started and electric heaters maintain 60 degrees at night. The coolers maintain a winter daytime high of 80°F.

— J&G Johnson

(Eastcentral US) I'm a home grower and keep my phals in the warmest room in the house. I control temperature by insulating windows and keeping doors closed. Keep plants at least 6 inches from windows during the winter.

— K. Kehew

(Florida Caribbean US) Our phal house is heated by two 350,000 Btu stainless steel heaters. They distribute the heat through 24-inch plastic tubes, 100 feet long. Because of our humidity and varying hot temperatures in the winter, we must adjust the control thermostats very often. Once January arrives, we have rather cool nights until about 20-25 February.

— W. Kelly

(Holland) Thermo-electrical central heating system.

— H. Kronenberg

(Central California US) When the daytime temperature rises above 85°F, which it can very readily here in the San Joaquin Valley, I increase the humidity by fogging the air and plants. This takes the stress off the plants. The higher the temperature, the more water I use. We use evaporative coolers to hold temperatures down.

— B. Livingston

(Florida-Caribbean US) Wet pads and fans keep temps about 80 degrees with no problem in the summer. During the winter the temp is set for 58/60 degrees nighttime low and daytime is generally around the 70/80 mark.

— L. Lodyga

(Queensland Coast Australia) Our houses are heated by electric fan heaters that are ducted along both sides of the house, well above the plants. The metal ducts have holes at intervals so that the heated air is blown down at an angle into the house. Temperature is controlled by thermostat.

— J. Mackinney

(Texas Gulf Coast US) I use a vented gas heater with a supplemental electric heater in case it gets really cold. I also cover all windows and Kool Cell with heavy plastic for most of the year.

— J. Margolis

*(Mid-Atlantic Coast US) Under artificial lighting...Plants are grown under normal home temperatures with the usual controls.

— E. Merkle

(California Coast US) Co-Ray-Vac infrared units.

— N. Nash

(Mid-Atlantic Coast US) Pneumatic thermostats.

— M. Owen

(Indian Coast South Africa) Should the natural coastal temperatures exceed 25°C (77°F) or the humidity go below 40%, we turn on misters. Our winter is mild enough not to require added heating, but we do close up the greenhouse with fibre glass side panels to stop cold winds.

— G. Paris

(Queensland Coast Australia) We don't heat our phal plants; however, in winter on rare occasions, when temperatures drop below 7°C (46°F) at night for any length of time, we cover the east and south sides of our shadehouse with clear plastic to protect the plants from cold winds.

— D&E Penningh

(Southeastern US) Boiler with copper pipes and aluminum fins (hot water). Overhead louvers to control heat in winter. Six-inch Cell Deck in summer with 48-inch suction fan, 2-speed.

— S. Pridgen

*(Northcentral US) Under artificial lighting...temperature is controlled by a window that opens automatically.

— A. Roberts

(Southcentral US) Electric heat in the winter; summer misting in the parts of the greenhouse away from the phal bench and under the phal bench. (The floor under the bench is quarry-tiled (unglazed red clay).

— P. Scholz

(South of England) Winter: solid fuel boiler with hot water pipes plus electric fan heater top-up when necessary (belt and braces). Lots of ventilation (bottom and top) when temperature rises to 75°F during the day.

— P. Seaton

(North of England) With a special 'aspirator' screen. (This device appears to be an electronic, semiconductor temperature sensor with a very narrow range of response time to over- or under-temperatures. It has a photoelectric device which switches the daytime regimen to a nighttime regimen automatically. ed.) The screen is really good and with the alarm box in the house one feels very secure in the knowledge that all is well in the greenhouse. Note: because the aspirator screen is so sensitive to temperature change, I have to have a microswitch on the first-to-open vent...automatically preventing the heating system from coming on when unwanted.

— D. Shuker

(Pacific Northwest US) I use thermostatically-controlled electric heat pads for seedlings.

— S. Skoien

(Midlands of England) Gas-heated hot water system with thermostatic control and electric fans are switched on at all times. Control through independent thermostats.

— F. Smith

*(Northeastern US) Under artificial lighting...To cope with the problem of excessive heat from transformer-type fluorescent ballasts, we switched to the cooler electronic ballast fixtures.

— D&D Strack

(Midlands of England) Heating is by natural gas boiler, heating large cast-iron radiators. The radiators are placed in a near-horizontal position under the bench rather than the conventional method of placing them vertically. This provides a larger heating surface. A greenhouse area of 25 x 12.5 feet is heated by eleven 3- x 3-foot radiators. Water temperature is controlled on the boiler. Circulation is controlled by a simple thermo plug (switch) wired into the water pump.

— H. Taylor

*(Northeastern US) Under artificial lighting...Temperature is controlled thermostatically and with a proper amount of shading. Shading is done with a chalk-based paint for the hot summer days.

— J. Vella

QUESTION 2(c) DO YOU INTENTIONALLY VARY THAT TEMPERATURE AT TIMES? IF SO, WHEN AND BY HOW MUCH?

(Southeastern Australia) No, I have no commercial reason to control flowering.
— M. Black

(Central California US) I 'set' flower spikes by delaying turning on the electric heaters until my phals have been exposed to 50/55°F ambient nighttime temps for about 3 weeks. I do not use my swamp (evaporative) cooler for nighttime cooling and I accept nighttime temps as they occur. Frontal (weather system) passages through the central California valley are very mild in October and nighttime temperature dips are very slight over an extended period. Once buds have formed, however, I set thermostats to maintain 63°F minimum throughout the blooming season.
— R. Buchter

(California Coast US) Yes, October and November temperatures are lowered to 55° at night to help initiation of flower spikes.
— E. Carlson

(Western Australia) I intentionally lower the temperature in January-February, <u>our hottest months</u>, (my emphasis. ed.) to 12-16°C (53-60°F) to initiate spiking.
— K. Clarke

(Indian Coast South Africa) In the past we've tried dropping temperatures in the autumn for about a week to set flower spikes, but have found they do just as well without trying to shock them and we are not really impressed that this really does bring them into spike quicker.
— C. Coll

(Southern California US) Yes, by moving plants from a Warm House to a Cool House.
— D&R Cowden

(Holland) Only in wintertime, when we have sometimes a lack of light, we will lower night- and daytime temperatures to only 18°C (64° from 68°F). In this way we bring the growth and flower development of the plant to a level of the availability of light. If we don't, we may lose buds or flowers may collapse.
— a major commercial grower

(California Coast US) No.
— H. Freed and others

(Mid-Atlantic Coast US) 50°F at night in the fall to induce flowering.
— R. Griesbach and others

(Northeastern US) A period of three weeks of 60-degree night temperature seems plenty to activate blooming for me. I get this much naturally during any cool spell in the summertime. Since my heater is off in the summer, I don't have to do anything to produce such cooling. I rarely would get three solid weeks of 60-degree lows; they would be scattered over the summer.

— D. Grove

(Southeastern US) In the fall (September through October) I intentionally do NOT turn on the heaters when the outside temperature falls to 45 degrees F minimum. (If colder, I fire them up keeping temperatures in the greenhouses above 50 degrees.) Greenhouse temperature drops to 50/55 degrees F without heat. For 3-5 consecutive nights I permit this to occur. By then the cold (weather system) front has passed and outside night temperatures return to 60 degrees plus. Thereafter, the heaters keep the minimum temperature at 68°F for the mature plants. If I do not get sufficient spiking, I'll intentionally drop it at night to 55 for 2 to 3 nights. This is usually not necessary since spikes continue to form readily.

— T. Harper

(Southern California US) The temperatures are varied on mature plants when they are chilled to 55°F for a couple of weeks to initiate spikes.

— E. Hetherington

(Southern California US) No. We do not intentionally vary temperatures at any time.

— D. Hirsch

(Midlands of England) The amount of heat given to my mature plants is not intentionally varied.

— P. Hirst

(California Coast US) If cool, dark weather persists, I raise the minimum temperatures to 65°F.

— T. Koike

(France) We can drop the temperature in order to get the blossoms. If we keep on under 13°C (55°F) each night during 3 week's time, we get the flowering stalk starting out 2 months after.

— Marcel LeCoufle

(Central California US) I don't intentionally vary temperatures, other than when I want to initiate flower spiking.

— B. Livingston

*(Mid-Atlantic Coast US) Under artificial lighting...Phals produce the best growth with warm temperatures and seem to need a wide day/night temperature variance to initiate good blooming. Many phal growers take advantage of cooler temperatures in early fall to initiate

the blooming season by giving their plants night temps in the 50's. I have not found it necessary for phals to experience low temperatures in order to produce spikes. My plants never get that cool.

During the winter months my indoor temps usually vary between 72 degrees during the day and 65 degrees at night; a 7-degree difference. During the summer the difference is usually greater because our air-conditioning units often cannot keep up when we have 95 + degrees outdoors and hot fluorescent lamps indoors. Although the overall room temperature may then go as high as 80°F, the plants may see a temperature in the 90's directly under the lights. When the lights are off at night, the air-conditioning is able to catch up and the temps will drop to 68 or so by morning. I believe this 22-degree spread in day/night temperatures is the main factor which causes most of my phals to begin their spiking in June and July instead of November and December.

Under these circumstances, the temperature factor works toward causing a summer blooming period. It should be understood, then, that temperature 'seasons' as well as controlled light-period 'seasons' can be manipulated by the grower to cause blooming when desired. I do not intentionally manipulate temperatures, but I am taking advantage of the circumstances to promote early blooming.
— E. Merkle

(Please note Mr. Merkle grows under artificial lighting. This kind of control would be difficult under other conditions. ed.)

(California Coast US) Drop to about 55°F nights/70°F days 12-16 weeks prior to desired blooming for about 2 weeks. Keep on the dry side.
— N. Nash

(California Coast US) No, I try to bloom my plants as late in the season as is possible...April and May.
— M&J Nedderman

(Mid-West US) In **March and April** (editor's emphasis. Possibly to initiate summer bloomers such as violacea, amboinensis, and venosa?..if summer bloomers are induced by lowered temperatures and not by longer days as some think. ed.) I let the temps drop to 58°F at night for about 3 weeks. I find dropping the temp will spike even the small plants. The dips in temp do not hurt the plants as they are growing dryer and their maximum growth cycle is just starting.
— R. Pallister

*(Northcentral US) Under artificial lighting.....summer temperature is whatever nature gives us. I have two 18x36-inch windows that are totally open from May to October.
— A. Roberts

(Southcentral US) I allow a natural cool spell in the fall to induce flowering. These occur in Louisiana about the end of October.

— P. Scholz

(North of England) Nights only. I lower the temperature from a norm of 65°F to 60°F about the first of October for a week; to 55°F for the next three weeks; up to 60°F for the next two weeks; and finally back to the 65°F norm thereafter. The heating system is a small, gas-fired boiler with tilting radiators. I have stand-by electrical fan heaters which come on automatically if temperature falls below 53°F at any time.

— D. Shuker

(Midlands of England) For the health of the plants and not to induce flowering, I like to see a 20° differential between day and nighttime temperatures. It is easy to get this difference in the summer when such a difference is natural, but, with the relatively low daytime highs and inflexible nighttime minimums, it is quite impossible on most days.

— H. Taylor

*(Northeastern US) Under artificial lighting...I don't have an active cooling system and when we have one of those heat waves in July or August here in the city, I turn on a one and a half ton air conditioner. When that didn't work, in the past I've used blocks of dry ice to cool things off.

— J. Vella

(California Coast US) I let it dip to 58°F in the fall to initiate spiking.

— J. Watkins and others

(Texas Gulf Coast US) We let temperatures drop to 50°F for 2 weeks in November.

— C&J Wilson

SECTION THREE
WATER/FOOD

(a) Do you keep the potting medium of mature plants moist...or allow it to dry out periodically? (b) What humidity level do you maintain for mature plants? (c) How often do you fertilize mature plants and with what nutrients?   (d) Do you vary the feeding program at times during the life of the plant?   (e) Do you use any special nutrient additives besides those in commercial fertilizers?

SECTION 3.1 WATER/FOOD CONSENSUS AND OPINION

Q 3(a) DO YOU KEEP THE POTTING MEDIUM OF MATURE PLANTS MOIST...OR ALLOW IT TO DRY OUT PERIODICALLY?

The majority favored damp roots, but a few said they allowed their plants to dry out occasionally. None of these gave a reason. Maybe they were listening to the Greek philosopher who advocated 'all things in moderation'. (I'll buy that. I stop drinking wine every now and again just to prove to myself I don't need it. Not for very long though, mind you.) DRYING OUT IS NOT RECOMMENDED FOR PLANTS GROWN IN NEW ZEALAND MOSS. Dried moss becomes waterproof.

Jim Kilgannon's comment summarizes well: "In arid areas, don't let the medium dry out; it may be OK in the maritime or more humid growing areas."

Terry Koike points out that, even in an arid area, he allows his pots to dry out a little in rainy weather. Makes sense, because you wouldn't want to water in wet weather, anyway.

In the natural situation, there is a drying-out period just prior to flower spike induction. For that reason, I ease up a little on watering during autumn before the spikes emerge. I water less in the winter anyway because of lessened evaporation on cooler days. I also lower humidity to decrease probability of pseudomonas cattleyae problems.

All agreed that the medium should be kept moist during spiking.

Q 3(b) WHAT HUMIDITY LEVEL DO YOU MAINTAIN FOR MATURE PLANTS?

I'm suspicious of humidity levels above 60% unless accompanied by an increase in air circulation. For the degree of air circulation I have in my greenhouses, 60% RH is the critical point; above that, I have problems with crown rot and Botrytis in flowering season. Below that, OK.

From 50 to 70% relative humidity seems to be the choice of most, irrespective of climate, with some raising it a few points during flower opening. Makes sense.

Higher humidities do permit longer intervals between watering if air circulation is not excessive, but in my arid climate, I couldn't raise the humidity even with a fire hose in the summer. I feel a little silly with the misting system, which is set at 60%, going while I'm in the greenhouse watering. I thought my humidistat was faulty, but realize now that the cooler blows out the moist air as fast as it is created by the misters. (I'll bet Don Shuker and Patrick Lindsay in the North of England really feel sorry for me with this problem.)

The 'dry mist' or high pressure misting system that Jim and Georgia Johnson use in Phoenix, Arizona, would help. Those systems are used locally to cool down searing-hot summer afternoon patios in the open. They change a 110°F/5%RH patio into 80°F/40%RH right now!

Q 3(c) HOW OFTEN DO YOU FERTILIZE MATURE PLANTS AND WITH WHAT NUTRIENTS?

WATER QUALITY: From the responses, it should be apparent that thinking phal growers should be aware of the content and quality of the water they put on their plants.

Respondents repeatedly indicate they adjust macro- and micro-nutrients to the needs of their plants and to what is or is not provided by their water supply. I think they are saying YOUR NUTRITION PROGRAM STARTS WITH A WATER ANALYSIS. (My city water department analyzes our water every 2 years and is happy to pass the results over the phone when I call.)

PLANT NEEDS: The next logical question would be, "Now that I know what the water has in it, what do my phals need?" Good question. Unfortunately, we do not know, because no one (to my knowledge) has ever done a study on the subject. The Plant and Soil Labs that do your leaf tissue analyses are probably guessing, too. A soil scientist-friend suggested posing phal's needs as a thesis for a graduate plant science student. Until the analysis is done, we can only arrive at a compromise analysis by trial and error.

NITROGEN NEEDS: There is a consensus that the phals need nitrogen when they are growing rapidly and little or none when they are not. No big surprise here.

What should be known to all, but often isn't, is the plant's nitrogen need is generally determined by the amount of light the plant is getting. More light, more nitrogen. Less obvious is opposite: less light, less nitrogen. This rules out the year-round use of the same fertilizing schedule and mandates a fertilizer schedule tied to seasonal changes.

More specifically, nitrogen needs are tied to temperature because temperature determines growth rate: bright light and high temps call for more nitrogen, but bright light and lower temps do not. Low light should be accompanied with lowered temps and a reduced nitrogen diet. Underlying all this is nitrogen's role as the basic determinant of growth. When the plant is growing fast, it needs more nitrogen.

Q 3(d) DO YOU VARY THE FEEDING PROGRAM AT TIMES DURING THE LIFE OF THE PLANT?

As above in general, and more specifically in cloudy weather, temperatures should be reduced and nitrogen withheld to slow growth. The alternative is a soft growth and a proneness to disease. This is the basis for the consensus on low or no nitrogen in winter.

Phalaenopsis ARE NOT HEAVY FEEDERS. 100 to 150 parts per million of nitrogen for periodic feeding is the range most experienced growers favor. That comes to an ounce of 20-20-20 per 10 gallons of water or slightly over half a teaspoon per gallon. The dosage is lower (may be zero) in winter.

Q 3(e) DO YOU USE ANY SPECIAL NUTRIENT ADDITIVES BESIDES THOSE IN COMMERCIAL FERTILIZERS?

As is the case in any inexact 'science', there is a flourishing market for orchid plant additives, the need for which is only vaguely established. A good parallel is the vitamin market in the United States. We all hope for a magic ingredient that will cure all our ills...but the only one those potions correct is the worry over what to do with our money.

It is my belief that if the trace or microelements of magnesium, sulfur, boron, copper, iron, manganese, molybdenum, and zinc are present in a fertilizer...and there are no special added local needs...then, no additives are needed. If local water supplies have elements in such quantity they antagonize the uptake of any other element, then perhaps additives are warranted. The same applies if acid is added to water to lower the pH.

However, SuperThrive, a trace element additive, seems to have widespread use among the American growers, even commercial growers who have an eye fixed on the bottom line...maybe I'd better get some.

EPSOM SALTS: An exception running through these responses, though, is the seasonal need for magnesium sulfate or Epsom salts. Virtually every experienced grower recognized the need for added magnesium sulfate, either as Epsom salts or as dolomite lime, during the flower spike formation period.

The opinions of the few who indicated dosages used ranged from 2 to 8 pounds of Epsom salts per 100 gallons of water. A number of respondents use Epsom salts year-round.

— editor

SECTION 3.2 WATER/FOOD: SELECTED RESPONSES

QUESTION 3(a) DO YOU KEEP THE POTTING MEDIUM OF MATURE PLANTS MOIST... OR ALLOW IT TO DRY OUT PERIODICALLY?

(Indian Coast South Africa) In Durban we don't have a dormant season where growth comes to a standstill, so feeding goes on through the year. I grow in charcoal and do not apply a drying-out period.

— A. Adriaanse

(California Coast US) Plants are watered once a week, except in cold, rainy weather. They probably stay moist in winter, but may dry out in summer during warmer weather.

— L. Batchman

*(Mid-Atlantic Coast US) Under artificial lighting...Moist during the active growing season and when buds are enlarging; drier when trying to set spikes.

— M. Bowell

(Central California US) I keep potting medium moist year-round. I check pots daily and water as necessary; 2- to 3-day interval during hot weather (ambient temp 95/105°F) and 5- to 7-day interval during cooler winter weather.

— R. Buchter

(California Coast US) Moist.

— E. Carlson

(Mid-Atlantic Coast US) We allow them to dry out slightly.

— L. Clouser

*(Northeastern US) Under artificial lighting...I try to allow the medium to dry a little between waterings. Sometimes I think they get too dry, but it's better than being too wet.

— I. Cohen

(Southern California US) Moist; we water twice a week.

— D&R Cowden

(South Australia) Yes; always keep the potting medium moist.

— M. Dennis

(Gulf Coast US) Always slightly damp. Never bone dry.

— J. Eich

(Rome Italy) Normally, I water the plants on Saturday and fertilize on Sunday, but I always let the compost be the indicator of whether it is too damp or too dry. I prefer to keep the medium always humid.

— A. Fanfani

(Holland) Moist.

— A major commercial grower

(California Coast US) Moist to near dry; never dry.

— H. Freed

(Maui Hawaii US) Yes, always moist.

— R. Fukamura

(South Australia) Plants are watered when the top of the pot gets dry.

— D&J Gallagher

(Arizona Desert US) Moist, but our very low humidity in the Phoenix area drys the plants out quickly, so I mist daily in the summer in addition to twice weekly waterings.

— E. Goo

(Mid-Atlantic Coast US) Dry out.

— R. Griesbach

(Atlantic Coast US) We keep plants damp to wet at all times, especially seedlings just out of the flask.

— K. Griffith

(Gulf Coast US) I do not keep potting medium moist at all times.

— J. Grimes

(Northeastern US) Yes, moist.

— D. Grove and others

(Southeastern US) I like to keep the potting medium moist at all times. However, it does dry somewhat between waterings, but never bone-dry. An extended period of cool, damp weather will create havoc with a watering schedule. We often experience these in the November-December and February-March seasonal changes.

— T. Harper

(Indian Coast South Africa I only use charcoal for all plant stages and do allow it to dry out on occasion.

— A. Harris

(Southern California US) We allow our potting medium on mature plants to dry out moderately between watering.

— E. Hetherington

(Midlands of England) Kept moist, particularly with plants in spike.
— P. Hirst

(Arizona Desert US) We try not to let our phals dry out. They are watered every 3 days when temperatures rise to 90+ °F and once a week for the rest of the time.
— J&G Johnson

(Florida Caribbean US) We grow all our plants in New Zealand sphagnum moss and we keep it quite moist.
— W. Kelly

(Southeastern Australia) This is the most difficult aspect of phal culture as judgments regarding the conditions involved are quite subjective and any error of judgment may lead to severe problems such as Botrytis, leaf rot or loss of the roots in the growing media. Aerial roots will be OK with too much water, but cannot survive in an active condition if left without water in low humidity conditions.

For a hard, semiporous medium, I would aim at damp. Knowing that the medium has good moisture retention, I then know that free water will drain out of the pots, but the medium will retain residual absorbed water for an extended period even with high daytime temps and a drop in humidity. I do not let media dry out especially during periods of low humidity or the plants will suffer loss of active root tips and leaf shrivel. The amount of permanent damage is a product of the total conditions experienced. In our climate (Sydney, NSW), it would be quite serious, but in total maritime areas such as Florida, New Zealand, or the Philippines, the damage would not be expected to be as severe.
— J. Kilgannon

(Southern California US) Moist, but drier when the weather is rainy.
— T. Koike

(East Java Indonesia) I keep the potting medium moist by watering every 2 days. I mount the plants with a kind of sphagnum moss, which is actually the roots of certain ferns similar to some kinds of New Zealand sphagnum moss, about one-half inch or one-inch thick on top of the phal roots. The temperature inside the roots increases.
— A. Kolopaking

(Holland) We allow it to dry out periodically.
— H. Kronenberg

(France) We water all the year-round, but less in winter. No real rest period. We keep the media always moist or slightly moist and we water with nutrient solutions especially made for us. We use town water which is especially treated. In the past we have used rainwater kept in tanks beneath the benches, but we fear they may encourage viruses.
— Marcel LeCoufle

(Central California US) I try to keep the plants moist all the time, but not soggy wet. I try not to let them dry out as is done with other genera of orchids.
— B. Livingston

(Florida-Caribbean US) We water our plants about twice a week which would keep them slightly moist.
— L. Lodyga

(Northeastern US) Potting medium is kept moist all the time during the summer. This means watering twice a week for hanging baskets and once a week for pots. In winter, the plants must dry out between waterings because it's so cold.
— B&C Loechel

(Queensland Coast Australia) In the summer months we tend to keep the potting media moist all of the time but, in the winter, we allow the media to more or less dry out between waterings.
— J. Mackinney and others

(Luzon Philippines) We grow them on twigs wrapped with osmunda fibers and keep them moist at all times except when fungal or bacterial diseases come in. Then we keep them dry until new growth, roots and shoots, become evident.
— D. Mendoza

*(Mid-Atlantic Coast US) Under artificial lighting...I keep the potting medium evenly moist at all times and prefer it not dry out. I believe that phal roots are much healthier when kept this way. The whole plant seems to do better when its growing 'momentum' is kept 'rolling' by constantly available moisture.
— E. Merkle

(Southern California US) Never allow them to dry out.
— J. Miller and others

(California Coast US) Most of the time the medium is kept evenly moist but, in the winter, plants are allowed to dry out about once every 4 weeks.
— M&J Nedderman

(Editor's note: there is a school of orchid thought that advocates allowing potted plants to dry out periodically to interrupt the life cycle of some fungi and bacteria present which require constant moisture. In the natural situation, the plants do, indeed, dry out (at least on the surface) and interrupt the life cycles of the microorganisms; but, it is a brief process...and happens frequently, like daily.)

(Mid-Atlantic Coast US) Allow to dry slightly between waterings. More so in October-January.
— M. Owen

(California Coast US) Moist, if our grower does what we want him to do. Water is too saline/alkaline to allow full drying.

— N. Nash

(Note: the reason for not allowing the medium to dry out completely where water is saline, as Ned Nash of Stewart Orchids comments, is that saline solutions, as they dry, become more concentrated and can cause greater injury to roots than they might if kept wet. Lesson: if you have a high salt content in your water, do not allow your potting medium to dry out completely. Heavy use of fertilizers can have the same effect as salty water. The old belief that you can't over-fertilize because the plant will only take what it needs is false. The plant can and will poison itself with too much fertilizer. Periodic flushing is a safety measure.

While most growers have gotten the message to leach fertilizer salts out of their pots by flushing with water periodically, a refinement on the practice is to flush a second time, a few hours after the first, to remove slow-dissolving salts. Use a quart or so for a 6-inch pot with each flush.

Symptoms of salt poisoning are wilted leaves in the daytime when the medium is moist. ed.)

(North Central US) I keep my plants a little on the dry side.

— A. Roberts

(California Coast US) I try to keep the medium moist, but not soaked, at all times. I use pots that are 'holey'. . . with at least ten 3/8ths-inch holes in the bottom and sides of a 6-inch pot.

— F. Robinson

(Mid-Atlantic Coast US) Medium usually retains some degree of moisture.

— E. Rutkowski

(South of England) The medium does dry out between waterings. I find under my conditions that keeping phals too moist is a mistake.

— P. Seaton

(North of England) Whilst I keep plants moist at all times, I do like to feel that they are coming to the dry point on the day I water/feed. I will leave until the next day if we have had a few wet days 'on the trot'. I will also reduce the misting from 11-second bursts to 3-seconds if necessary to enable me to keep to my water/feeding program. I also increase air movement by increasing fan running time.

— D. Shuker

*(Mid-Atlantic Coast US) Under artificial lighting...we had a hot/cold water bathroom shower mixing valve installed at the beginning of the water line that serves both the basement growing area and the 10 x 20-foot greenhouse. With this mixing valve, we use slightly-less-than tepid water year-round. We water one day, spray the next, feed on the third day and on the fourth day, spray again.

— K&M Smeltz

(Midlands of England) Allowed to dry out but, more often that not, they are watered weekly.

— H. Taylor

*(Northeastern US) Under artificial lighting...Moist, most of the time.

— J. Vella

(California Coast US) I can't control it. There are always some too dry and some too wet when I water.

— J. Watkins

Timer setup to shut misters off before sundown...and reduce Botrytis problem. 24VDC power supply is interupted by the timer. Use a plastic wire bundle tie to secure.

QUESTION 3(b) WHAT HUMIDITY LEVEL DO YOU MAINTAIN FOR MATURE PLANTS?

(California Coast US) 50%. I keep the plants on racks over dishpans of water and mist them as necessary.
— W. Adams

(Indian Coast South Africa) Optimum is 70 to 95% RH (relative humidity), but in full summer, it will run up to 100% and sometimes more! The plants seem to love high humidity.
— A. Adriaanse

(California Coast US) We keep humidity at about 70% during the warm part of the day by a fog system. Plants are allowed to dry off in the evening.
— L. Batchman

(Southeastern Australia) I don't allow humidity to fall below 60%, although I experience some difficulty in reducing it in our winter (Doncaster, VIC) to a figure below 90%.
— M. Black

(Central California US) 50 to 70% RH. The floor of the greenhouse is covered with 6 inches of medium-sized 'trap rock' (gravel) which I hose down morning and noon on dry, warm days. During winter or foggy weather, I ventilate the greenhouse after watering with portable fans until plants and walkways are dry. This sometimes takes 6 to 8 hours. I water only on sunny, clear days in the winter.
— R. Buchter

(California Coast US) Average 60%. For the home grower, humidity can be added to the atmosphere surrounding the plant by placing the pot on a shallow dish or tray containing pebbles and water. Keep the level of the water just below the top level of the pebbles. Never let the water touch the bottom of the pot because capillary action will take place and cause water to rise into the pot. This will create a soaked condition of the bark surrounding the roots which then will soon rot.
— E. Carlson

*(Northeastern US) Under artificial lighting...Around 70%.
— I. Cohen

(Southern California US) 50%.
— D&R Cowden

(South of England) 75 to 90%
— R. Dadd

(South Australia) 80%, if possible.
— M. Dennis

73

(Rome Italy) I try to maintain between 60 and 100% humidity in the greenhouse.
— A. Fanfani

(Holland) If possible, around 70% RH.
— a major commercial grower

(California Coast US) Around 60%.
— H. Freed

(Mid-Atlantic Coast US) In order to improve humidity for aerial roots, which are often the most active and the most receptive to fertilizer, I place the plants close together and try not to move them. Aerial roots will grow between the pots and do extremely well in an atmosphere of 80-90% humidity. Such a humidity level in the greenhouse generally would make the plants extremely susceptible to disease. I also mist under the benches in order to humidify the roots growing down out of the pots.

For windowsill growers, a way to increase humidity is to aim a small fan at a tray of water on its way to the plants. Be sure the fan intake is from a warm air source or the 'wind chill' factor from cold, damp air will stress the plants.
— M. Frier

(Maui Hawaii US) We have a natural 65% or so humidity.
— R. Fukamura

(Southern California US) I think 60% RH is quite adequate for good culture of Phalaenopsis, at least where I live in semidesert conditions. I'd like to be able to keep it higher during the brightest part of a summer day to be better able to cope with the high lighting (1,500 to 1,600 fc) I'd like to give my plants, but there's always the bugaboo of Botrytis and crown rot.

A flaw in most misting systems (humidity control) that complicates the problem of delivering ideal humidity is their failure to anticipate the end of the day. Most systems keep on wetting things down right up to the set point on the humidistat...as the daytime high temperature is coming down and the relative humidity is rising. A problem here is there is a lag in the point where the water is misted and the point where the mist is converted to the water vapor that influences the humidistat...and the result is an over-shoot of the relative humidity in the evening hours. I suspect this is when the Botrytis proliferates.

The solution to the problem may be a timer that cuts off the power to the misting system solenoid valve 3 hours or so earlier than if the system was left on. I set a timer to return power to the system after the humidistat has opened and shut off the water; this resets the system for the following day. (Set the 'off' for 3:00PM or so, and 'on' for 10:00PM.) This arrangement would permit high humidity during the day when it is needed and shut it off in time to prevent an overshoot in RH during the evening hours.

74

I have a 24 VAC-operated solenoid valve (from a lawn sprinkling system) in the misting system, so I mounted the 24 VAC power transformer on a household timer, and the timer interrupts its power supply. If you have a solenoid valve in your misting system, put the timer between the solenoid valve and its power supply. You could also use the timer to operate a relay in the power lead to the solenoid. My arrangement was the cheapest solution I could come up with. Total cost for the modification: less than US $10.00. . .for the timer.
— editor

(Northeastern US) I aim for 70 to 80% RH with lots of good air movement around each and every plant. . .or else you get lots of bacterial rot and fungi.
— D. Grove

(Florida Atlantic Coast US) Being located in North Florida and on a large river, our humidity stays at 70% or better year-round.
— C&L Hagan

(Southeastern US) Humidity is maintained at 60% for mature plants and seedlings. There is a considerable variation in the relative humidity, however. Night humidities in summer can go to 80 + %, while days are sometimes 15/20% in the winter on cold, bright, dry days. (Spider mites can be a real problem then.) Wet pads do the job in summer. A misting system over the floor does it in the winter. Both of these are on humidistats and timers.
— T. Harper

(Indian Coast South Africa) Ambient conditions seem to be adequate, but I do have my pots standing on a layer of stone which tends to collect excess water. This would be inclined to increase the relative humidity.
— A. Harris

(Southern California US) Mature plants, 50 to 85% RH.
— E. Hetherington

(Arizona Desert US) We control humidity with a dry misting system (high pressure) set at 65% RH.
— J&G Johnson

(The 'dry mist' system produces a fog so fine it does not settle to the ground and functions effectively also as a cooling system in at least two greenhouses in Phoenix, where 115°F summer temps are not unusual. ed.)

(Southeastern Australia.) Regarding the ideal humidity for phals, I work on the assumption that in a glasshouse the plants have two root systems to consider:

Firstly, there are the roots growing within the medium in the pot. These roots require an environment that is mainly damp. The medium will take up water and still allow excess water to drain away. I like media to have an open texture through which air can, to some extent, be free to circulate. The moisture level of the solids of the medium will be drawn out by the roots and it will gradually become dry. There is also a basic drying-out by the atmosphere, this being determined by the relative humidity in the growing area.

The second system is the free roots that prefer not to penetrate the medium, but wave in the breeze or adhere to the wooden bench tops.

The first system requires a low relative humidity to ensure that excess moisture is removed as soon as possible after watering in order to reduce the likelihood of bacterial or fungal rot. The low relative humidity will stress the leaves and the exposed roots...which I consider more effective and important in a glasshouse situation than those in the pot.

As a compromise, therefore, a relative humidity of 60 to 70% is desirable in our area (Sydney), but moving up in very hot conditions.
— J. Kilgannon

(Southern California US) Whatever can be maintained by wet wall pads and misters under the benches.
— T. Koike

(Central California US) I try to keep 50-60% humidity. It can vary, though, just as it does in nature.
— B. Livingston and others

(Florida Caribbean US) 50% or higher.
— L. Lodyga

(Texas Gulf Coast US) 70% and up. Houston is very humid.
— J. Margolis

(Luzon Philippines) Estimate 80 to 85% RH. (natural environment)
— D. Mendoza

*(Mid-Atlantic Coast US) Under artificial lighting...A home atmosphere in the temperate zones tends to be dry, especially during the winters when heating systems can drive humidity levels down to 10%. I keep the humidity directly around my plants at about 60% by lightly spray-misting them most mornings and by growing them on top of plastic 'egg crate' grates placed over trays containing an inch or so of water. The water in the trays evaporates and produces a local rise in humidity that is satisfactory to the plants. At one time I kept moist gravel in the trays, but algae and various critters multiplied quite rapidly in there, so now I use straight water with some Physan added to control any algal growth.
— E. Merkle

(California Coast US) Ambient. We're about one mile from the Pacific Ocean coast, but we try for 50% RH minimum. We don't measure it...we feel it.
— N. Nash

(California Coast US) Normally about 50%, but higher during blooming times.
— M&J Nedderman

(Mid-Atlantic Coast US) 60 to 90% optimum. System controlled with a humidistat and centrifugal humidifiers.
— M. Owen

(Southeastern US) 62% with under-bench, automatic misters.
— S. Pridgen

(Florida Gulf Coast US) We don't have to control humidity. We usually have all we want and more.
— J&M Roberts

(Queensland Coast Australia) Natural coastal humidity is satisfactory.
— R. Robinson

(Southcentral US) 30%. Fluctuations in humidity (so long as the plants are properly watered) seem to produce healthier plants.
— P. Scholz

(South of England) I maintain a high, unmeasured RH in my greenhouse, but I also allow the potting medium to dry out before watering. I think it is important to make that distinction because the two are interrelated. I maintain the high humidity by damping down the concrete floor, under-bench gravel, and staging. I think the moist staging is important because of the need to keep moist air near the plants.
— P. Seaton

(North of England) I try to maintain the humidity at around 70% using an automatic misting system.
— D. Shuker

(British Columbia Coast Canada) I have three large water dishes with rocks in them and plants on them for humidity. I keep these filled with water.
— L. Slade

*(Mid-Atlantic Coast US) Under artificial lighting...we have a cabinet-type humidifier in the basement of the house with the plants and operate it when needed during furnace-running time. Under the majority of the bench area, we have a layer of 'Terragreen' (baked clay). This porous material absorbs and holds water. This entire system allows us to maintain 50 to 60% RH most of the time.
— K&M Smeltz

(Midlands of England) 60-80%.
— F. Smith

*(Northeastern US) Under artificial lighting...Summer 60%; winter 40%.
— D&D Strack

(Oahu Hawaii US) Don't control it. It's natural.
— R. Takase

(Midlands of England) 80-90% relative humidity.
— H. Taylor

*(Northeastern US) Under artificial lighting...I keep the humidity set at 50-65% of saturation.
— J. Vella

(California Coast US) 40 to 60% RH.
— J. Watkins

(Mid-Atlantic Coast US) Between Nature, watering and the humidifiers, I keep between 80 and 90% RH the whole time.
— J. Webster

QUESTION 3(c) HOW OFTEN DO YOU FEED MATURE PLANTS AND WITH WHAT NUTRIENTS?

(Indian Coast South Africa) I feed once every seven days with a balanced compound which I make myself.
— A. Adriaanse

(California Coast US) I fertilize the plants at each watering with a home-mixed 30-12-12 fertilizer made from urea, mono-ammonium phosphate and potassium nitrate with a small amount of trace element supplement added. Fertilizer composition is not varied throughout the year.
— L. Batchman

(Southeastern Australia) On the basis of probable paucity of fertiliser in nature, mature plants are fertilised only once in 6 to 8 weeks.
— M. Black

(Central California US) I fertilize every 3 weeks using ROMEO-brand 24-10-18 (cheaper than Peters). Prior to this year I was using Peters 30-10-10 and 10-30-20. I'll let you know next year how this works out!
— R. Buchter

(Southern California US) I limit the total dissolved solids in the fertilizer water to 1,000 PPM. Local tap water is about 200, so I divide the remaining 800 PPM equally among nitrogen, phosphorous and potash in an 18-18-18 fertilizer. This necessitates using the fertilizer at one-half the recommended rate on the package (full strength = 473 PPM nitrogen).
— E. Campuzano

(California Coast US) Every watering with a 30-10-20 formula.
— E. Carlson

(Western Australia) I fertilize twice weekly in summer and once every 2 weeks in the winter. The only nutrients I use is Nitrosol and, when spikes appear, I add a little potash.
— K. Clarke

*(Northeastern US) Under artificial lighting...I fertilize weekly, rotating among various brands. I use more nitrogen in the spring and summer.
— I. Cohen

(I find Osmocote 14-14-14 very useful for feeding seedlings, especially those just out of the flask. They go very well with the already good accommodation of New Zealand moss for the little ones, because with the moss you water (feed) less often. The slow-release nature of Osmocote suits the seedlings just fine, but keep the beads out of seedling crowns. The beads are hygroscopic, that is they attract moisture, and act as a lightning rod for crown rot. ed.)

(Southern California US) I fertilize when we repot and again 6 months later with 18-18-18 Osmocote (slow release pellets).
— D&R Cowden

(Mid-Atlantic Coast US) We feed every 3rd or 4th watering in spring and summer and every 5th or 6th watering in fall and winter.
— L. Clouser

(Indian Coast South Africa) We calculate the amount of feed needed in a 7-day period, break that amount down into one-seventh the concentration and apply it **daily** to the plants and potting material with a 10-litre, hand-pumped spray. Since our phalies are grown under controlled conditions, the only exception to that feeding schedule is very wet, rainy days. The plants don't get wet from the rain, but because we're right on the sea, the humidity is very high. On these days, we don't feed.

We feed with 19-8-16 plus trace elements.
— C&I Coll

(Southern California US) I use a commercial fertilizer (20-20-20), year-round, every other time I water.
— W. Cousineau and others

(South Australia) Weekly with 30-10-10 from October to May (summer Down Under) and Blossom Booster (high phos) from May to September, alternating feeds weekly with blood-bone liquid feed (Nitrosol).
— M. Dennis

(Mid-Atlantic Coast US) I fertilize with every watering with an injection-type proportioner. I find Peter's 20-20-20 to be a good, general purpose fertilizer.
— R. Drejka

(Florida Gulf Coast US) Twice monthly: May through August with 30-10-10. September through April with 20-20-20. Trace elements are added to all fertilizer solutions.
— J. Eich

(Holland) With every watering except when plants have just been repotted.
— A major commercial grower

(California Coast US) Usually twice each month with a fertilizer formula recommended by a Soil and Plant Lab (derived from leaf tissue analysis).
— H. Freed

(Maui Hawaii US) I fertilize seedlings every week with Peters 30-10-10, one teaspoon per gallon. Mature plants get Peters 20-20-20, one teaspoon per gallon. In winter, I feed every other week.
— R. Fukamura

(Mid-Atlantic Coast US) With every watering — 100 parts per million nitrogen from 20-20-20 fertilizer with trace elements.

— R. Griesbach

(Atlantic Coast US) Seedlings just out of the flask are fed once a week with 27-15-12, one teaspoon per gallon. Mature plants are fed the same in the spring and summer, then in the fall we go over to 10-30-20. Mature plants are fed twice a month in the spring, summer and fall and only once a month in the winter.

— K. Griffith

*(Gulf Coast US) Under artificial lighting...I usually feed with Peter's fertilizer, ¼ teaspoon per gallon, once a week. I use a balanced fertilizer in the summer and early fall and 10-30-10 in the late fall to late spring. Occasionally use a small amount of trace element supplement.

— J. Grimes

(Northeastern US) Every week or two during period of most active growth, scaling down to once monthly during cold, gray periods in the winter. I use a balanced fertilizer most of the time, with occasional use of 30-10-10 in the spring and summer. Also, I occasionally use a high phosphate fertilizer, so-called 'Blossom Booster', when plants begin to spike. I am not very systematic in my choice of fertilizers.

— D. Grove

(Florida Atlantic Coast US) Various Peters fertilizers, twice a week; once a month we add fish oil.

— C&L Hagan

(Southeastern US) Fertilizer is provided with each watering at the rate of one teaspoon per gallon. I use the modest Hozon Syphonex with very good results. (why pay more?)? I presoak my bark with various additives, including urea fertilizer, then provide the regular feed of 20-20-20 plus SuperThrive (one tablespoon per five gallons) plus one tablespoon of Sequestrene (a chelated iron additive).

I've been considering the following change in my method of feeding: Bark presoak with 20-20-20 plus dolomite lime plus Physan. Then, I'll use 30-10-10 during the growing season and change to 10-30-20 during the blooming season. In this way, the balance of the nutrients would always be available for the plant, and a boost from the watering fertilizer would provide the extra nutrients to meet the needs of the plants for the season. Makes sense to me. What do you think?

— T. Harper

Tom, I favor the use of fertilizer in presoaking <u>seedling</u> mix only. I agree with the rest of your program other than that. The nitrogen won't last too long, because it leaches out quickly, but while it does, it will provide a nutrient soup for microorganisms on the surface of the bark...and accelerate the breakdown. This is also the case whenever an excess of nitrogen is used in the feeding program. With the poor grade of fir bark we've been getting recently, that could mean a significant shortening of the medium's useful life. With seedlings, life of the bark is less important, because they're usually repotted every 6-12 months, anyway.

With the use of dolomite lime, you may not need to use Epsom salts. Dolomite contains magnesium as well as calcium; the regular grade of limestone flour contains only calcium. The orchid's need for magnesium has been established, but what has not been established is when they need it. Most annual crops do well with magnesium added to the soil when it is prepared for planting rather than during the life cycle. Most contributors here agree the time for Epsom salts is autumn.

— editor

(Indian Coast South Africa) Once weekly, mainly with 18-18-18.
— A. Harris

(California Coast US) We (Rod McLellan Co.) have a periodic tissue analysis done by an outside laboratory in order to vary our fertilizing program to meet current needs of a mixed orchid collection. Based on this lab's recommendation, we use an average amount per plant of 1/8th teaspoon of magnesium sulfate (Epsom salts) with every watering as a source of magnesium. This is a secondary nutrient not often considered by other growers. This recommendation, of course, relates to our particular water quality (source: South San Francisco municipal water supply), our potting media (bark), and other cultural factors.
— S. Hawkins

(Southern California US) We feed mature plants every ten days to two weeks at a rate of one pound of 30-10-10 fertilizer to 100 gallons of water.
— E. Hetherington

(Southern California US) In summer, every 2 weeks; in winter, about monthly using Peter's 30-10-10 with a small amount of phosphoric acid added to lower pH to under neutral.
— D. Hirsch

(Midlands of England) A 20-20-20 fertiliser is applied at half-strength with almost every watering during the period of March through October.
— P. Hirst

(Florida Caribbean US) Plants are watered twice a week on a 15-minute cycle. While they are being watered, an injection system supplies fertilizer at a ratio of 1/8th gram per liter of water. (1 ounce to 62.5 gallons; or about 1 teaspoon in 10 gallons; or 125 PPM of nitrogen) We use a commercially-made liquid delivering a 10-10-10 ratio. No chlorine is added. We can adjust the feed rate in summer for added growth. Once a month we withhold all chemicals and flush out the pots. Aqua-Solv is also injected constantly to keep our heavy lime deposits in suspension.
— W. Kelly

(Southeastern Australia) During the summer to early autumn I apply quarter-strength balanced fertilizer on a weekly basis. Nitrogen can be increased in bark-based media. Experience alone can guide the grower to the amount of fertilizer needed because the amount and the quality of the sunlight received is going to determine that. More specifically, the range and amount of each wave band through from the infrared to ultraviolet will control the feed consumed. The plant must not be allowed to become too 'luxuriant'. This is akin to a human being overfed and under-exercised. Balance the nitrogen to give a hard yellow-green leaf, but a fast, new leaf growth rate. Judge the rate of growth by observing the progression of the wettable powder fungicide marks left in the base of the new leaf.

I believe that automotive emission buildup over a city cuts out a lot of the useful light energy. Long periods of overcast weather during the 'wet' season require a cutback in fertilizer to prevent the growing medium from becoming sour. Buildup of chemicals under these conditions causes 'starvation' as it lowers the osmotic pressure of the moisture in the potting medium, stopping transfer of moisture to the roots.
— J. Kilgannon

(East Java Indonesia) Nutrients with Gandasill once a week. When they receive more sunlight, they get more nutrient.
— A. Kolopaking

(Holland) In the growing season, once per month, 28-12-10 at the rate of 1 gram per liter. In the winter, no feeding.
— H. Kronenberg

(Central California US) I fertilize every time I water, full strength, flushing out the pots with water (no chemicals) every 5th watering. We mix our own chemicals. We use ammonium nitrate, calcium nitrate, phosphoric acid, muriate of potash, magnesium sulfate and iron chelate. These chemicals are used in two formulas and I alternate them. The compounds were formulated for use with our local water.
— B. Livingston

(Florida Caribbean US) We use Peters 20-20-20 year-round. We use Bloom Booster (10-30-20) in the late summer/early fall once a month till spikes are showing.
— L. Lodyga

(Queensland Coast Australia) In spring we apply slow-release 18-2.6-19 fertilizer. Since the manufacturer of this fertilizer raised the iron content to .15%, we've noticed stronger growth.
— J. Mackinney

(Luzon Philippines) We fertilize every other day during watering time at the rate of one tablespoon to three gallons of water with:

    30-10-10...after blooming for 2 months.

    18-18-18...thereafter for 4 to 6 weeks.

    10-20-30...thereafter until blooming and the cycle is repeated.

          — D. Mendoza

(Southeastern Australia) We fertilise weekly alternating Aqua-sol, Wuxul, and Nitrosol.

          — A. Merriman

(Queensland Coast Australia) Fertilize usually once per week with a foliar fertilizer. About once each month I apply a drench of filtered liquid cow manure through a Syphonex.

          — R. Merritt

(Southern California US) We fertilize once every two weeks in summer and once a month and even less in winter. We use Peters 20-20-20 at a concentration of 150 parts per million of nitrogen with no further additives or variation of formula.

          — J. Miller

(Southern California US) Every other week with 20-20-20.

          — H. Moye and others

(California Coast US) Feed, with every watering, half-strength fertilizer. We use 30-10-10 for three waterings, 6-30-30 once and then back to the 30-10-10.

          — N. Nash

(California Coast US) I fertilize with quarter-strength 20-20-20 weekly. About every 6 weeks the pots are flushed to prevent salt buildup.

          — M&J Nedderman

(Mid-Atlantic Coast US) One time every two to four weeks with 20-20-20 from March through August. Monthly with 10-30-20 through October. One time every six weeks with 15-15-15 November through February.

          — M. Owen

(Mid-West US) I use Peters 30-10-10 from March through September, 10-30-20 from September through November; and I do not fertilize December through March. I fertilize every two weeks at 150 ppm of nitrogen with the water adjusted to a pH of 5.8 to 6.0 (slightly acid) with phosphoric acid. I add four tablespoons of Epsom salts to the fertilizer in my Merit Proportioner.

          — R. Pallister

(Queensland Coast Australia) We fertilize every week in the summer and every 3 to 4 weeks in the winter.

          — D&E Penningh

(California Coast US) Fertilize weekly with half-strength 20-20-20, except in the winter months of December and January, when I use half-strength 15-30-20.
— F. Robinson

(Mid-Atlantic Coast US) I use a uniform feeding program with slight fertilization with every watering throughout the year, with no special additives.
— E. Rutkowski

(Southcentral US) Every other watering alternating 20-20-20 and 10-20-30.
— P. Scholz

(South of England) During active growth most of the year I feed with two of every three waterings. I use no fertiliser in the third watering because I'm told it is useful to flush out accumulated salts, but I'm not convinced of that. As orchids are relatively slow growing, I use half-strength of a balanced fertiliser in spring and summer and begin to use 5-5-10 from the end of July onwards to stimulate flowering and 'harden' growth.
— P. Seaton

(North of England) February through early autumn: two consecutive feedings with 20-20-20, followed by one of 12.5-25-25 and then flush with plain water. Late autumn through February: two consecutive feedings with 10-30-10 followed by a flush with plain water on the third watering.
— D. Shuker

*(Mid-Atlantic Coast US) Under artificial lighting...we use either Peters or Millers 30-10-10 much of the time. During autumn and sometimes in the spring, we use 20-20-20 or 10-30-20. We use an M&P proportioner with a 50:1 dilution factor that gives us about 100 PPM nitrogen in the final feed solution.
— K&M Smeltz

(Oahu Hawaii US) At least once a month during June, July and August with high nitrogen. Other months, 12.5-25-25.
— R. Takase

*(Northeastern US) Under artificial lighting...Every 20 days with 30-10-10, 20-20-20, or 15-30-15 at half- or quarter-strength.
— J. Vella

(Mid-Atlantic Coast US) I try to use fertilizers that have little or no urea. The incidence of pseudomonas seems to me to be directly proportional to the amount of urea in the fertilizer. I believe fertilizing should be reduced during times of seasonal temperature changes because the plants seem to show softer growth (or stress) and are more susceptible to infection at these times. I lose more plants than I should during these times.
— M. Werther

(Texas Gulf Coast US) We feed every week, year-round, three times with 30-10-10, then once with 9-59-8.

— C&J Wilson

QUESTION 3(d) DO YOU VARY THE FEEDING PROGRAM AT TIMES DURING THE LIFE OF THE PLANT?

(Southeastern Australia) For mature plants, no, but I feed juvenile plants in perlite/peat every 5 days.
— M. Black

(Central California US) I always flush pots with clear water the day before fertilizing to leach out any accumulated salts and ensure the velum coating on the roots is spongy and receptive to nutrients.
— R. Buchter

(Southern California US) I sprinkle dry MagAmp (slow-release 7-40-6) directly on top of the medium in the fall.
— E. Campuzano

(Indian Coast South Africa) Every second month we add 1 kg of Magsulphate (Epsom salts) to a 100-gallon drum of water and all plants watered on that day are fed.
— C&I Coll

(Mid-Atlantic Coast US) Sometimes an application of MagAmp (7-40-6, slow-release) will encourage a plant to flower almost continuously from the main spike on through a secondary spike. After the last flower dies, I remove the flower spike from below the first flower scar. This seems to encourage a secondary flower spike.
— R. Drejka

(Editor's Note. REGARDING THE USE OF MAGAMP, ANY HIGH PHOS FERTILIZER OR PHOSPHORIC ACID to lower the pH of water used for feeding your phals:

"The unusually high level of phosphorus in MagAmp can result in the reduced availability of iron, manganese, copper, and zinc in the root media. Careful attention should be paid to the micronutrient fertilizer program as a result. This fertilizer also contains 12% magnesium (Mg) which is high enough to antagonize the uptake of calcium in some plants and result in serious nutritional problems. Special care should be exercised to maintain calcium at a moderately high level in the root media to avert a deficiency. This problem is particularly important in areas where the water supply has a low calcium content. MagAmp at one-third the normally recommended rate supplemented with periodic liquid fertilizer is suggested in New England."
— (Nelson, 1981)[1]

---

[1]. Nelson, P., 1981 Fertilization. Greenhouse Operation and Management. Reston Publishing, Reston, Virginia 22090

(The PureGro Company, West Sacramento, CA makes a supplement to compensate for the problem Mr. Nelson refers to above; Leaf Life Complexed [11%] Copper-Iron-Manganese-Zinc. ed.)

In the book reference above, Mr. Nelson also details some common 'antagonisms', or rooting medium situations in which an excessively high level of one nutrient can cause a deficiency in another. These include:

NUTRIENT IN EXCESS	INDUCED DEFICIENCY
Nitrogen	Potassium
Potassium	Nitrogen
Potassium	Calcium
Potassium	Magnesium
Sodium	Potassium
Sodium	Calcium
Sodium	Magnesium
Calcium	Magnesium
Calcium	Boron
Magnesium	Calcium
Magnesium	Iron
Iron	Magnesium

(Holland) Yes.
— A major commercial grower

(Mid-Atlantic Coast US) No.
— R. Griesbach and others

(Northeastern US) No, but perhaps I should use 30-10-10 in a weak solution more often for small plants.
— D. Grove

(Southeastern US) Presently, I do not vary the supply of nutrients to the plants. However, I do water without chemicals every fourth watering to flush out the pots. I believe that consistency pays off when it comes to watering.
— T. Harper

(Southern California US) We do not feed during cold weather. Sometimes during the growing season we vary two or three times with the 10-30-30 and once with 6-30-30.
— E. Hetherington

(Southern California US) Yes. We use 10-30-20 to induce flowering in December and January.
— D. Hirsch

(Southeastern Australia) Yes, I replace the NPK (nitrogen-phosphorus-potassium) fertilizer with Epsom salts (magnesium sulfate) for 4 to 6 weeks prior to and during flower spike initiation. I also give extra potash and drop the nitrogen level during spike growth and the early part of the flowering season.

— J. Kilgannon

(Texas Gulf Coast US) About every 5 or 6 weeks I leach with water, rainwater, if possible.
— J. Margolis

*(Mid-Atlantic Coast US) Under artificial lighting...During active growth I use a high nitrogen fertilizer to encourage good tissue substance and to discourage the plant from blooming.

— E. Merkle

(California Coast US) Rarely. Only if the plants look a bit soft and aren't producing spikes do we stop the 30-10-10 and go to all 6-30-30 for 2 to 4 weeks.
— N. Nash

(California Coast US) In the late fall and winter, I use 6-30-30 to help flowering and spike formation.

— M&J Nedderman

(Indian Coast South Africa) We do not alter our fertiliser for spiking or leaf growth as we find that our phals do well left alone.
— G. Paris

(Queensland Coast Australia) No, but perhaps we should.
— R. Robinson

(Southcentral US) After August 15, I use 10-20-30 only.
— P. Scholz

(Pacific Northwest US) For seedlings we use 30-10-10 and we use it more often than for mature plants. Near flowering, we use 10-30-20.
— S. Skoien and others

*(Northeastern US) Under artificial lighting...Mature plants are switched to 10-30-20 in late winter.

— D&D Strack

QUESTION 3(e) DO YOU USE ANY SPECIAL NUTRIENT ADDITIVES BESIDES THOSE IN COMMERCIAL FERTILIZERS?

[Note: see numerous references to the use of Epsom salts (magnesium sulfate) in the preceding question, 3(d). Magnesium will be considered a macronutrient for the purpose of this text and will be discussed in both sections.]

(Indian Coast South Africa) I do not use tap water straight, but pump from lily ponds with a good fish population, so there is a fairly good supply of trace elements and minerals. If some addition has to be made, I use the standard preparations.
— A. Adriaanse

(Southern California US) Phosphoric acid, 1 ounce per 100 gallons of water (local water is about pH 8.0); Epsom salts, 4 pounds per 100 gallons of water for two feedings in late September.
— E. Campuzano

(California Coast US) Epsom salts applied at the rate of one tablespoon per gallon during the winter months will increase the plant's resistance to cool temperatures. I feed my plants twice a month with Epsom salts October through February and thereafter once each month for the rest of the year. I also use zinc, copper and iron chelates.
— E. Carlson

*(Northeastern US) Under artificial lighting...I use seaweed once a month and SuperThrive almost every week. I always use a brand of fertilizer which contains trace elements and use Miracid every few months to compensate for our hard water.
— I. Cohen and others

(Mid-Atlantic Coast US) I use calcium nitrate and Sequestrene 330Fe [an iron chelate to correct iron deficiency] as supplements, especially during active growth periods.
— R. Drejka

(Northeastern US) Yes — trace elements such as Peters STEM (Soluble Trace Element Mix) or chelated iron. Also SuperThrive or Best Grow. I don't know if the trace elements and SuperThrive do any good. Maybe they merely help to make me feel 'I care'.
— D. Grove and many others

(Florida Atlantic Coast US) SuperThrive.
— C&L Hagan and others

(Southeastern US) SuperThrive and iron chelate (Sequestrene). Like many others, I've admired the quality of Zuma Canyon's plants and wondered why mine don't grow like that. Do you

think they are growing them 'in the dark' as seedlings (reduced light with high nitrogen fertilizer), then initiating spikes with a cool shock?
— T. Harper

I also admire the quality of Zuma Canyon's plants Tom, but they certainly don't grow their seedlings in the dark. I've never noticed anything different about their greenhouses from the norm...other than cleanliness. They're some of the cleanest I've ever seen. Perhaps they pay more attention to the basics than most of us do.

We may never know the Vasquez's secret, but the Malibu Coast has nearly perfect Phalaenopsis in-culture conditions. Temps are cool and stable; breeze is constant; humidity is moderate with the Pacific Ocean less than a mile away; and insolation, or the amount of sunlight reaching the earth, is unparalleled. Ever wonder why the movie stars buy property there? Now you know. [The only property values I know of that even come close to those of Malibu, though, are in downtown Tokyo.]

It sure beats hell out of the edge of the Mojave Desert where I live; but then we don't have high surf, forest fires, rockslides, traffic jams on the Pacific Coast Highway and tourists by the ton, either. Amado's 40 years of experience and natural talent with phals are probably the answer.
— editor

(Indian Coast South Africa) In the summer I feed with a weak solution of liquid fowl manure.
— A. Harris

(Southern California US) Phosphoric acid as an additive to fertilizer at the rate of one-half ounce per 85 gallons of water...all year-round.
— D. Hirsch

(Midlands of England) About one ounce of calcified seaweed (lithothamnium calcarium; contains minerals and trace elements. ed.) is added to each 20 litres of compost. One salt-spoon of this product is also sprinkled onto each pot on two occasions during the summer period.
— P. Hirst and others

(Eastcentral US) I put the used-up charcoal from my fish tank (fresh water) filters into potting mix. Phals seem to like it.
— K. Kehew

(Florida Caribbean US) We inject SuperThrive weekly.
— W. Kelly

(Holland) In the potting medium, we add some chalk and minor (trace) elements, both at a rate of 1 gram per kilogram.
— H. Kronenberg

(Queensland Coast Australia) We add Wuxal at half-strength once a fortnight during summer and once a month during winter. We intend using a fertilizer with a higher iron content in future as it has been proved that any wood- or bark-based potting medium requires extra iron, up to 0.2% or even as high as 0.25%. We did use slow release iron for a period and found much stronger leaf substance and less bacterial rot.
— J. Mackinney

(Texas Gulf Coast US) Four times a year I give my plants fish emulsion (fertilizer). With every watering I add SuperThrive and Medina D+E.
— J. Margolis

(Southern California US) Every 3 months I add a half teaspoon of Terra Vite (trace elements).
— M. McCooey

(Southeastern Australia) Extra iron chelates and magnesium are added to the commercial preparations.
— A. Merriman

(California Coast US) Nope.
— N. Nash

(California Coast US) I add calcium nitrate and chelated iron to the standard 20-20-20 formula. This, I think, prompts better growth, especially during summer and spring when phals can be grown rather rapidly. It also prevents yellowing when plants are grown with more light.
— M&J Nedderman

(Queensland Coast Australia) I leave that to nature.
— R. Robinson

(Southcentral US) I add calcium nitrate three or four times a year because our water contains little calcium.
— P. Scholz

(Midlands of England) I add Sea Gold, a calcified seaweed, in large quantities to my potting mix. The compound contains trace elements which are, in my opinion, essential to good growth.
— H. Taylor

*(Northeastern US) Under artificial lighting...Iron sulfate and SuperThrive, every other month, for a strong root system.
— J. Vella

(California Coast US) Occasionally add trace elements and vitamin B1.
— J. Watkins

(California Coast US) Sequestrene 330FE (iron chelate).
— J. Wilson

SECTION FOUR
AIR CIRCULATION

(a) To what degree do you circulate air around your plants? (b) Do you vary the amount of air circulation and, if so, how much, how and why? (c) What do you see as the reason for circulating air in a phal growing area?

SECTION 4.1
CONSENSUS AND OPINION

Q 4(a) TO WHAT DEGREE DO YOU CIRCULATE AIR AROUND YOUR PLANTS?

The need for air movement around phalaenopsis plants was almost universally supported. Two who did not agree were, oddly enough, Dutch. The major commercial grower, who asked that their name not be printed, cited 'bad culture' as the only reason for moving air in a phal greenhouse.

I think I can understand that. It is a preventive measure against the possibility of bacterial and fungal problems...and in very large greenhouses I imagine the cost of the systems to move air would be substantial and may not be economically feasible when plotted against the cost of a few lost plants. Large volume greenhouses, too, are likely to have their own convection currents, perhaps enough to offset the need for mechanical help. Given their sales volume of one million flowering phals each year, it seems likely they have a complete disease prevention program that leaves few problems left to be solved by air circulation. It may also be significant that two of the biggest growers of phals in Florida, Jones & Scully and Orchid World International, both use greenhouse air circulation systems.

Ned Nash points out that vents provide all the air circulation needed at Stewarts-Carpinteria (formerly Armacost and Royston). Their greenhouse ceilings are very high and I wonder if convection currents aren't providing all the air circulation they need when the vents are closed.

Many growers reduce air circulation at night and on cloudy days.

Note that Andy Adriaanse hangs all his plants. No benches. That's one way to keep snails and slugs from hiding underneath.

Walt Cousineau just rolls up the sides of his greenhouse and lets the breeze blow through. The walls of his greenhouse are inflatable plastic tubes that are erected by a compressor...that is controlled by a thermostat. He waters frequently, though, in the dry southern California summers.

Still, since I entertain no notions that I am in complete control of growing environment for my phals, I think I'll stick to the fans. They're cheap insurance.

More than one grower mentioned they do not direct moving air onto the plants; vertical fans are usually directed above the plants and horizontal fans are directed upward, away from the plants in both cases. My own experience is that plants in the path of briskly moving air are dried out sooner than those not and require special attention.

Q 4(c) WHAT DO YOU SEE AS THE REASON FOR CIRCULATING AIR IN A PHAL GROWING AREA?

Prevention of disease, redistribution of heat, drying the plants, removal of plant waste products, replenishment of the supply of carbon dioxide, replacement of stale air, a 'buoyant atmosphere', duplication of the natural habitat, and John Watkins' suggestion that it 'homogenizes' the temperature and humidity of the air.

Andy Adriaanse and others caution the effects of too much air circulation...that of too-rapid drying of the medium and its effect on the plants.

There is a message coming across: Some air circulation is good for most Phalaenopsis greenhouses, but don't get carried away. (Note the other warnings against using too much air circulation.)

I think air circulation in an orchid greenhouse has at least two advantages: First, the conventional wisdom of drying surface water off the plants and, thereby, reducing the likelihood of fungal or bacterial infection. But, I see a second advantage (and in the case of our near-desert growing conditions in San Bernardino, California, perhaps a more important one.)

Briskly moving air in a phal greenhouse redistributes heat from the hot pockets throughout the house, reduces the damage done by overheating, and keeps the environmental envelope of the plants in a more nearly optimum growing range. More rapidly moving air around a plant will permit it to tolerate a higher level of light...which will permit the plant to grow faster. That higher light level will also develop a tougher epidermis on the plant and lower its susceptibility to disease. It also does a better job of evaporating moisture on the underbench gravel, raising the greenhouse humidity...just as I want it to do.

It also disperses gaseous waste products from the plant and delivers carbon dioxide needed for growth. And last, but certainly not least, in the winter, it reduces energy-wasting stratification of air in the greenhouse. Vertical, ceiling (or Casablanca) fans are most efficient for this last purpose. (For long life, spray the wooden blades with a water-proofing agent.)

I'm willing to accept the drying effect of brisk air movement to achieve these advantages and a more uniform growing condition, one devoid of hot and cold spots. I can water more often, but I can't flit around warming the cool plants and cooling the warm ones.

It is my practice, therefore, to speed up the greenhouse fans whenever outside temperatures are either (1) above normal or (2) below normal. Several respondents pointed out, and I agree, if a breezy growing location near the top of a tree is good enough for the Grand Design in nature, it's good enough for my greenhouse, too.

To hold down the redistribution of bacteria and fungus by a vigorous air circulation system, I spray dirt floor areas of the greenhouses periodically with a bactericide/fungicide. That is, after all, the primary source of the bad stuff.

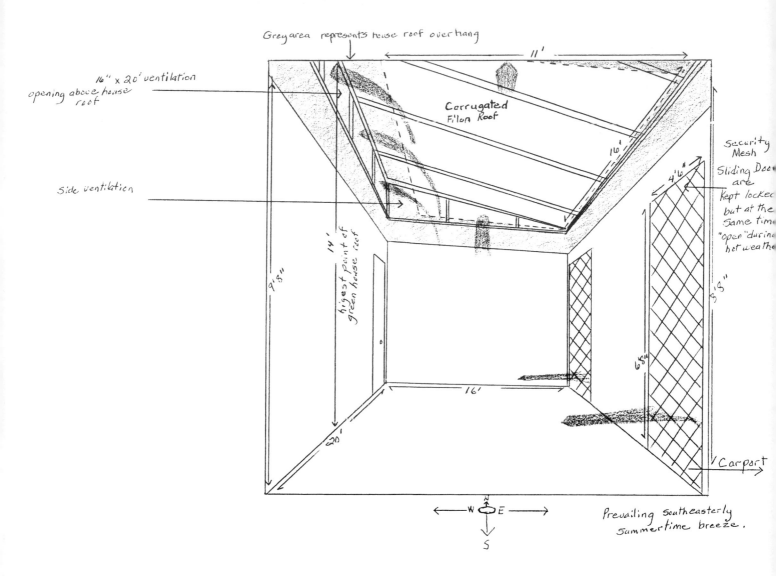

Grey area represents house roof overhang

16" x 20' ventilation opening above house roof

Side ventilation

Corrugated Filon Roof

highest point of greenhouse roof

14'

9'8"

20'

16'

11'

16'

Security Mesh

Sliding Door are kept locked but at the same time "open" during hot weather

4'6"

5'5"

6'5"

Carport

W ← → E
N
S

Prevailing southeasterly summertime breeze.

Clerestory roof on Pamela Scholz' greenhouse which makes use of the chimney effect to provide free ventilation. For more on this, see page 106.

SECTION 4.2   AIR CIRCULATION: SELECTED RESPONSES

QUESTION 4(a) TO WHAT DEGREE DO YOU CIRCULATE AIR AROUND YOUR PLANTS?

(Indian Coast South Africa) This is a subject full of contradictions. If there is no stale air then I only open a door. All slides stay closed because there is no need to over-ventilate. All pots are suspended from wires attached to overhead supports, so there is already an optimum of circulation. If benches are used you will need more ventilation. The misting system runs 20 cm (8 inches) above the floor and the plants are hung 80 cm (32 inches) above the floor.
— A. Adriaanse

(California Coast US) Air is moved continuously at plant level at a velocity of about 0.5 feet per second.
— L. Batchman

(Southeast Australia) I use a 12-inch ducted fan located above the plants (8 feet from the floor), directed slightly downward, and turning fast enough to float cotton threads suspended from each side of the house above the plants.
— M. Black

(Mid-Atlantic Coast US) Swaying flower spikes.
— M. Bowell

(Central California US) I believe air circulation is essential to the health of the plants, especially fresh air. I use a 20-inch box fan with a rotating grill near the eave of the house to provide air circulation 24 hours per day. On days when weather permits, I open a wall louvered-vent and use a portable box fan in the opposite wall vent to ensure air circulation and exchange.
— R. Buchter

(California Coast US) Air is circulated only during the time the heaters are running or the vents are open.
— E. Carlson

(California Bay Area US) Very high circulation except during flowering; then more gentle.
— W. Cecil

*(Northeastern US) Under artificial lighting...At least one fan is going all the time.
— I. Cohen

(Southern California US) We use a fan-jet (for a greenhouse 32'x 90') which moves 20,000 cubic feet per minute, enough to cause spikes to barely move.

— D&R Cowden

(Central Atlantic Coast US) We use a common (household) window fan, hanging from the roof of a 20x35-foot greenhouse, running at low speed.

— L. Clouser

(Indian Coast South Africa) We have the usual arrangement for air circulation of a fan with a long, sock-type arrangement of a plastic tube with holes made at various intervals and the air blows through this continuously day and night. We have one other fan which is set high up towards the roof (a rotator fan) which blows all day and all night and this is just an ordinary household fan that we have rigged up to just give a little more air circulation. It is a rotating fan which moves from side to side and is directed towards the roof and so gives a very gentle breeze all the time.

— C&I Coll

(Southern California US) During the past 3 years I have developed an 'open air movement' for my orchids by using 'Poly-Vent' closures on the ends and sides of the 95-foot square house. Poly-Vents are 9-inch, connected, flexible-plastic tubes that can be inflated with a small electric air compressor on demand. When the temperature drops below 70°F, the compressor comes on and inflates the stack of plastic tubes that rise to fill the gap between the ground and the lower part of the greenhouse roof...effectively closing up the greenhouse that had been open all around to a height of about 6 feet.

In this part of southern California it gets warm enough almost every winter day to open the system and flood the greenhouse with fresh, cool air. Accumulated moisture and stale air are swept out and the plants love it. We have almost daily breezes blowing in from the ocean a few miles away carrying moisture that cools the houses. I use no air coolers or fans to cool or dry my orchids. The breeze does that for me. I have an overhead misting system to cool and moisten plants on really hot days.

With the system I have eliminated crown rot and fungus on my phals. I have not sprayed with a fungicide or bactericide in 2 years.

— W. Cousineau

(South of England) Internal circulating fans move air around the house 3 feet above the plants...in a racetrack pattern.

— R. Dadd

(South Australia) We have three fans to move the air in the greenhouse and one extractor fan to change the air. Good air movement is essential for healthy plants.

— M. Dennis

(Central Atlantic Coast US) All the plants receive circulated, fresh air even in the winter as long as the sun is shining to warm the greenhouse regardless of the outside air temperature.
— R. Drejka

(California Coast US) Fans are positioned for a gentle, tumbling effect of the air.
— W. Eckberg

(Rome Italy) In the summer when I want faster drying, I turn on an air conditioner. An evaporative cooler and ventilator fan provide normal air movement.
— A. Fanfani

(Holland) None. (The reason cited for circulating air in a phal growing area is 'bad culture'. ed.)
— major commercial grower

(Maui Hawaii US) The house for mature plants is open to the breeze and needs no further help. In the seedling house, and enclosed glasshouse, I use a fan on a hot day. We have a strong breeze blowing almost every day, so all I have to do for air circulation is to open the door.
— R. Fukamura

(Central Atlantic Coast US) About 2 miles per hour.
— R. Griesbach

(Atlantic Coast US) Good air circulation is a must. We use convection tubes placed down the middle of the greenhouse over the plants. I believe a tube down under the plants would be especially useful during the winter.
— K. Griffith

(Gulf Coast US) I keep at least two fans running at all times; the plants need a lot of air circulation.
— J. Grimes

(Florida Atlantic Coast US) We have a large fan at the end of the greenhouse and air turbines on the roof.
— C&L Hagan

(Southeastern US) In winter: a variable speed device on a fan-jet controls the air movement. If plants are wet from watering, more air is circulated; less when plants are dry. On warm, sunny days, I most often turn it off to prevent the hot, dry air from blowing on the plants.

In summer: The fan-jet is off during the day. It is run on low each night to provide air movement and to prevent Botrytis. During the day the fan-wet pad system provides the cooling and air movement.
— T. Harper

(Indian Coast South Africa) My greenhouse allows a small amount of air circulation as certain small parts of the walls and door are open to the elements; so, any outside wind would create air movement inside the greenhouse.

— A. Harris

(Southern California US) We have evaporative coolers which circulate a generous amount of moist, cool air on hot days.

— E. Hetherington

(Midlands of England) Air circulation around my phal plants is almost continuous throughout the year, taking two forms. During the favourable, warm, damp days...louvres at bench level in the gable end of the greenhouse are opened and so is the greenhouse door in the opposite end. The fan may or may not be left running. During the colder part of the year, this single large capacity fan runs continuously. Apart from air recirculation it also helps minimise the amount of condensation which forms on the polyethylene liner inside the greenhouse.

— P. Hirst

(Florida Caribbean US) We have eight 52-inch fans in our 100- x 200-foot Phalaenopsis house. Four circulate air under thermostat control. The other four come on at a higher temperature and start up the cool-pad system. They stop inversely.

— W. Kelly

(Southeastern Australia) I find we get better growth and less disease if we have a large slow fan moving the air along the house above the plants. Do not have the air current blowing directly onto the plants. The movement cools the plant by increasing evaporation. Water lightly to prevent too much dryout, but do not let heavy media become too wet. The air circulation system can be used to induce small amounts of outside air to modify conditions undesired in the growing area.

— J. Kilgannon

(Southern California US) Convection tubes distribute air prior to exhaust fans coming on.

— T. Koike

(East Java Indonesia) We give as much air circulation as is possible. So, we grow them **three metres above the ground.** (emphasis is mine. ed.)

— A. Kolopaking

(France) In some greenhouses we have the same cooling system you use in the US and, in others, we have the old opening at the top of the houses which are opened by hand when the temperatures outside and inside allow it to be done.

— Marcel LeCoufle

(North of England) Vents open in pleasant weather and two fans for gentle air movement.
— P. Lindsay

(Central California US) We use a University of Connecticut air circulation system, developed by them a few years ago. (U of C system features racetrack air courses within the greenhouse) The fans run continuously. We've found the system to be very effective; air temperature at floor level is the same as it is well above the plants.
— B. Livingston

(Florida-Caribbean) The air in the greenhouse is constantly moving with inside fans or the large exhaust fans. Depending on the temperature in the greenhouses, the exhaust fans are automatically programmed to go on when the inside temp goes above 75°F.
— L. Lodyga

(Queensland Coast Australia) We have louvre windows at one end of the greenhouse and an exhaust fan at the other. Additionally, the heat duct system is used to circulate air when temps rise above 28°C (83°F). We also place the plants on wire mesh benches with good spacing between plants.
— J. Mackinney

(Southern California US) Good air circulation is the most essential element in growing spray orchids, particularly Phalaenopsis.

Makers of circulating systems have calculations for how many times per minute there should be a complete change of air in a greenhouse. But, I do not like to sacrifice my humidified air (sometimes heated, too) and I have worked out a compromise.

I use a 24-inch convection tube attached to a side-vented evaporative cooler **which is installed inside the greenhouse.** The convection tube draws outside air through the top vents and doorway and also a venturi over the door. This mixes with the inside air so there is a constant mixing rather than a complete exchange. At night the door and top vents are closed so the convection currents pick up the hot air from under the bench and circulate it with a circular motion from top to bottom picking up moisture from the ground and under the bench.

As for the amount of circulation, I again follow the intuitive method of what looks and feels correct. Generally speaking, the flowers and spikes should be observably waving in the breeze. There should be no cold drafts of air which will cause bud drop.
— J. Miller

(California Coast US) None. Air circulation is provided by venting our greenhouses...which have 20 some-foot high ridge lines.
— N. Nash

(California Coast US) I think, ideally there should be a barely detectable light breeze in the greenhouse. If there is too much air moving, some buds and flowers will be dehydrated.
— M&J Nedderman

(Southeastern US) Two overhead 24-inch fans; one high and one low.
— S. Pridgen

(California Coast US) I believe Phalaenopsis should have <u>continuous</u> air movement around them, whether provided by a fan or any other means.
— F. Robinson

(Northcentral US) In a Wardian case. . .air exchange is crucial, so I have a computer 'muffin' fan mounted on top which comes on with the lights.
— Randy Robinson

(Southcentral US) Mild general air circulation in the greenhouse during the winter.
— P. Scholz

(South of England) In a 10- x 15-foot greenhouse, two fans are suspended from the roof half-way along either side, blowing in opposite directions.
— P. Seaton

(North of England) I use small 14-watt fans (sometimes called 'computer' or 'muffin' fans) which are hung at 6-foot intervals all around the greenhouse. They create a gentle air movement and their angle is altered several times a week. They are connected to a quarter-hour time switch which operates the fans for 15 minutes 'on' and 15 minutes 'off'. When the temperature rises above 75°F, the fans operate until it comes back down.
— D. Shuker

(Pacific Northwest US) Lots of moving air. Fans blow <u>around</u>, not on the plants.
— S. Skoien

*(Central Atlantic Coast US) Under artificial lighting. . .I can't emphasize the need for good air circulation strongly enough for anyone who grows phals indoors. We have a 15-inch floor fan and three 5-inch 'muffin' fans going 24 hours each day. Without these we would have much crownrot and Botrytis <u>cinerea</u>. We speak from both our own experience and that of others.
— K&M Smeltz

(Oahu Hawaii US) The sides of the greenhouses are screened to let air pass through.
— R. Takase

(Midlands of England) Circulating fan operating daytime only. I have never used air circulation at night and have not had any trouble with spotting on the flowers, not even whites.
— H. Taylor

*(Northeastern US) Under artificial lighting. . . I circulate about 2,400 cfm around my plants and under the benches.
— J. Vella

(California Coast US) Not enough! I have five or six small fans running constantly and one larger fan which brings in fresh air when the greenhouse temperature rises above 75°F.
— J. Watkins

(Mid-Atlantic Coast US) I grow other orchids in addition to the phals, but I keep the phals grouped together where I can fertilize them and ventilate them as a block. Phals require at least twice the air movement of other orchids. Air movement below the benches is very useful because it does not dry the plants out so quickly.
— M. Werther

(Mid-Atlantic Coast US) We have large fans in the ceilings of our greenhouses. They run continuously, but I often wonder why. I recently had a greenhouse operate for a year without moving the air and saw no difference between it and the other houses. (If the volume of the house is large enough, it could be that efficient thermal convection currents are set up and serving the function of fans. See Consensus and Opinion above. ed.)
— C. Williamson

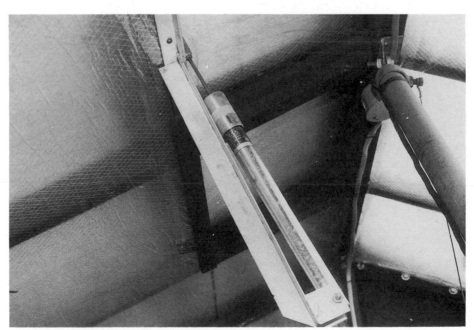

Greenhouse ridgeline vent operated by a freon-gas heat motor. Gas in the cylinder expands when heated and operates the piston, opening vent. Knurled collar adjusts operating temperature.

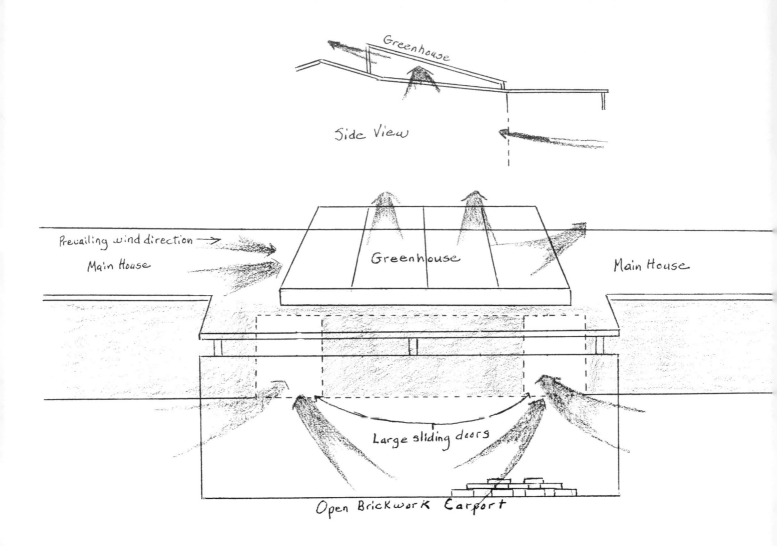

Side View

Prevailing wind direction →

Main House

Greenhouse

Main House

Large sliding doors

Open Brickwork Carport

Greenhouse

Pam Scholz' answer to the problem of greenhouse ventilation: a clerestory, which is a window placed high in a wall near the eaves or projecting vertically from a roof's surface. It not only permits chimney-effect ventilation, but also allows light gain during the winter when the sun's angle is low.

QUESTION 4(b) DO YOU VARY THE AMOUNT OF AIR CIRCULATION AND, IF SO, HOW MUCH, HOW AND WHY?

(Indian Coast South Africa) If the air is 'close' or heavy, I ventilate by opening sliding windows top and bottom. There is no direct air stream over the plants.
— A. Adriaanse

(Mid-Atlantic Coast US) I might be careful not to have a plant at the stage of flower enlargement too close to fast-moving air. Too much transpiration.
— M. Bowell

(Central California US) During the summer I use an evaporative cooler which greatly increases the air exchange and air circulation in my greenhouse.
— R. Buchter and others

*(Northeastern US) Under artificial lighting…More air circulation at night.
— I. Cohen

(Southern California US) During the winter we move the phals to the warm house where the air circulation is greater.
— D&R Cowden

(Florida Gulf Coast US) We always have air movement in the greenhouse, but less in the winter.
— J. Eich

(Northeastern US) No.
— D. Grove and others

(Midlands of England) Yes. During the shorter, warmer summer nights a small fan — of about one-tenth the capacity of the one normally used — is considered adequate for night use and for dull, cool day use.
— P. Hirst

(Holland) On days when the temperature rises above 25°C (77°F) an extractor fan comes on.
— H. Kronenberg

(Texas Gulf Coast US) At night, only 3 of the 7 fans run.
— J. Margolis

(Luzon Philippines) We normally do not vary the air circulation as we depend on natural conditions. However, in the event of strong winds, we protect the plants by providing net covers.
— D. Mendoza

(California Coast US) After watering I increase the air movement by turning on an additional fan. This may be left on only as short as a few hours (summer) or as long as 2 days in the winter.

— M&J Nedderman

(California Coast US) I increase air circulation whenever the temperature in the greenhouses rises above 85°F to prevent leaf burns. It also keeps moisture from standing on the leaves and axils of the plants, thus discouraging fungal disease.

— F. Robinson

(Southcentral US) I direct additional fans on the phals after watering. The greenhouse is constructed with one side fully open and a 2-foot opening around the other sides immediately under the roof. The arrangement is opened in the summer and creates a natural chimney effect. (Anyone growing in a warm, moist area like Louisiana, take note of the greenhouse innovation. Sounds like a terrific idea. See the sketch of how it's built. ed.)

— P. Scholz

(North of England) I have under-bench vents and these are opened for a short time daily (one hour) and this is combined with the opening of one roof vent during the colder months. (October 1st through the end of April). From the 1st of May until the end of September the under-bench vents are left open day and night with the roof vents opening automatically above 78°F.

— D. Shuker

*(Northeastern US) Under artificial lighting. . . In the cooler months, I reduce fan operation by 50%.

— J. Vella

QUESTION 4(c) WHAT DO YOU SEE AS THE REASON FOR CIRCULATING AIR IN A PHAL GROWING AREA?

(Indian Coast South Africa) Ventilation has its place, but over-ventilation seems to have an adverse effect. If one investigates the areas where the species come from, then it appears that the plants are protected by other vegetation or rock walls. In full summer, when the weather bureau predicts good weather, I leave all the windows open.
— A. Adriaanse

(California Coast US) Moving air helps dry plants off and reduces the chance of disease.
— L. Batchman and others

(Southeastern Australia) To reproduce logical, natural conditions and to even out distribution of heat, when artificial heat is needed.
— M. Black

(Central California US) Air circulation is essential to elimination of plant diseases caused by air stagnation around the plants. During winter months I monitor wind direction and flow closely when neighbors are using their wood-burning fireplaces!
— R. Buchter

(California Coast US) Air circulation is a necessity if plants are grown under very damp or humid conditions...to prevent bacterial and fungal diseases.
— E. Carlson and others

*(Northeastern US) Under artificial lighting...To prevent diseases and dry the plants off, especially in the area of the crown. Air circulation also improves the supply of carbon dioxide and prevents disease spores from landing.
— I. Cohen

(South of England) To keep oxygen, carbon dioxide, and ethylene! at even concentrations around all plant surfaces.
— R. Dadd

(South Australia) Stops fungal and bacterial diseases by drying the leaves off. Also fresh air must be drawn through daily to replace stale air.
— M. Dennis

(Florida Gulf Coast US) They thrive in this type (breezy) of atmosphere. It holds down problems with fungus and bacterial infections, provides more uniform drying, etc.
— J. Eich

(Southern California US) Air circulation reduces disease and thermal stress.

— R. Engel

(Holland) Bad culture.

— a major commercial grower

(California Coast US) To prevent crown rot...and give the fan dealers extra business. Crown rot and other diseases can thrive with poor ventilation. We started with 12" fans under the benches. However, the constant watering of the plants rusted the fan blades and the rusted part would finally fall off until the blades were ineffective and had to be constantly replaced. Parts of the greenhouse had dead air and this added to the chance of crown rot or other diseases. We finally replaced all of the fans with fewer overhead fans and never had any more problems.

— H. Freed

(Mid-Atlantic Coast US) I have seen many home greenhouses where small circulating fans are supposed to do the work of cooling the greenhouse in summer. What they do instead is interfere with the natural draft of hot air out the top vent and push hot air into the corners of the greenhouse. A better solution would be to put an exhaust fan near the top of the ridge and have properly-sized air inlet louvers at the bottom of the greenhouse. (See article on solar chimneys at the end of this section. ed.)

— M. Frier

(Central Atlantic Coast US) Prevent bacterial growth.

— R. Griesbach

(Gulf Coast US) Much air circulation helps prevent crown rot and more nearly duplicates conditions found in the natural habitat.

— J. Grimes

(Northeastern US) Phals need high humidity and can tolerate vigorous air movement; bacteria and fungi (at least those that bother phals) also need high humidity, but they cannot tolerate constant, vigorous air movement. All portions of the plant need to be swept by the air flow. Also, air movement is the easiest way to get water out of the crowns after watering or misting the plants (along with raising the thermostat).

— D. Grove

(Florida Atlantic Coast US) To control leaf temperatures and to dry crowns out and prevent crown rot.

— C&L Hagan

(Southern California US) Helps keep down the spotting of flowers caused by Botrytis.

— D. Hirsch

(Midlands of England) I am not convinced that continuous air movement around Phalaenopsis plants under all weather conditions is necessary.
— P. Hirst

(California Coast US) Botrytis is the #1 reason.
— T. Koike

(Holland) I am not sure that fans are really needed in phal culture.
— H. Kronenberg

(Central California US) Air circulation allows transpiration to take place, keeps stale air areas from forming, and prevents moisture from standing on leaves. . .which helps control bacterial and fungal problems.
— B. Livingston

(Luzon Philippines) I would say it is to dry up excess moisture and thereby cool off the plant. In some cases, it prevents too much accumulation of ethylene which tends to stimulate flower fading and death.
— D. Mendoza

(California Coast US) The main reason for air circulation is to prevent diseases such as bacterial and fungal rots in winter and to prevent heat buildup in summer in the succulent leaves of Phalaenopsis. It also prevents hot and cold spots in the greenhouse.
— M&J Nedderman

(Western Australia) Air movement is a natural and essential ingredient of plant welfare. I use a 900mm (36-inch) ceiling fan for this purpose, the blade tips of which have been modified to act as a turbulator. The blades have been turned up to force air in a horizontal direction toward the greenhouse walls and thence down over the plants. Fan speeds are increased during the main flowering season to minimize Botrytis spotting of the blooms and again during the summer to reduce heat build up.
— K. Rex

(South of England) Firstly: to reduce the boundary effect, wherein carbon dioxide next to the leaf becomes depleted and limits growth. Moving air replaces this 'boundary air' with a fresh supply. Secondly: the cooling effect due to the increased rate of transpiration. Thirdly: it prevents the 'spotting' of blooms with fungal colonies. This can become a problem during several consecutive days of wet weather — not an unusual occurrence in England!
— P. Seaton

(North of England) I consider air circulation very important for the well-being of Phalaenopsis, for even distribution of carbon dioxide together with other nutrients present. It also keeps the temperature at a more stable level.

I used to have the fans running 24 hours a day, but since using a 15-minute on/off timer, there seems to be a more 'buoyant atmosphere' with no bloom damage whatever.
— D. Shuker

(Midlands of England) I do not like humid, stagnant air as I am sure this causes rotting from the crown.
— F. Smith

(Midlands of England) Air is circulated to try to keep a buoyant atmosphere.
— H. Taylor

(California Coast US) It 'homogenizes' the temperature and humidity of the air.
— J. Watkins

(Texas Gulf Coast US) Better growth and less disease.
— C&J Wilson and others

Solar chimney installation. The chimney on the left is mounted on the greenhouse at the left. Note: more than one chimney may be used on a greenhouse.

Solar chimney air inlet: the dark patch at the top center of the end wall of the house.

SECTION 4.3
LET THE SUN COOL YOUR GREENHOUSE

(Ventilating with solar energy)

The energy of the sun can be used to ventilate orchid greenhouses at no recurring cost to the grower. The more sun you have, the more ventilation you can have.

Moreover, the method we're going to discuss has the sterling benefit of operating even when nothing else does. It costs nothing to operate and works even in a power outage. And it's easy to build. You're skeptical? Read on.

The principle of the chimney effect is an elegantly simple one: warm, rising air that is contained will draw replacement air into the bottom of the container..in this case a vertical pipe. That 'draw' is our means of removing unwanted hot air from the greenhouse. The chimney or stack will boost natural convection currents and if the air is heated in the chimney, the process can go on as long as the heating continues. It only works when sun is shining...but then, that's the time you need the ventilation most, isn't it?

How to heat air in a chimney? That's where the solar energy comes in. We will heat air in a chimney with the sun's rays and sustain the vertical movement of air in the chimney...and the suction at the bottom...which is going to provide extraction of the hot air...which is what we want. Neat. The whole greenhouse or solarium is, in effect, a solar chimney. We take in cool air, heat it and convect it out through the stack.

What that means to us as orchid growers is that a simple structure called a solar chimney is going to cool our greenhouses with no outside help. It turns itself on as the greenhouse heats up...and turns itself off when the greenhouse cools down. The hotter it gets in the greenhouse, the harder it works. Sound too good to be true? I know it does, but it works, folks. And, although it has for a couple of thousand years, some of us have gotten into the habit of looking on anything that is cheap as being unworthy. Not so.

Now don't turn the page and say I can't build things, so this is not for me. If you really can't build things, find someone who can and have them make you one. It will be worth the small expense. The pay back on the investment, incidentally, is fastest in the hot, sunny regions.

Solar chimneys can be used to ventilate greenhouses, sun porches, homes, shops, barns, and almost any other structure they can be bolted to and where the sun shines.

BUILDING THE SOLAR CHIMNEY

The structure is basically a box, a foot square and 8 feet long. The four 2x2's, which are the skeleton, are attached to a base and covered on three sides with clear, corrugated fiberglass-reinforced plastic. The fourth side faces away from the sun and can be covered with 3/8'' exterior plywood. The base provides rigidity and a means of attaching the chimney firmly to the greenhouse structure. The guy wires are optional, but recommended in windy areas.

Hung inside the wood and fiberglass-box is a seven and a half-foot (three 30-inch sections) length of 12'' stovepipe, painted flat black. (High temperature, flat black paint suitable for our purposes is available in auto supply stores. It's used for painting exhaust manifolds and barbecues, among other things. 3-M Black Velvet is good.)

This stovepipe is the source of the magic the solar chimney produces. Sun shines on the pipe, warming it and causing the air inside to begin rising. The hotter the sun, the more heat produced and the greater the chimney effect. The stovepipe is topped with a 12'' attic vent turbine to improve the air extraction and to keep rain out of the chimney. The plastic 'skin' keeps the heat from being dissipated by the wind.

A small door at its base. . .to isolate the chimney during the cool evenings of fall and spring. . .will prevent unwanted loss of accumulated heat. When nighttime temperatures stay above 60°F. the chimney can be left open or ''on''. Cabinet hinges and a magnetic catch will work just fine. I use a 3' long piece of stiff wire, attached to the door, to open and close it; long reach.

An opening in the greenhouse wall must be provided to allow a source of fresh air from the outside to replace warm air exiting through the chimney. One and one-half to two square feet of opening will do if the opening is unscreened. Double that area if insect screening is used. . .as it should be in most areas. Several distributed small openings are better than one large one. (See detail for a neat energy-saving gadget.) Do not count the area of input from an evaporative cooler in this required opening.

Locate the cool-air inlets low and at the end opposite the chimney for best circulation of air inside. Effectiveness of the chimney is going to depend in large measure on the vertical distance between the cool-air inlet and the top of the chimney. Greater difference means greater effectiveness. Intake low and exhaust high for best results.

INSTALLING THE CHIMNEY

Attach the completed chimney with its bottom opening at the highest point possible on the end of the greenhouse. The reason is simple: we want to draw off the hottest air in the house and that means the highest.

A ceiling or turbulator fan which mixes air in the greenhouse probably will reduce the efficiency of the chimney somewhat, but we've got to have them, so don't worry about the loss. A gee-whiz feature of the system comes into operation if power goes off in hot weather.

The heated air in the house stratifies with the hottest air at the highest point in the greenhouse. . .and this gives the best possible performance of the chimney.

The 'feet' of the chimney must be strong enough to support the weight of the whole structure, so don't skimp on material dimensions here. The 'feet' stand on a solid greenhouse member and should be firmly attached with either bolts or lag screws or both. Vertical height of the base is not critical and can be adjusted for best attachment to a solid greenhouse part. If none is available to mount the chimney to, make and install one.

A lower external brace from bottom of the chimney to either the ground or a hip molding on the house will relieve strain from other parts of the chimney and promote longer life.

For all the macho men out there: get some help raising the chimney in place. It's awkward and dangerous, particularly if there is a breeze blowing when you put it in place. (I know, but the scars from my hernia operation have almost faded now.)

OPERATING THE CHIMNEY

Open the hatch when you want ventilation. Close it when you don't. That's it.

AFTERTHOUGHTS:

The chimney has three noteworthy effects: first, the running time of your cooler (if you use one) will be shortened; second, you can probably unplug your wall ventilating fan (if you use one); and third, if used in conjunction with a heat-motor vent and an emergency overhead sprinkling system. . .it could save your collection in the event of a power outage or cooler malfunction on a hot summer day. (For more information on these latter features, see Coping With a Power Outage, Culture of the Phalaenopsis Orchid, Laid-Back Publications, 276 E. Shamrock, Rialto, CA 92376.)

This system, using a 12-inch stovepipe and an 8-foot high box, probably won't provide all the ventilation needed for many greenhouses, but it will skim the hottest air from <u>any</u> structure in which it is used.

For that purpose it is an inexpensive, cost-effective and reliable option worthy of an orchid hobbyist's consideration.

— editor

Solar chimney air inlet: closeup.

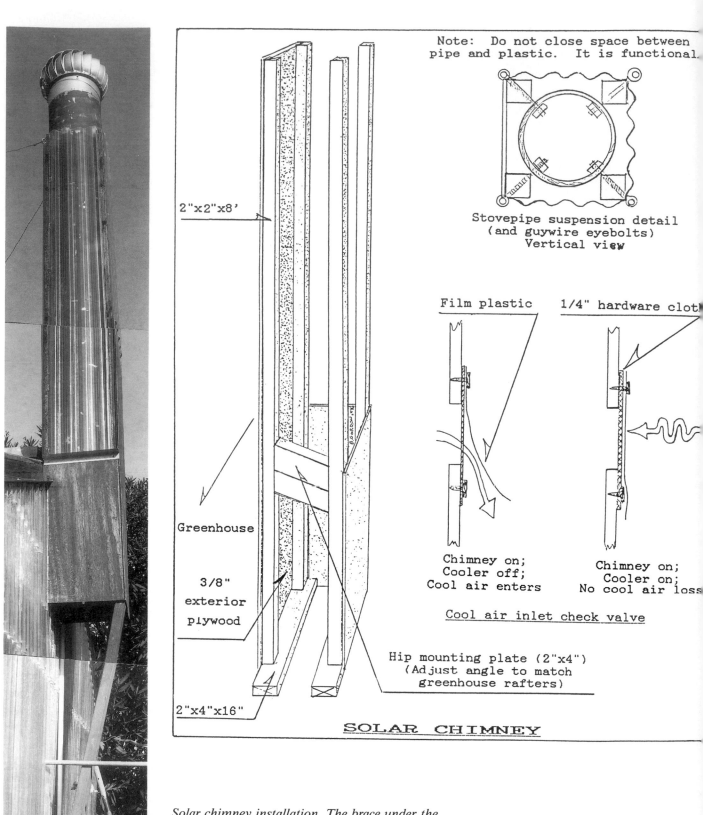

Note: Do not close space between pipe and plastic. It is functional.

Stovepipe suspension detail
(and guywire eyebolts)
Vertical view

2"x2"x8'

Film plastic   1/4" hardware cloth

Chimney on;   Chimney on;
Cooler off;   Cooler on;
Cool air enters   No cool air loss

Cool air inlet check valve

Greenhouse

3/8"
exterior
plywood

Hip mounting plate (2"x4")
(Adjust angle to match
greenhouse rafters)

2"x4"x16"

SOLAR CHIMNEY

Solar chimney installation. The brace under the chimney is secured at the bottom to the hip molding of the green-house. The view is to the north (in California, US).

SECTION FIVE
ROOTING MEDIUM

(a) How do you determine when repotting is necessary? (b) Do you use any available pot type or do you prefer ones with extra drainage such as 'azalea' pots? (c) Does the condition of the potting medium affect watering intervals? (d) What medium do you use and how often do you normally repot?

SECTION 5.1 ROOTING MEDIUM: CONSENSUS AND OPINION

Q 5(a) HOW DO YOU DETERMINE WHEN REPOTTING IS NECESSARY?

Although a number of very logical tests for the need for repotting are cited, most of the respondents (like the rest of us) repot at some selected time in the calendar year. Fortunately for most phal hobbyists, the best repotting time lines up with summer vacation time and that's when most is done. The tests are used to gauge the general condition of the medium in the collection and have the additional use of identifying individual plants in need of repotting.

My own feelings on when to repot are that phals should be repotted before they show signs of needing it. I'm sure most fir bark will last longer than 1 year, but I repot then on the presumption that it is about to break down anyway. (Seedlings every 6 months) I'm sure my situation is not typical, because I have the time. Another benefit flows from this philosophy: I cull out the junk relentlessly to keep from having to repot it. One last item on this personal view: My wife, Nancy, does most of our potting.

I like Terry Koike's test for repotting plants grown in fir bark: when the bark loses it's sharpness to the touch. Good point. Note that some of the respondents say they repot when the plants get too big. I read that to mean that the medium is not the limiting factor. Several responses said they repot when the aerial roots get long. To me, that usually means that the medium has broken down and, invariably, the long aerial roots are the only live roots the plant has.

Ernie Campuzano brought up the old standby of repotting when the plant roots are growing actively. If you have a choice in the matter and not too many plants to do, this probably would be a good guide...but not too practical for commercial growers or hobbyists with more than a few hundred plants.

DICK BUCHTER'S POIGNANT REMARK THAT MEDIUM IS THE CHEAPEST STUFF IN HIS POTS... SHOULD BE CHISELED IN STONE.

Q 5(b) WHAT KIND OF POT DO YOU USE?

The majority of respondents reported using the stubby, 'azalea pots, supporting Mary Carol Frier's and Dr. Edmund Rutkowski's contention that phals like to be under-potted. If you can handle a more frequent watering schedule, this practice makes sense because the plants will need it.

Extra drainage was preferred by most growers. Some made extra drainage holes in already well-drained pots.

POT SIZE: Regarding pot size, I agree with the point made by Bill Livingston, Phil Hirst and others that root ball size is the determining factor in how big a pot will be used. It is my practice to trim root balls to fit the smallest pot size feasible...that is one that will hold enough wet bark to last the plant a week and won't let it fall over when a big spike arches over the side. (I have a supply of fist-sized riverbed stones on hand for that emergency.) I believe **the roots should touch the sides of the pot when centered and before refilling with new medium...otherwise, the pot is too big.**

I rarely use pots over 6 inches in diameter for phals. My experience has been that <u>every time I use a bigger pot, I find the roots of that plant gone when I repot it next.</u> If the root ball of a big white, pink or gigantea-violacea hybrid won't fit into a 6-inch pot, I trim it until it will. Before kissing this one off, try it. It seems as though the more roots you cut off, the faster they grow back.

CRITICAL MEDIA VOLUME: I'm beginning to think there is such a thing as a 'critical mass' in phal pot media volume. Water in the center of the medium in big pots just doesn't dry out between waterings, at least not on my watering schedule. It probably would if given long enough, but watering intervals in most orchid greenhouses are not established on the needs of the big horses...but rather on those of the little 3- or 4-inch pots. Right? That's the way it is in my greenhouse, so I'd have to remember to water the big pots only every second or third watering if I wanted to use

them. Keeping track of that sort of thing makes my head hurt, so I don't do it.

And I don't mix pot sizes in a given area on the bench. All the two-and-a-halfs are together; all the fours are together; and all the sixes are together. The blocks of six-inchers are watered separately when they're lighter than they ought to be. Everything else gets watered on the seasonal schedule, either by hand or automatically by the overhead system.

Wetness of the medium is a product of medium porosity, watering frequency and volume of the pot. The volume of a 7-inch 'azalea' pot is one and one-half times the volume of a 6-inch 'azalea' pot. Crunching the numbers, going from a 6-inch to a 7-inch, you increase the volume by 50%, but the evaporative surface by only 36%. Humidity has only a minor effect. Using a large volume, 7- or 8-inch pot for a phal has the same effect as using a finer medium or increasing the watering frequency. Wetness of the core of the medium is not offset by the larger root ball, at least <u>not</u> in my experience.

Nothing over a 6-inch pot for phals.

Azalea pot dimensions: Pot height ranges from 75 to 85% of the pot width in the commonly-used sizes.

WATER TABLE: After watering, the bottom of an orchid pot is, in effect, the plant's water table since water can't seep down any farther than that. The medium in shallow pots allow the roots to approach the water table and stay in the wettest part of the pot.

You with me?

Phals like moist roots. So, they also like shallow pots. Seedlings also like moist roots and are happiest in shallow trays or flats. But because the roots are so close to the water table, the growing condition is close to that of a swamp...shallow water table. To cope with that, we need to drain it more efficiently than we would have to drain a deep pot. (Watering seedlings grown in flats is very tricky business...because, in effect, they're growing in a swamp.)

So phals like the moist roots that shallow pots give them, but those pots need more drainage than the deeper pots because we all know that phals don't like wet roots. Right? Shallow pots with lots of drainage. 'Azalea'. Phals.

The preference for under-sized pots with over-sized drains makes a statement for the need for quick draining by phals.

Q 5(c) DOES MEDIUM CONDITION AFFECT WATERING INTERVALS?

There is some agreement that watering intervals should be lengthened as the medium ages, but there is a reticence to do it.

Many feel that they need to water more often immediately after repotting, but Marcel LeCoufle notes they allow their plants to dry out a little to encourage new roots and give the older, damaged ones a chance to heal.

Bill Livingston's comment on the need to group plants by pot size is one that few hobbyists adopt. Maybe it's more obvious when you have lots of plants as the commercial growers have. It makes a lot of sense because when you have a shorter watering schedule for seedlings, they can be done without over-watering the larger pots.

Note that Dr. Dorotheo Mendoza waters his plants on slabs 4-5 times each day!

Ned Nash and John Watkins observe that bigger root balls in faster growing plants will use up water faster than a slow-growing plant potted a shorter time will...and tend to even up the drying-out time. I see this happening in my greenhouse, but only to about half of the collection.

Q 5(d) WHAT ROOTING MEDIUM DO YOU USE?

This has got to be every phal grower's favorite subject, but as some point out the function of rooting medium is to keep the plant upright and help keep roots moist...and a lot of different materials will do that admirably. (I know a grower who uses the pink fiberglass home insulation for his phals. The roots, what there are of them, look like hell, but the flowers are good, so who am I to criticize.) I'm in favor of using whatever is acceptable to the phals, convenient, and cheap...in that order.

Please take note of Jim Kilgannon's point that any rooting medium is OK so long as it holds the plant upright and SO LONG AS YOU ADJUST YOUR WATER/FEEDING PROGRAM TO IT. I think you'll agree with the wisdom of his statement when you see the variety of materials used successfully by the 125 or so growers represented here. Apparently, the quality of organic media is a problem worldwide. A disciplined approach to watering and repotting would be to put a mental quality label on each batch of medium used and at least be aware that its life will probably be short, long or average...and schedule watering and repotting accordingly.

SEGREGATING GOOD/BAD BARK: A good many growers report floating the good portion of a batch of bark off the bad. Good stuff floats; bad stuff sinks. I used to do that, too, but found it unnecessary when I repot every year. Floating off the good stuff would permit me to go longer than a year between pottings, but not 2 years. So I said to hell with it and now I just sift the bark through a quarter-inch sieve, sterilize it, use it...and repot every year.

Ernie Campuzano has a 4' x 6' x quarter-inch sieve supported on concrete blocks and just pours a bag of fir bark in and rakes it around to get rid of the fines. Neat.

DOLOMITE LIME: Several respondents said they soaked their bark in dolomite lime before using it. Sounds like a good idea because (1) it raises the pH of the bark from a norm of 4.0 to 4.5 to a level more acceptable to the phals and (2) it adds magnesium needed especially during spike induction...just a couple of months after repotting.

I like Steve Pridgen's idea of putting rocks in the bottom of the pots of large plants...

or those with long spikes that tend to tip a plant over when in bloom.

NEW ZEALAND SPHAGNUM: New Zealand sphagnum moss holds just about the right amount of moisture for the right length of time for phals. Eric Goo's comments on its use are timely and are worth reading before you use the moss.

An article in the October 23, 1987 issue of the Wall Street Journal indicated a Canadian firm, St. Raymond Paper Company, will spend 15 million to convert a pulp mill to a facility that makes a new super-absorbent, paper-like material from sphagnum moss. The company did not indicate its plans for the new material which was 12 years in development. The article went on to point out that some species of sphagnum moss absorb and retain 35 times their dry weight of water and synthesize sphagnol, chemically akin to phenol and somewhat effective as an antiseptic. Maybe we're looking at a hi-tech substitute for NZ moss.

The popularity of the New Zealand sphagnum moss, evident here, will probably drive the price up and out of sight in the near future. It is a limited resource. It's already in short supply. In the meantime, I'll use it only for seedlings coming out of flask and for my sick ones.

But sphagnum's value as a seedling medium won't come as any big surprise to the Hawaiian growers, particulary Ben Kodama, who has been using coarse Canadian sphagnum mixed with perlite for years...with marvelous results.

The rush over the use of cork as a potting medium seems to have died down. It lasts much longer as an open-air slab than it docs as contained pot medium.

I thought we'd hear more of the classical argument in favor of the inorganic media in the questionnaires, but it didn't happen. There were a number of positive comments on the use of charcoal, but almost all who used it, used it as a supplement. Feeding phals grown in inorganic materials is a squirrely process because the medium adsorbs (rather than absorbs) fertilizer and the plants see only feast or famine. It's true that inorganic media last longer, but there was little support for its exclusive use.

Worth reading, or re-reading on this subject, is judywhite's essay, Media Mania — Surveying the Mixed-Up Realm of Orchid Potting Materials, on page 488 of the May 1986 issue of the AOS Bulletin (Vol 55, Number 5).

There appear to be valid arguments on either side of those who support a short repotting interval and those who support a longer one. Timing for the long interval is usually based on obvious need and that of the short interval is based on the calendar...to prevent the plant from experiencing a need.

Commercial growers, as you might expect, support the longer interval. Hugo Freed and Marcel LeCoufle, neither of whose credentials are in question, note that a large plant gets comfortable when left alone for several years and shows its pleasure in lavish flower production.

Phals are not the only orchid to do that. If you can get good flower production without losing the roots, terrific, go for the longer interval. If not, join the short-interval group. There is little dispute that THE MEDIUM'S CAPACITY TO RESIST BREAKDOWN IS THE FACTOR THAT DETERMINES THE POTTING INTERVAL.

There was a consensus to repot during the summer and the earlier the better. The reason for early repotting is to put as much stabilizing time as possible between repotting and spring spike induction. Late repotting, within 2 months of spike induction, lays the two heavy burdens of induction and post-potting recovery on the plant at one time and spring flower quality will suffer. There is little doubt that the early repotting is going to adversely affect summer spikes, though, so take your choice on where you want the best flowers. It's a tradeoff.

IF YOUR REPOTTING SCHEDULE IS TIED TO THE SUMMER SEASON AS NOTED ABOVE, YOU HAVE FEW CHOICES OF INTERVALS BETWEEN 1 YEAR AND 2. I like to repot in the summer and the bark I use seldom will last longer than 18 months, so I repot annually. When I bit the bullet and started annual repotting, my head stopped hurting, so it must have been a good move.

Most commercial growers repot the year round for economic reasons.
— editor

SECTION 5.2 ROOTING MEDIUM: SELECTED RESPONSES

QUESTION 5(a) HOW DO YOU DETERMINE WHEN REPOTTING IS NECESSARY?

(Indian Coast South Africa) If you use a medium which can decay rapidly, then 2 years is about the limit. If your medium is an (relatively) inert material such as charcoal, then you have the advantage of being able to overpot a bit and this should give you 3 years or so.
— A. Adriaanse

(California Coast US) Repotting is done when the potting mix starts to break down and may be done at any time of the year; when in spike, if necessary. Normally, plants are repotted every 2 years.
— L. Batchman

(Central California US) I routinely repot every year. I like to check on my roots. Medium is the cheapest stuff in my pots!
— R. Buchter

(Southern California US) When the medium is soft, roots are hanging over the sides of the pot and there are new, green tips on the roots.
— E. Campuzano

(California Coast US) After the bark starts to break down; about 15-18 months.
— E. Carlson

*(Northeastern US) Under artificial lighting...When the mix appears soggy; when the growth rate or roots are poor; when the plant is more than 3 times the diameter of the pot; when it is 'necky' or coming out of the pot.
— I. Cohen

(Central Atlantic Coast US) We repot when the plant obviously outgrows the pot or when the mix begins to deteriorate and stays too wet.
— L. Clouser

(Indian Coast South Africa) At least every 12 to 15 months.
— C&I Coll

(Southern California US) I handle primarily phal seedlings and their growth is so rapid in my 'open greenhouse' that I repot them when they seem too large for the pot. I repot mature plants at intervals of up to 2 years if the plant and roots seem strong.
— W. Cousineau

(South of England) I repot to lower mature plants in their pots as they grow and to contain wandering aerial roots before they get too long and invade other pots! (Nonsense. That never happens! ed.)

— R. Dadd

(South Australia) By the look of the plant and the medium.

— M. Dennis

(Central Atlantic Coast US) ...on an average of every 2 years, usually in the late spring or early summer.

— R. Drejka

(Florida Gulf Coast US) We repot every year. Our plants grow that fast.

— J. Eich

(Southern California US) Examination of the roots.

— R. Engel

(Rome Italy) When new roots are showing and when the flower spikes are no more than 4 to 6 inches long.

— A. Fanfani

(Holland) When plants are flowering size, every third or fourth year.

— a major commercial grower

(California Coast US) The time to repot Phalaenopsis seedlings or repot mature plants depends on the season and the need for repotting. At Malibu we started about the middle of March and continued through September. Repotting should be avoided in the winter unless necessary. This is due to shorter daylight hours and less light intensity. However, if a plant is crowding the outside of the pot and there are plenty of roots, there is a way out.

Pot the plant, pot and plant together, in a larger sized, plastic pot...it should also be deeper. Put enough fresh bark at the bottom of the larger pot, so that when you place the smaller pot inside, the top will be about a half inch below the rim of the larger pot. Center the smaller pot in the larger one and let the surface roots dangle over the edge of the smaller, but inside the larger. Fill the empty space with bark, tamping it down firmly, but not heavily. You now have a plant that can be allowed to continue to grow (or show. ed.) without any problems. Around March or April, repot normally.

Also, if a plant has good, established roots above the top of the pot, (an inch or two) you can cut off the whole plant just below these roots and replant it in another pot. The original plant will form new roots and soon send up a new growth. This should be done only from around April to August.

— H. Freed

(Maui Hawaii US) When plants are growing well, I never repot. When the leaves start to drop or shrivel, <u>then</u> I repot.

— R. Fukamura

(Arizona Desert US) The best way for me to determine when to repot is by watching for new root tips to emerge. When they do, it is a good time to repot. Consideration must be given to the condition of the mix and the time of the season.

One year, I repotted almost everything in September and was disappointed with the poor flowering results. Another group I repotted in June were in much better shape and I'm led to believe that September is too late in the season.

Incidentally, I've had very poor results with cork as a potting medium. It breaks down rapidly and turns into a muddy substance. I once found an earthworm in broken-down cork bark mix.

— E. Goo

(Atlantic Coast US) We repot mature plants every year and seedlings twice a year. Phals always respond well to repotting and if we had time we might repot more often.

— K. Griffith

(Northeastern US) By inspection, but, ideally, it should be done once each year. Every 18 months is usually adequate if the potting material was in good condition at the outset (often not in the case of fir bark). Going past 18 months is neglect which some plants will show more quickly than others. Over 24 months is an invitation to disaster which may or may not strike, but growth and blooming will be far below the plant's potential.

— D. Grove

(Florida Atlantic Coast US) By inserting my finger into the medium. (My stand-by. If it won't go or comes out clean, the medium is still OK. If it comes out dirty, repot. ed.)

— C&L Hagan

(Indian Coast South Africa) Probably not very scientific, but I tend to repot only when the plant either outgrows the pot or is obviously unhappy with its circumstances.

— A. Harris

(Southeastern US) For mature plants I repot every 2 years minimum or when the bark breaks down. An examination of the plant and its medium will tell me when repotting is necessary.

— T. Harper

(Southern California US) We repot when the plant is excessively large for the pot size or the mix has broken down.

— E. Hetherington

(Midlands of England) Generally when a potting material is spent, it is very easy for me to insert a finger deep into the compost.

— P. Hirst

(Southern California US) When bark stays too wet and loses its sharpness to the touch.
— T. Koike

(East Java Indonesia) I slab-mount my phals and determine the sphagnum moss replacement by their color from brown to lesser brown, about 6 months every time.
— A. Kolopaking

(Holland) If plants are too far above the compost.
— H. Kronenberg

(France) Young plants are repotted every year. Adult plants kept in full benches for the cut flowers (which we get all the year round) are potted every 3 years.
— Marcel LeCoufle

(North of England) Annually, when the plant has outgrown its pot, or when it has too many aerial roots.
— P. Lindsay

(Central California US) When you can press your thumb down into the bark, it's time to repot.
— B. Livingston

(Northeastern US) In pots and baskets, we repot about every 2 years in bark.
— B&C Loechel

(Texas Gulf Coast US) I repot each year whether the plants need it or not. An overactive seedling may get repotted twice a year. Phals respond well to fresh medium.
— J. Margolis

(Southern California US) When the roots fill the pot, when the medium breaks down or when the plant looks sick.
— M. McCooey and others

(Puerto Rico US) We repot every year in July.
— R. Melendez

(Luzon Philippines) We normally look and examine the condition of osmunda fibers. With time (12-14 months) it deteriorates and clogs the circulation of water and air around the roots when decomposed.
— D. Mendoza

(Mid-Atlantic Coast US) Because phals grow best in fresh medium, I repot every 12 months. Some beginners tend to repot when the roots grow over the edge of the pot, but this is a

mistake, because phal roots normally wander a bit. I've seen pictures of mature phals in the wild with 6- to 10-foot long roots.
— E. Merkle

(Queensland Coast Australia) If the plants look distressed, we repot them immediately.
— R. Merritt

(California Coast US) At root initiation at plant base (usually late March/April).
— N. Nash

(California Coast US) To determine when repotting is required, every plant is marked with the last repot date. Plants are repotted every year for seedlings and sometimes more often for rapidly growing crosses. Mature plants are repotted every year to 2 years. If a Phalaenopsis plant begins to show a lack of vigor they are repotted and roots checked for problems. If the medium (fir bark) is in good condition, other causes are suspected, e.g. virus, incipient crown rot, etc.
— M&J Nedderman

(Central Atlantic Coast US) Usually by condition of the mix. Occasionally by the growth of the plant up too far and out of the pot.
— M. Owen

(Northcentral US) When aerial roots become so numerous that they become an eyesore or the area is a complete root mass.
— A. Roberts

(California Coast US) After blooming is over I repot all plants at 18-24 month intervals. If plant is growing roots profusely out of the pot, I may repot sooner.
— F. Robinson

(Puerto Rico US) For a potting mix of two parts of fir bark to one part of styrofoam (with a little dolomite lime), I repot every year.
— R. Rodriguez

(Central Atlantic Coast US) Repotting is done at intervals of 3 months to 2 years, depending on growth rate, desire to 'push' plants, and available time; normally yearly intervals at a minimum. We tend to underpot compared to most growers, so growth is usually the determining factor for repotting (6 months for smaller plants and annual for larger).
— E. Rutkowski

(Southcentral US) I stick a tag in the pot marked with the month and the year when repotted last. In between repottings, I watch for signs of sogginess or mold.
— P. Scholz

(South of England) I repot routinely annually, but will repot any plant at any time if it appears sickly. Annual repotting allows me to see if the medium is breaking down and I may reuse part or even all of the old medium if it is in suitable condition. This, of course, reduces problems of wetting a fresh batch of compost. I am always surprised that despite 'good tops' the occasional plant will have very little root. I would then 'pot down', THE SIZE OF THE POT BEING DETERMINED BY THE ROOT SYSTEM, NOT THE TOP OF THE PLANT. (Emphasis mine. Also see Bill Livingston's remarks in Q 5(e) to the same effect.) I find that the quality of bark can be very variable, and annual inspection of the compost is valuable for that reason. Annual repotting also allows you to inspect your plants for pests.
— P. Seaton

(North of England) When I was using bark as my principal potting medium, I repotted every 18 to 24 months providing the plant was growing normally. But because of the poor quality of bark available in England today, I have not used bark for some time. I still have a few plants in bark and these will be repotted soon and in a different medium.
— D. Shuker

*(Central Atlantic Coast US) Under artificial lighting...The presence of external root growth, size of the plant vs size of the pot, and the condition of the potting medium determine when we repot.
— K&M Smeltz

(Midlands of England) My phals are potted every year, irrespective.
— F. Smith

(Mid-Atlantic Coast US) When the plant falls over from top-heaviness or after 3 years, whichever comes first.
— M. Steen

(Gulf Coast US) When the roots talk to me.
— B. Steiner

*(Northeastern US) Under artificial lighting...Adults are repotted annually and seedlings every 6 months.
— D&D Strack

(Oahu Hawaii US) Depending on the rate of growth, a plant is left in its pot for 2 to 3 years. When plants get too tall, they are topped off and replanted.
— R. Takase

(Midlands of England) At present, I repot only when time permits. For mature plants that means every 3 to 4 years. I try to repot the seedlings every 6 months. I'm quite sure the young plants appreciate repotting.
— H. Taylor

(Mid-Atlantic Coast US) We mainly repot when the plants are large enough to look nice in the next larger size pot. But remember, we are commercial and try not to either over- or under-pot because of appearance. We suggest to our customers that they do the same.
— C. Williamson

(Texas Gulf Coast US) Yearly, if the medium doesn't break down sooner.
— C&J Wilson

Pruning roots: proportions of plant size, root ball size, and pot size. Pot is five and one-half inches at the rim.

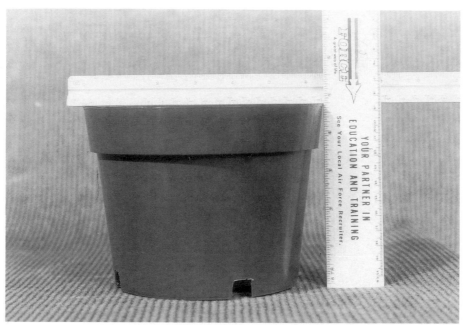

'Azalea' pot of a type best suited to phalaenopsis culture. Height of pot is 75-85% of the width of the top. See text. This pot is five inches high by six and one-half inches wide at the top.

An 'azalea' pot with a crescent-shaped section of the rim removed to allow phal leaves to droop. . . draining the crown. Crown rot insurance courtesy of John Miller.

130

QUESTION 5(b) DO YOU USE ANY AVAILABLE POT TYPE OR DO YOU PREFER ONES WITH EXTRA DRAINAGE SUCH AS 'AZALEA' POTS?

(California Coast US) Plant size determines size of pot used; 4-inch square, 6-inch 'azalea', or 8-inch standard. Plastic pots are used exclusively. Extra drain holes are preferred.
— L. Batchman

(Southeastern Australia) Standard plastic pots.
— M. Black and others

(Central California US) I use new or cleaned/sterilized plastic pots. All bottom drainage holes are enlarged using an electric drill equipped with a countersink. I check and trim all drain holes of any plastic debris that could interfere with optimal drainage.
— R. Buchter

(Southern California US) For both bark and New Zealand moss I use plastic pots with slots cut half way up the sides and half way to the middle with a power table saw. I use a silicon carbide blade with a kerf about 1/8th inch wide. I used to use clay pots with New Zealand moss, but found that the roots died wherever they touched the clay. Inside the root ball was OK.
— E. Campuzano

(California Coast US) I prefer plastic pots with bottom and side drainage and not tall.
— E. Carlson

(California Bay Area US) I make my own well-drained pots.
— W. Cecil

*(Northeastern US) Under artificial lighting...I like plenty of holes. For smaller plants I use 'azalea' or squatty pots; for larger plants 6-7'' I use bulb pans.
— I. Cohen

(Southern California US) We use regular pots with four to eight holes in them.
— D&R Cowden

(Central Atlantic Coast US) We use 'azalea' clay pots. The plastic pots seem to stay wet too long.
— L. Clouser

(Indian Coast South Africa) We use plastic pots with the usual number of drain holes, but we use a circular saw to make vertical and horizontal cuts into the pot at its lower end on four sides. The length of the cuts depends on the size of the pot, of course, but in the main they are half the height or half the width of each pot.
— C&I Coll

(South of England) One standard make of black, plastic pot of relatively short depth. No extra drainage.

— R. Dadd

(South Australia) Always use pots with good drainage holes.

— M. Dennis

(Central Atlantic Coast US) I use 6- and 8-inch standard plastic pots, preferably white, for mature phals.

— R. Drejka

(Florida Gulf US) Always with extra drainage.

— J. Eich

(Holland) Only plastic containers with normal drainage in the bottom.

— a major commercial grower

(California Coast US) Prefer extra drainage.

— H. Freed

(Mid-Atlantic Coast US) I think phals should be under-potted. The reason is the interior of a large pot hardly ever dries out. Big pots are okay, I guess, where the climate can be controlled so the rate of evaporation is the same every day. (Only on trees in the southwestern Pacific. ed.) It isn't possible here in New Jersey and the plant is likely to lose its roots if an oversized pot is used.

— M. Frier

(Central Atlantic Coast US) 'Azalea' pots only.

— R. Griesbach

(Atlantic Coast US) We use Kord plastic pots of the 'azalea' type.

— K. Griffith

(Gulf Coast US) I usually use plastic 'azalea' pots. I melt additional drainage holes in the bottom and sometimes in the sides of the pot. Also, I invert a much-slotted 2-inch pot over a large center drainage hole to form an air-cone in the bottom of the big pot before filling it with medium.

— J. Grimes

(Northeastern US) I prefer extra drainage holes. Contrary to my favorite Phalaenopsis Guru, I prefer standard-sized pots over the 'azalea'-type for two reasons: First, they help keep roots above the deteriorating medium, which always starts at the bottom of the pot; delays in repotting are in that manner less damaging (Dr Grove, like many phal growers travels a good deal. ed.); and second, the taller pots keep the ends of the leaves above the bench surface. This, in turn, permits more light and air movement around the ends of the leaves.

Moreover, for plants which have long, arching inflorescences, the taller pots provide better balance, visually, in my opinion. Of course, if you hang your plants on a wire netting or set of pipes, my arguments wouldn't hold (except for the last one, when the plants are removed for exhibition,) but most growers grow their plants on benches.

— D. Grove

(Florida Atlantic Coast US) I use only clay 'azalea' pots.

— C&L Hagan

(Southeastern US) 'Azalea'-type pots are the best for phals. The new ones made of flexible plastic with bunches of bottom holes are just great. They work well and give a clean outward appearance without the drainage holes showing on the side of the pot. 'Azalea' pots also have a low profile using less potting medium, and allow for good drainage. For large plants I use 2/3-gallon Polytainer-type pots with large, hard styrofoam 'peanuts' in the bottom for improved drainage.

— T. Harper

(Southern California US) We use stubby pots in 4-, 5-, and 6-inch sizes on the average.

— E. Hetherington

(Southern California US) We use pots with extra drainage provided by drilling holes.

— D. Hirsch

(Midlands of England) Plastic pots are preferred for Phalaenopsis culture. If pots larger than 6-inch are required, additional drainage holes are made in the sides.

— P. Hirst

(Arizona Desert US) We prefer the plastic pots with extra drainage. If we can't get them, we use an old soldering iron to poke additional holes until we're happy with them.

— J&G Johnson

(Southeastern Australia) For any given set of conditions of growth and management, there is an optimum size and shape of the plant container. The diameter/depth ratio is very important as this controls the amount of water takeup, the evaporation rate and the residual water/air content about the roots of the plants. The coarseness of the mix also has to be accounted for in this judgment. The amount of deterioration of the organic solids has to be continually monitored and, if necessary, repotting undertaken to ensure the health of the pot-bound roots and, thus, the plant. Uniformity of the potting mix throughout the house is very desirable to maintain even moisture in the pots.

— J. Kilgannon

(California Coast US) Usually the 'azalea'-type pots.

— T. Koike

(Holland) Normal stone pots.
— H. Kronenberg

(Central California US) We use 6-inch Scotch (squat) pots, 4-inch pots with side and bottom drain holes, 3 1/4-inch and 2-1/2-inch pots with the same drain holes.
— B. Livingston

(Florida Caribbean US) We use plastic pots with plastic 'peanuts' for extra drainage.
— L. Lodyga

(Northeastern US) We use plastic 'azalea'-type pots, but I heat a piece of 1-inch copper tubing with a blow torch and put extra holes in them. It's cold here in the winter (Cape Cod, Massachusetts) and we have lots of air through the mix to prevent rotting. It works, too.
— B&C Loechel

(Queensland Coast Australia) We use squat plastic pots without making additional drainage holes, but we buy the ones that have the best drainage.
— J. Mackinney

(Luzon Philippines) We are not using pots although they are aesthetically and functionally good. If our plants are under 2 years of age, we maintain them on twigs. Thereafter, we move them to slabs; 1-inch thick, 6-inches wide, and 8-inches long. You may even put a frame around the sides... to make a nice-looking specimen Phalaenopsis plant.
— D. Mendoza

(Mid-Atlantic Coast US) I use 'azalea' pots and check every one to make sure the drain holes are clear. Phals love a mix that is evenly moist, but will quickly reject a mix that becomes stagnant when the drain holes are blocked. Without good air circulation in the medium, roots quickly die and the plant suffers.
— E. Merkle

(Queensland Coast Australia) We use standard squat pots, 165mm (6.5-inch) for adult plants. As plants are repotted, extra holes are drilled in the sides and bottom.
— R. Merritt

(Southern California US) For mature plants we use Scotch (stubby) pots. For seedlings we use small, standard-drainage pots.
— J. Miller

(Southern California US) Any available pot.
— H. Moye

(California Coast US) All pots used for phals are short and with good drainage.
— N. Nash

(California Coast US) Pots are the 'azalea'-type or pots with additional holes added. In a large collection I think it is important to use the same type of pot for each size. This will make watering easier; when plants dry out, they all need watering at the same time.
— M&J Nedderman

(Central Atlantic Coast US) We use three-quarter 'azalea' clay pots.
— M. Owen

(Mid-West US) I use National Plastics pots with the extra slots.
— R. Pallister

(Southeastern US) 'Azalea' pots altogether.
— S. Pridgen

(Northcentral US) I use 6-inch, 'azalea'-type pots exclusively on all adult plants.
— A. Roberts

(California Coast US) I use any available pots, but add drainage holes with a drill or soldering iron. I prefer not to use the 'gallon'-type since they are too deep and use too much medium.
— F. Robinson

(Queensland Coast Australia) We grow species on natural cork slabs with a wad of Deuynaria fern fibre attached. Hybrids are grown in pots.
— R. Robinson

(Central Atlantic Coast US) Pots used are squares up to 4-inch and 'azalea' pots from 4-inch up.
— E. Rutkowski

(Southcentral US) I prefer pots with holes in both the sides and the bottom.
— P. Scholz

(South of England) Standard plastic pots. They are easy to use and to clean. I incorporate plenty of drainage.
— P. Seaton

(North of England) I use only black, plastic pots, full-depth up to and including the 5-inch size. Over this size, I find it best to use what we call 'three-quarter depth' pots. I've not yet found a pot with sufficient side or bottom drainage, so I set to work with a soldering iron. The hot iron leaves a 'fast' (a ridge of plastic? ed.) on the inside of the pot which I prefer not to remove since it discourages roots from exiting the pot through the holes.

(from photographs it appears that Mr Shuker increases the drainage on standard pots by about 100%. On 'azalea'-types he increases the drainage by 25% or so. ed.)
— D. Shuker

(Midlands of England) Standard plastic.
— F. Smith

(Northeastern US) Under artificial lighting...Prefer Farand squares up to 4 1/8th-inch size, then 'azalea'-types for larger.
— D&D Strack

(Midlands of England) My preference is for the black, polythene pots. I do not increase the standard drainage, although I once carried out calculations to determine the ratio of the area of drainage hole to the volume of the pot. YOU WILL NOT BE SURPRISED TO FIND THAT AS THE POT VOLUME INCREASES, THE RATIO (SIZE) OF THE DRAINAGE HOLE DECREASES VERY MUCH. (Emphasis mine. Good point. ed.) My preference is for the three-quarter (squat) pot as this provides a bigger base area and more stability to the pot.
— H. Taylor

*(Northeastern US) Under artificial lighting...I slab-mount on my own handmade mounts made of mixed osmunda and redwood fiber. (2 parts osmunda to 1 part redwood fiber)
— J. Vella

(Mid-Atlantic Coast US) I invert small pots inside the big ones to improve drainage and ventilation.
— J. Webster and others

QUESTION 5(c) DOES THE CONDITION OF THE POTTING MEDIUM AFFECT WATERING INTERVAL?

(Indian Coast South Africa) The condition of the medium will <u>determine</u> the watering pattern. A coarse, open medium is more beneficial to plants having better aeration and leading to less root decay.

— A. Adriaanse

(California Coast US) The condition of the potting medium does not affect the watering schedule.

— L. Batchman

(Southeastern Australia) So long as the material is still in good condition, no.

— M. Black

(California Coast US) Yes; as the bark gets older and breaks down, more moisture is held in the pots. Therefore, plants are watered at less frequent intervals.

— E. Carlson and others

(Southern California US) No, because the mix doesn't break down in the year interval we have between repotting.

— D&R Cowden

(Florida Gulf Coast US) Yes. As the (organic) medium ages, less frequent watering is required.

— J. Eich

(Holland) Yes.

— a major commercial grower and others

(Maui Hawaii US) Yes. For different media, you water different ways. You should always check the condition of the growth, then decide if you are over- or under-watering.

— R. Fukamura

(Indian Coast South Africa) No.

— A. Harris and others

(Southeastern US) Technically, it should, but with thousands of plants to repot and care for, when one gets watered, they all do...with very few exceptions.

— T. Harper

(Southern California US) We have to water whole houses at one time, so we cannot customize watering.

— E. Hetherington

(Arizona Desert US) We do not vary the watering schedule because of the condition of the medium. We just repot the plant.
— J&G Johnson

(France) We keep more dry after the repotting, awaiting the start of the new roots.
— Marcel LeCoufle

(Central California US) Condition of the potting medium does have an effect on the watering interval, but probably keeping pots grouped according to size is more important in determining the watering interval. Smaller pots need more frequent watering than do the larger sizes. A 6-inch pot may need watering once a week or 10 days according to the weather. Smaller pots need watering every few days.
— B. Livingston

(Florida Caribbean US) As the medium deteriorates, the interval of watering is lengthened.
— L. Lodyga

(Luzon Philippines) If you grow on slabs, more frequent watering is needed. We water our slab-mounted plants 4-5 times a day.
— D. Mendoza

(Southern California US) Yes, as the medium gets older, it needs less water.
— H. Moye and others

(California Coast US) A leading question obviously, but in an older mix, a plant will usually have a fuller root ball, which compensates for increased water retention.
— N. Nash

(Central Atlantic Coast US) The size of the bark used is adjusted so the entire greenhouse is watered at the same time.
— E. Rutkowski

(Southcentral US) Yes, fresh medium needs more frequent watering.
— P. Scholz

*(Northcentral US) Under artificial lighting...It should, but it doesn't.
— W. Schumann

(California Coast US) Fresh bark drys quicker; however, if the plant is growing quickly, the roots will dry in a large pot with older bark just as quickly. For convenience, I water everything at once, but hit the small pots and newly-repotted plants as needed.
— J. Watkins

QUESTION 5 (d) WHAT ROOTING MEDIUM DO YOU USE?

CHARCOAL (Indian Coast South Africa) There are many creations of mediums. I look at it this way: no epiphitic plant needs potting medium. The main factor is anchoring the plants and keeping them in the proper position. I use charcoal to pot all my phals, from seedlings to mature plants. It is easy to clean, gives you a chance to overpot a bit, and, as the material is inert to a high degree, you can wash through the medium freely. No salt deposits stay in the pots to burn the roots. Plants can remain in the same pot for a longer time (than with less inert media). It offers good aeration. There is, however, one disadvantage: it requires a higher level of humidity for the plants. (I grew on logs for a number of years, but logs are hard to get now.)
— A. Adriaanse

FIR BARK (California Coast US) We use medium fir bark, exclusively.
— L. Batchman

PINE BARK (Southeastern Australia) One-half to three-quarter inch pine bark from very aged trees or bark from aged dead trees. This material will last for about 6 years. Occasionally pots are soaked in limewater as a sweetener, especially after 3 years or so, to offset the effect of accumulated salts.

I grow PLANTS OUT OF FLASK in perlite and peat and will give you a fertiliser recipe that makes them grow while you watch.

8 ounces of Zest/Thrive/Aquasol (probably not known to you under these names, but use your version of a complete fertiliser that dissolves completely in water).

1 pint of Nitrosol (same as above.)
2 ounces of fungicide (Captan or Natriphene).
2 ounces of iron chelates.
4 ounces of Epsom salts.
1 level tablespoon of phosphoric acid.
1 level tablespoon of copper sulfate.
1 level tablespoon of complete trace elements.
10 drops of Formula 20 (root growth promoter).

Dissolve in 50 litres of water and dispense through a 16:1 Hozon gadget through a hose, twice a week.

When the babies are up to 3- or 4-inch pots, revert to bark and feed much less.
— M. Black

PROMIX/BARK/TREE FERN (Eastern Texas US)

Three gallons of Pro-Mix (Peat moss, vermiculite, dolomite lime, and other things)
Two gallons of small fir bark
One gallon of perlite
Two gallons of shredded tree fern
One half cup of Osmocote 14-14-14
Two cups of ground oyster shell*

*Two reasons for the oyster shell: (1) if there is a problem with sodium in the water, usually the calcium will combine with it to produce sodium sulfate, a solid that can be leached from the potting medium; and (2) it will allow a better ion exchange, making the fertilizer more readily available to the plant.

— T. Brown

FIR BARK (Central California US) I use steam-cleaned, sifted, medium-sized fir bark.

— R. Buchter

FIR BARK/NEW ZEALAND MOSS (California Coast US) Three-quarters of my plants are in bark. The remaining are potted in New Zealand sphagnum moss. Any plant that is the least bit distressed is potted in the moss. Once a plant is started in moss, I leave it in the moss from then on. When time comes to pot up, I unpot the root-moss ball, wrap additional moss around it to fit it to the larger pot and stuff it in. I do not remove the old moss from the plant. It isn't necessary. The old moss may crumble, but it is still good and the plants love it.

The moss should be packed loosely around the root ball when repotting. Watering interval for phals in moss is 10 to 14 days, even in dry southern California. Use a wetting agent solution on the surface of the moss annually to break down the algae which can reject water and lead to a desiccated plant.

Store New Zealand moss damp to keep it growing and vital.

— E. Campuzano

FIR BARK (California Coast US) Plants are repotted every 15-18 months in fir bark. From 2- to 4-inch pots, I use fine bark (1/8'' to 1/4'') and 6-inch or larger are potted in medium bark (1/4'' to 5/8'').

— E. Carlson

AUSTRALIAN PINE (Western Australia) I use Australian pine which is readily available in local forests. I collect the large pieces, put them through a Muncher and sieve thoroughly to clean out dust and small particles. We collect from fallen trees which I estimate have been down for 1 to 2 years. I use no other bark.

— K. Clarke

CHARCOAL/TREE FERN (Central Atlantic Coast US) We are using a mixture of 50% #2 charcoal and 50% coarse shredded tree fern.
— L. Clouser

FIR BARK (Northeastern US) Under artificial lighting. . .Fir bark mix. Repot adults about every 2 years. A layer of styrofoam plastic 'peanuts' is useful on the bottom of the pot for drainage.
— I. Cohen

BARK/CHARCOAL/and. . .(Indian Coast South Africa) Rooting medium is 7 parts bark, 1 part charcoal, 1 part peat or perlite, 1 part vermiculite, 1 tablespoon of Dolomite lime, and ½ teaspoon of iron chelate. (No quantities of first four ingredients given. ed.)
— C&I Coll

FIR BARK/PERLITE (Southern California US) For years I used a combination of charcoal, cork bits and man-made rock with exceptional root growth, but after adopting the 'open greenhouse' culture (super-ventilated), I found I could not keep the potting mix moist. I have recently reverted to fir bark with 20% quarter-inch perlite with good results.
— W. Cousineau

MISCELLANEOUS (Southern California US) We use a mix of 1 part coarse peat moss, 1 part fine fir bark, 1 part medium fir bark, 1 part #3 pumice, 1 part ground redwood shavings and 1 teaspoon of 18-18-18 Osmocote (slow release) fertilizer per gallon of medium.
— D&R Cowden

ROCK WOOL (South of England) Grodan water-repellent rock wool of loose, granular type, medium grade, mixed with perlite. Initially wetted with 6 drenches after potting with water containing 20 ppm wetting agent. Repot about once each year. (Bob Dadd has an experiment underway on a potting mix of rock wool and a dedicated feeding formula. . .specifically for phals and has already seen a good bit of success with it. He should have some definitive results in the spring of 1988, about the time we go to press on this book. . .so it won't be included here. Contact him for comments then. Perhaps he can be encouraged to write a short piece for submission to the Orchid Review on his findings. ed.)
— R. Dadd

BARK/CHARCOAL/et al. (South Australia) American fir bark or similar. . .red gum charcoal. . .blue stone (large). . .isolite. Equal parts. Repot when necessary from 2 to 4 years.
— M. Dennis

FIR BARK (Central Atlantic Coast US) I use medium grade fir bark for mature plants.
— R. Drejka and others

COARSE FIR BARK or TREE FERN (Florida Gulf Coast US) I use coarse fir bark with plastic pots. . .and a mix of tree fern and redwood bark with clay pots.
— J. Eich

FIR BARK AND STYROFOAM CUBES (Southern California US) One-third styrofoam cubes (one-half inch) and two-thirds fir bark. Repot every 2 to 4 years. (Dr. Engel has about 2,000 plants in this medium and they grow beautifully . . . but require more frequent watering. ed.)

— R. Engel

ASSORTED (Holland) One, a mixture of german peat and styropor; two, a mixture of rock wool with styropor; or three, oasis. (The green, crushable plastic foam used by florists for arrangements, but in shredded form.)

— a major commercial grower

WHATEVER IS ON-HAND (Maui Hawaii US) I use all kinds of media such as hapu (tree fern); bark; and cinder mixed with 1/3rd bark, 1/3rd peat moss (and 1/3rd cinders) and with plastic peanuts on the bottom of the pot. In Hawaii (Maui) this last is the best mix.

— R. Fukamura

NEW ZEALAND MOSS (Arizona Desert US) Seedlings immediately out of flask appear to grow more rapidly in New Zealand moss than their contemporaries in fine fir bark. I suspect the more rapid growth can be attributed to the moss' efficiency in holding moisture and its antiseptic qualities. The considerable moisture held by the moss seems to be evenly distributed so that there are no wet or dry spots in the medium. The antiseptic quality seems to prevent fungus from growing regardless of how wet it is and, with the salts on the surface of the medium, the roots in the moss seem to grow faster (and die slower).

Regarding the issue of how tightly to pack the moss in a pot with a plant: a compressed sponge holds less water than one that isn't, but I don't know if this matters. Phals can tolerate a drenching or soaking. It only becomes unhealthy if it is too wet too long. So, the duration of the wetness is more important than the degree of wetness.

While an un-compressed sponge holds more water than one that isn't, it is also capable of holding more air. Which would dry out faster, a bucket tightly filled with wet sponges . . . or one loosely filled with wet sponges? I don't know, but the moss seems to work better for me when it is loosely packed. To those just beginning to use the New Zealand moss, I would recommend potting with a layer of gravel on the bottom, for ballast when the moss dries out, and the use of shallow pots with extra drainage holes. All of this is to prevent the moss from staying too wet, too long.

Note: if you use clay pots the gravel isn't needed.

Some observations on the use of New Zealand moss:

1. Plants in NZ moss seem to do better in smaller pots than if potted in bark.

142

2. When repotting, I do not remove the old moss. I just add enough new moss to fill up the pot.

3. Algae will grow on the surface if you are doing things right. Do not let the algae growth bother you and do not try to prevent it. Drenching it with a Physan solution seems to break the moss down and screws up its water retention properties. (Dr. Jack Fowlie suggests these blue-green algaes will fix atmospheric nitrogen into amines, a form useable by orchids. Dr. Forrest Robinson uses a thin layer of charcoal on top of the moss to prevent the algae formation. ed.)

4. The moss will come with a few fine twigs and leaves. These should be removed when encountered. Fungus will form on them, but not on the moss.

5. THIS IS VERY IMPORTANT: Before using the moss, fluff it up by adding about a half-gallon of hot water per kilo of moss. It just doesn't seem to work right if you skip this step.

6. When the moss is first used, it is a little hard to get wet and can get very dry, very fast. The drier it gets, the harder it is to get wet again. When this happens, I water or mist it every day until the moss wets again, then go back to a normal routine.

7. Since I do not remove the old moss when repotting, the plants experience little damage or transplant shock. The practice also allows you to repot any time of the year that the plant is actively growing.

8. NZ moss doesn't work equally well with all phals. Some like it better than others. For this reason, I do not recommend changing a whole collection over to the moss at one time.
— E. Goo

FIR BARK (Central Atlantic Coast US) Three parts medium fir bark (1''), 1 part seedling fir bark (1/4''), 1/4 part perlite.
— R. Griesbach

ROCKWOOL/CHARCOAL/STYROFOAM (Atlantic Coast US) Our medium is half rockwool, quarter charcoal and quarter styrofoam. We use this for new seedlings as well as for mature plants. Mature plants are repotted every year and seedlings every 6 months.
— K. Griffith

CHARCOAL (Gulf Coast US) By far, the best potting medium for mature plants and larger seedlings for me is charcoal. I repot when the plant outgrows the pot.
— J. Grimes

FIR BARK (Northeastern US) Fir bark alone or a mixture of fir bark, tree fern, coarse perlite and sometimes a little charcoal thrown in as well. The potting mix is less important than other elements of culture. I have seen all kinds of mixes used by good commercial and amateur growers in various parts of the world with equally good results when other cultural practices were appropriate. The message is not the medium (groan! ed.), but what the grower does with it.
— D. Grove

COCONUT FIBER/FIR BARK (Florida Atlantic Coast US) I use some fir bark, but mostly coconut fiber. I repot in bark every year; in the coconut fiber, every 2 to 3 years.
— C&L Hagan

CHARCOAL (Indian Coast South Africa) Charcoal, and I am able to repot between the second and third years.
— A. Harris

FIR BARK (Southeastern US) I use medium fir bark (Sequoia) for 6-inch pots and larger; fir bark seedling mix for smaller sizes, community trays (10x20''), and half-flats.

> MEDIUM BARK PREPARATION: Each batch of bark is soaked (actually floated) in water for 24 hours minimum. I use a 100-gallon galvanized tub. The gunk settles to the bottom and the good stuff floats and is skimmed off, spread out on the ground and allowed to dry for 2 to 3 days. Usually the sun will dry it, but I sometimes use a fan to blow over it to dry it faster, especially in damp, cloudy weather. The dried bark is then returned to the empty tub and doused with a combination of fertilizer, dolomite lime and Physan in 5-gallons of hot water for four cubic feet of bark.

[Tom Harper advises that he found the use of detergent and insecticide in this mix unnecessary, something I had recommended in an earlier phal culture book. I agree that the detergent is not necessary when Physan is added, but the insecticide is still a recommended practice...and one of the few ways I know of to conveniently remove bush snails from fir bark as it comes from the forest...and come from the forest they do!

Another way that is practical only in a hot climate is to put the bark in a dark-colored plastic trash container, add the insecticide, cover it...and set it out in the hot sun. Instant 130°F. Malathion has the handy quality of running out of zip in about 6 hours, so it can be handled after a short soak. To avoid getting Malathion on your hands when potting, Tom, scoop the treated bark up with a 4-inch square pot. Piece of cake. ed.]

SEEDLING BARK (1/8-1/4'') PREPARATION Because of its size, I just add the same premix to 4 cubic feet of bark, with no pre-floating. This year I'm adding sponge rock to help aerate the bark because of its tendency to pack too tightly. I use sponge rock instead of perlite because of its larger size (about the same size as the bark.)

I've had excellent growth in fir bark. Good green color and more flowers per spike are characteristic of the plants. This all make sense when you look at the soilless mixes used by pot plant growers.

— T. Harper

FIR BARK/CHARCOAL. (Southern California US) We use three parts fir bark to one part of #1 grade charcoal.

— D. Hirsch

PEAT (Midlands of England) A peat-based compost is used for all plant sizes and is prepared from prepacked scottish sphagnum peat blocks which are broken down on a kitchen cheese grater. To each two parts of peat is added one part of recycled polystyrene beads and 1/4 part charcoal and 1/4 part of fresh sphagnum moss. Repotting needs to be carried out at 12-18 month intervals for adult plants.

— P. Hirst

FIR BARK/PUMICE (Arizona Desert US) Our medium consists of 8 parts fir bark and 3 parts (volcanic) pumice rock. (The desert southwest of the US is a dormant volcano area. The volcanic pumice is a locally-available material which is handy, cheap and works well. I see this use of local materials running through many of the responses. ed.)

— J&G Johnson

FIR BARK (California Coast US) Medium fir bark; we repot normally about 2 years on cut flower stock.

— T. Koike

ASSORTED (Southeastern Australia) Obtaining suitable components for the media is a problem experienced by most growers at some stage. At present sphagnum moss, pinebark, pinechips, charcoal and polystyrene granules are available here and can all be used in mixes.

— J. Kilgannon

SOFT PEAT (Holland) I grow in soft peat lumps which stay for 3 years, at least. Transplanting normally after 2 years.

— H. Kronenberg

UNSPECIFIED (France) Our composts are indicated in our catalogues or in my book, ''Orchid'es Exotiques'', edited by la Maison Rustique.

— Marcel LeCoufle

FIR BARK (Central California US) We use Sequoia fir bark and try to repot once a year or <u>as needed.</u> Seedlings like to be repotted several times a year when they are small. I select pot sizes according to the size of the root mass of the plant. Never put a small plant in a medium or large pot.
— B. Livingston

NEW ZEALAND MOSS (Florida Caribbean) We used to grow in tree fern and then in bark mixes, but now we are moving all our plants into New Zealand moss as we've found this to be far superior to the other media. With this moss, we only water once a week.
— L. Lodyga

FIR BARK/CHARCOAL (Queensland Coast Australia) We pot in Sequoia orchid (fir) bark mixed with charcoal at a proportion of 5 parts bark to 4 parts charcoal in medium grade up to 5-inch pots and coarse grade for larger.
— J. Mackinney

CHARCOAL/PERLITE (Texas Gulf Coast US) Charcoal, perlite and a small amount of 'Metro Mix'. Styrofoam in the bottom.
— J. Margolis

NEW ZEALAND MOSS/BARK (Southern California US) I use New Zealand moss for pot sizes up to 4-inch. For larger pots, I use medium fir bark. If I start a small seedling in moss, then I can keep moving it up in moss up to a 6-inch pot.
— M. McCooey

SERVO (Mid-Atlantic Coast US) I used Servo exclusively for 5 years, but became dissatisfied with it for use with phals. I think it is wonderful for fast, luxuriant growth, but the stuff needs watering every other day and that much work wore me out. It also breaks down in about 6 months. I'm back to using fir bark.
— E. Merkle

PINE BARK (Southeastern Australia) I use half-inch sized pine bark with a small amount of shell grit and peanut shells.
— A. Merriman

NEW ZEALAND MOSS/STONE (Queensland Coast Australia) 50% New Zealand moss (I'd prefer german peat moss, but it's hard to get) and 50% water-worn river stone, all sizes from 1/8th to 1/2''. Usually repot between 18 and 24 months. (Ron, a New Zealand grower told me he couldn't get any NZ moss. It was all being exported. In California, we have a hell of time getting decent fir bark (from California forests.) Welcome to the wonderful world of foreign exchange. ed.)
— R. Merritt

NEW ZEALAND MOSS (Southern California US) We are having the best results with New Zealand sphagnum moss and the secret is to pot with moist, but not wet, moss firmly, but

not tightly or loosely packed, with a 2- or 3-inch layer of plastic 'peanuts' for drainage. Smaller pots dry out quicker and must be watered as necessary. Repotting must be done when the seedlings outgrow the pot or to 'pot down' when plants grow too large.
— J. Miller

FIR BARK (Southern California US) I use fir bark of the 'Pathway' (1/2 to 3/4'' size for mature plants and repot every year.
— H. Moye

FIR BARK (California Coast US) Three parts of medium size fir bark (3/8 to 5/8'') to one part of shredded redwood bark...and we repot every year.
— N. Nash

FIR BARK/TREE FERN (Mid-West US) I use coarse fir bark in the bottom third of the pot and a mix of one part medium tree fern and three parts fir bark seedling mix...on plants up to 6-inch pots. On larger than 6-inch pots, I add two parts of coarse fir bark to the seedling bark. I also put several pieces of redwood bark in each pot to control snow mold. This works quite well in Mid-America where frequent misting is necessary to keep up a 70% RH level.
— R. Pallister

ASSORTED (Southeastern US) Starting from the bottom: a layer of styrofoam peanuts, a layer of sphagnum, a layer of Pro-Mix BX (peat moss, vermiculite, perlite, limestone and nutrients), a layer of charoal and a layer of cut 2-inch lengths of Husky Fiber. Large pots have a few rocks added to the styrofoam peanuts for stability.
— S. Pridgen

AUSTRALIAN PINE The local (Perth) pine bark (Pinus radiata) in use for orchids is very good, readily available and considerably cheaper than peat moss.
— K. Rex

FIR BARK/CHARCOAL (California Coast US) For plants with a leaf span of up to 10 inches, I have been having good luck with a mix of 50% fine fir bark, 25% medium perlite, and 25% charcoal. For larger plants, 50% medium fir bark, 25% volcanic rock, 15% redwood bark, and 10% charcoal.
— F. Robinson

PERLITE/ISOLITE (Queensland Coast Australia) One part peat moss, one part vermiculite, 2 parts perlite and 2 parts isolite (finely shredded Coolite polyfoam). This mix is used for hybrids. Species are grown on cork slabs with a wad of Drynaria fern fibre.
— R. Robinson

FIR BARK (Southcentral US) Fir bark; one-third seedling grade and two-thirds medium grade. I repot at least once a year, twice to give a special or a sick plant an added boost.

SPECIAL NOTE: I dampen, not soak, the bark in Watch-Us-Grow (8-8-8 liquid fertilizer) for no more than 2 hours. In our very humid climate, any longer soak makes the bark 'age' too rapidly.

— P. Scholz

* BARK (Northcentral US) Under artificial lighting...Medium bark mixed with such things as cypress mulch, tree fern fiber, sphagnum moss, etc.

— W. Schumann

PEAT/CORK (North of England) Eight parts of 3/8 to 1/2" cubed peat, three parts each of 1/4 to 1/2" cork, three parts of 1/4 to 1/2' cubed polystyrene, three parts of chopped sphagnum moss and two parts of 1/4 to 3/8" charcoal.

— D. Shuker

FIR BARK/CHARCOAL/A COMMERCIAL MIX (Mid-Atlantic Coast US) Under artificial lighting...We've used Douglas fir bark with success, but must repot every 1 to 2 years. We like charcoal, but haven't had much experience with it. Looks good. For phal seedlings, we use Bud Mellott's (Pittsburgh, PA) paph seedling mix. It has 1/3 fir bark seedling mix, 1/3 seedling charcoal and 1/3 chopped polyurethane foam. It works well for us.

— K&M Smeltz

SPHAGNUM/STYROFOAM (Mid-Atlantic Coast US) Sphagnum and ground styrofoam, with the proportion of styrofoam ranging from 20% of the total in 4-inch pots to 50% of the total in 8-inch pots.

— M. Steen

FIR BARK (Oahu Hawaii US) My potting medium is bark; for mature plants, three parts of half- to 1-inch size and 1 part of quarter- to half-inch size in plastic pots.

— R. Takase

PEAT/PERLITE/CHARCOAL (Midlands of England) I use rough Finnish peat and perlite, used as a 2:1 mix (2 peat:1 perlite) together with a quantity of charcoal. To every bushel of the mix, I add about 3 handsful of Sea Gold, a seaweed compound. You can't overuse the Sea Gold because it does not burn the roots. I also often add a small amount of trace elements to the mix.

— H. Taylor

NEW ZEALAND MOSS...IN BASKETS (Mid-Atlantic Coast US) Phals grow well with a ball of NZ moss wrapped around their roots and the plant placed in an open-web strawberry container (a small plastic basket, cupsized).

— M. Werther

PREFER TREE FERN, BUT USE BARK (Mid-Atlantic Coast US) We think tree fern fiber is the best medium for growing Phals, but have changed to fir bark because our customers complain they cannot keep it sufficiently moist, especially in the winter. The addition of charcoal to the tree fern helps.

— C. Williamson

SECTION 5.3
THE SECOND MOST IMPORTANT THING IN GROWING PHALAENOPSIS WELL:
GOOD DRAINAGE

You've probably heard the advice that good drainage is essential to good orchid culture so many times you could just barf. Right? Me too. But, dreary as it sounds, it is true.

Adequate drainage is probably second only to adequate light as the most violated principle of good Phalaenopsis culture. Usually if a mature phal won't bloom in the first year of ownership, the reason is lack of light to meet its needs. That's probably true of a lot of orchids, but when a phal poops out in the second or third year, THE REASON IS ALMOST ALWAYS FAILURE TO PROVIDE THE NECESSARY DRAINAGE AND AERATION OF THE ROOTS.

The 'right' amount of moisture for phal plants' roots is a difficult notion to pin down. When potting medium is new the plant probably needs to be watered often, because new bark and tree fern have low capacities for water retention. That changes as the medium ages.

Good, new fir bark is nut-hard and absorbs very little water at first. However, as it ages and breaks down from microbial action, it holds an increasing amount of moisture. When it's rotten it does a great job of holding it...too good a job, because then it fills in the air spaces in the medium and denies air to the roots. And they die...followed shortly by the rest of the plant.

Fortunately, during most of its life, the water-holding capacity of fir bark remains fairly constant. If you need a number to work with, fir bark's useful life for phals is on the order of 18-24 months. But, for the first two months fir bark is used in a phal pot, it can be counted on to hold very little water. After that, though, and through the 18 to 24-month term, it will give you good service.

Don't plan on using fir bark as a phal potting medium any longer than 24 months. And don't let it go that long if it wasn't hard as a nut to start with...which it usually isn't. (An eighteen month-interval is a disaster if you're trying to do your re-potting at a fixed time each year, but it's better than letting things go 6 months past the time for re-potting. A lot of roots can go bellyup in that time.) Some growers reuse serviceable bark (that has been sterilized) in quantities up to 20% of the total volume to 'seed' new mix.

All right, the other aspect of the drainage problem, in addition to medium, is the pot itself or more specifically, the holes in the bottom of the pot.

MOST POTS, AS THEY COME FROM A SUPPLIER OR NURSERY, ARE NOT SATISFACTORY FOR USE WITH PHALAENOPSIS. Unless they are of the stubby, 'extra drainage' or 'azalea' type, they just do not do an adequate job of getting rid of standing water in the pot. They don't have enough or big enough drain holes. Small drain holes clog easily.

Even the ones with extra drainage are often not suitable because drain holes may be partially or completely covered over with extruded plastic films which result from worn pot molds in manufacture. And don't presume that since you got a plant from a good nursery that the pot will be OK. It probably isn't.

The solution to this problem is to clear clogged drainage holes and add new ones where necessary. You can drill, saw or punch the extra drains, but the easiest way is with heat. A 100-WATT SOLDERING IRON WITH A 3/8" DIAMETER COPPER DOES A GOOD JOB FOR BOTH CLEANING OUT CLOGGED HOLES AND MAKING NEW ONES.

A propane torch can be used to zap out films which are obstructing drain holes...but make it a quick shot or your pot will be a puddle of burning plastic. The new, instant-firing, piezo-electric propane torches are handy for this and sterilizing uses and should be a part of every serious orchid grower's tool kit.

PHALS IN A 4-INCH POT SHOULD HAVE ABOUT 1 SQUARE INCH OF DRAINAGE HOLE AREA OR ABOUT EIGHT OR NINE 3/8THS-INCH ROUND HOLES. Six-inch pots should have about 2 square inches of drainage or double that of a 4-inch pot.

When heating plastic to make or enlarge holes, work next to a fan which will carry away any smoke generated. Fumes from hot plastic can be hazardous to your lungs. Be careful, too, of touching melted plastic. It sticks to skin and can cause nasty burns. Allow pots to cool before stacking them because hot plastic can fuse a stack of pots into a single, solid mass. I've thrown away more than just a few new pots with this affliction.

In summary, good Phalaenopsis culture requires serviceable medium and adequate drainage. Add good light and you've just about got good phal culture wired.

— editor

SECTION SIX
PESTICIDES

(a) What pests affect your plants?   (b) What pesticides and in what strength do you use to control them?

SECTION 6.1   PESTICIDES CONSENSUS AND OPINION

Q 6(a) WHAT PESTS AFFECT YOUR PLANTS?

It's frustrating, but the more nearly perfect your growing conditions are for phals, the more nearly perfect they are for the 'vectors'. (Who the hell ever thought up a word like that for a disease carrier? 'Bug' is a much more sensible word.)

It probably won't come as any surprise that snails, scale, mealybugs and mites are the bane of phal growers world-wide. Fortunately, there are effective means at hand for dealing with these pests, both toxins and non-toxins.

A fellow in our orchid society was for a long time very vocal about never having had pests in his greenhouse. The last time I saw him he said he had for the first time, overnight, gotten an infestation of mites. That was in June...just about the time he got some new glasses. He is not alone.

MITES; AN INSIDIOUS PEST: I find mites to be the most insidious of Phalaenopsis pests. They're there and established before you can even see them...and unless you have sharp eyes, you may only see the leaves sustaining mysterious black pitting or even falling off. Since the microfungus is in vogue right now, many growers treat the black indentations with all manner of fungicides or bactericides. I really don't think those are going to get the mite's attention.

As John Miller and Woody Carlson point out in this section and in the next, it is important that you know that the microfungus damage is tan in color and some mite damage is black...with few other visual differences. And you need a 10-power glass to get close and look for yourself. The presence of live, dead and unhatched mites is unmistakable with that magnification. If you don't have a good mental image of what a mite looks like, get one. It's important.

Mites are to phals what fleas are to dogs. They've either got them, are about to get them, or are just getting rid of them. Maybe you think you haven't got them, but if you have any sort of warm, dry weather-damage that doesn't seem to have any source, suspect mites.

Whether you believe in prophylactic spraying for bugs or not, the practice is in order for mites. They're just too damned hard to detect. Better you should be the insidious one and lay in wait for them.

Growers under lights seem to have fewer pest problems than the rest of us. Artificial light may lack some wave length that the bugs need.

RESIDENT COLONIES: Many of us are given to wonder where the bugs come from, considering all the precautions we take. I think there are at least 4 sources to be considered by those of us unlucky enough to have pest problems: (1) resident colonies that aren't killed off by pesticides, either because they've developed an immunity or because they are out of range; (2) the potting medium, especially fir bark. Insecticide fogs or smokes may answer the first problem by getting under benches and leaves. Treatment of your potting medium with a pesticide before use will go a long way toward correcting the second source; (3) incoming plant material; and (4) for mites, incoming air.

I bought a battery-operated power sprayer and am convinced now that at least part of a persistent mealybug problem I had was due to poor coverage of the spray. At about US$300 each they aren't cheap, but, with 70 pounds per square inch operating pressure, the coverage is terrific...and I now can spray under the benches very thoroughly. The sprayer I have has a 5-gallon capacity, rolls on wheels and is super lightweight. Super. I still can't spray under the leaves of each of my 3,000 plants, but that's what the foggers and systemics are for.

I favor the treatment of bark with a pesticide before use. Herein is the principal avenue by which nasty little buggers get into our greenhouses. (See Bob Dadd's interesting comment that his phals in rockwool seem to be pest-free.) The bark was loaded with bugs in the forest and we have no reason to believe that anything changes before it arrives at our greenhouses. Some bark is steamed before packaging; some is tumble-dried before packaging; but, most gets nothing other than a sifting. A bark salesman at an exposition told me the only differences between the horticultural grade and the common garden-variety of fir bark

was the label...and the price. So, I think it makes sense to presume that those little brutes are in there and decide whether you want to treat them now...or later.

Note Hugo Freed's assessment of the most dangerous pest: humans.

I like Ron Merritt's down-home remedy for roaches and grasshoppers: a piece of rosemary herb.

Q 6(b) WHAT PESTICIDES DO YOU USE AND IN WHAT STRENGTH DO YOU USE THEM?

I don't think any of us needs yet another lecture on the hazards of the use of horticultural pesticides and their impact on the environment. Most orchid growers I know are lovers of the natural world in its pristine form, so few are likely to deliberately abuse the privilege of enjoying it. I say 'deliberately' because many growers I know do so unintentionally.

Growers occasionally use pesticides in concentrations that exceed those recommended by the manufacturer. It seems to me that the main reason why this happens is that the pesticide package labels are difficult for the lay person to read. The language used on pesticides sold in the United States is very carefully chosen to meet the requirements of the law and to protect the manufacturer from liability lawsuits. It appears that the language necessary to instruct on how to get best results from the material is of secondary importance. And herein is the problem.

Dosages are a problem, too. For example, the instructions on a bag of Kocide 101, a copper hydroxide fungicide, tell how to dispense the material for <u>aerial</u> delivery...and in pounds per acre. That doesn't help me much. But then, too, the material may or may not be US government-approved for use with orchids by hobbyists, either.

Manufacturers are hesitant to spend the large amount of money ($10-20 million per product) that is necessary to prove the product is safe for use with orchids, a very limited market. So the product doesn't get government approval for orchid use, even though it may be in common use in orchid culture. And the instructions for its use with orchids are not listed on the label. And professionals cannot recommend a material that they know to be safe for use with orchids...for fear of lawsuit by a disgruntled user or by the government for advocating a material that has not met their testing requirements.

A response by Ned Nash to a question on this subject in the September 1987 issue of the American Orchid Society <u>Bulletin</u> summarizes the quandary of orchid experts very well:

"I have been writing for the <u>Bulletin</u> and other orchid periodicals for more than 10 years. None of my articles has brought the response that the 'Question Box' answers have and none of the 'Question Box' answers has stirred the same response as the answer to the question about scale and Cygon. My reply to that question needs further clarification.

Cygon is, indeed, the best and most effective agent for use against Boisduval scale on cattleyas, but I cannot recommend it because it is not labeled for use on orchids. I am not a licensed pest control advisor, only a commercial grower working from experience and subject to the same federal and local regulations as everyone else. I have to be concerned not only with my own personal liability, but also with that of my company and that of the <u>Bulletin</u>.

The labeling of insecticides for particular crops is the responsibility of the manufacturer, overseen by the U.S. Department of Agriculture or whoever. Rarely is the financial benefit great enough for large chemical companies to label their products for orchids because of the expense and hassle involved. I hope that the above will clarify the answer originally printed."
— Ned Nash

Yet another unproductive jog in the course of our lives caused by fee-hungry tort lawyers...and the greedy people who hire them. (I read of <u>one</u> redeeming virtue of tort lawyers the other day, though...they're a good source of protein. Know what is brown and black and looks good on a lawyer? A Doberman. Shakespeare was right.)

Getting back to why people use pesticides improperly: The labels are somewhat confusing and, probably more important, some people just don't read them closely enough. (A friend with a doctorate in chemistry warned me of the bad effects of using a certain fungicide and, given his credentials, I listened closely. When I asked the dosage recommended, he couldn't remember. Turned out he was using twice the recommended dose.) Many will take the easier route of asking someone who should know...like friends or the experts cited in this book.

DO NOT TAKE THE ADVICE IN THIS BOOK ON PESTICIDE CONCEN-TRATIONS WITHOUT FIRST READING THE PACKAGE LABEL INSTRUCTIONS YOURSELF. I've seen some comments made in this section on the use of some pesticides that have scared me, particulary in regard to the use of systemics.

Some pesticides work best in an alkaline solution; others work best in an acidic solution; and still others work best at about neutral or pH of about 7.0. That kind of information is sometimes on the package. Yet another reason for reading the labels of pesticides.

Have we whipped this dead horse long enough?

My wife, Nancy, uses rubbing (isopropyl) alcohol to spritz mealybugs with and it works right now. It is effective, relatively innocuous, cheap and available. I've only been able to buy it in pint bottles and she uses a lot of it, so we get a lot of strange looks in the checkout line at the store when we buy 30-40 bottles at a time. I like to mumble something about 'party time' and walk away.)

In the line of home remedies, I've heard moth balls or crystals do a fair job of fending off flying insects, including whiteflies.

Some of the most innocuous treatments can sometimes be harmful to the plants. Ernie Campuzano reminds us that good old Physan is hard on seedlings and can kill off the little ones with no trouble at all. (In my experience, Natriphene is much safer for little seedlings right out of the flask.)

I'm hoping we will learn enough about predatory insects and their use as a biological pest control in the near future so we can include some more experience on what works and where they can be gotten. The problem with the present market is that packages of the predatory insects are available only in commercial greenhouse sizes, all big. Andy Adriaanse's and Don Shuker's commentaries are useful. (The WA Burpee Co of Warminster, PA 18974 USA is advertising predatory insects for sale in quantities small enough for hobbyist use.)

A relatively new predatory insect which we'll probably hear more from in the near future is a strain of nematode that attacks other underground pests and is innocuous to humans and plants. Several new predatory strains of the worm are being developed by Biosis, Inc in Palo Alto, California and they anticipate early development of aboveground operatives that will control termites and cockroaches, among other pests. Stay tuned.

Take note of Mick Dennis' statement that detergent should not be used on phals during the flowering season because it causes premature opening of buds and furling of the petals and sepals. I haven't heard or observed that, but it certainly makes a statement against the free use of a household detergent as a wetting agent for pesticides during flowering season.

I don't know the horticultural difference between household detergent and commercial-grade, non-ionic wetting agent, but the latter doesn't seem to have any ill effects on flowers.

An intriguing press release from a conference of plant scientists appeared in a local newspaper recently. The thrust was that extracts from bug-killing bacteria had been inserted into plants to create cotton, tobacco and tomatoes that produce their own insecticides. The plants can pass hereditary information on and the progeny can also be protected.

The bug-killing bacteria, Bacillus thuringiensis, has been used directly on trees and many crops for about 20 years, mainly to control caterpillars. The bacteria produce a protein called endotoxin, which kills insects by disrupting their ability to digest food, but which is safely ingested by humans.

Genes have also been engineered that can make plants safe from herbicides like Roundup <u>and from a number of viruses, some of which affect orchids.</u>

IS THERE ANYBODY OUT THERE WORKING ON THIS FOR PHALS?

I'd like to add an 'Amen' to Phil Seaton's thought that close observation is the best preventive insect control measure. **There is, quite simply, no substitute for frequent examination of the plants for bugs.**

In this section I have relied to a considerable degree on the counsel of John Niedhamer for comments and opinions. Some of the opinions are coded with his

initials. John is a southern California pest consultant and author of a new book on orchid pest control which should be in print late 1988. Hang on, we're finally going to get an orchid pest book that actually helps control pests.

— editor

Five-gallon power sprayer I've found useful.

SECTION 6.2 PESTICIDES: SELECTED RESPONSES

QUESTION 6(a) WHAT PESTS AFFECT YOUR PLANTS?

(Indian Coast South Africa) Indoors; scale and mealybugs. Outdoors; scale, mealybugs and aphids.
— A. Adriaanse

(California Coast US) Brown scale is the most common insect pest I have with Phalaenopsis. Snails and slugs are also a problem.
— L. Batchman

(Southeastern Australia) Only two: scale and mealybugs.
— M. Black

(Central California US) Slugs and mealybugs. Never have had scale.
— R. Buchter

(California Coast US) None. Before you go into shock, I should tell you that I have my greenhouses treated with Temik 10G (Aldicarb) twice a year. [See question 6(b).]
— E. Carlson

(Western Australia) My main pest is the Garlic snail which seems to flourish in greenhouses locally. I had no success in getting rid of them until I tried a dusting gun and powdered metaldehyde at weekly intervals for 3 weeks. I've had mealybugs this year for the first time, but got rid of them with malathion with a little white oil. I 'put paid to another visit by them' (Aussie for prevented recurrence) with a little Thimet sprinkled on each pot.
— K. Clarke

*(Northeastern US) Under artificial lighting...I don't think I've ever had a pest on a Phalaenopsis plant, but I don't put them outside in the summer, either.
— I. Cohen

(Indian Coast South Africa) Slugs are our only insect problem.
— C&I Coll

(Southern California US) I find scale and mealybugs are the real culprits.
— W. Cousineau

(Southern California US) Snails, slugs, scale (hard and soft), aphids, and spider mites.
— D&R Cowden

(Central Atlantic Coast US) We have very few pest problems, just an occasional scale or mealybugs or cockroach damage.
— L. Clouser

(South of England) Scale insects and very occasionally mini-slugs which come in on plants received in organic composts.
— R. Dadd

(South Australia) Mealybugs.
— M. Dennis

(Central Atlantic Coast US) The only insect problem I have with phals is 'oyster' scale.
— R. Drejka

(Florida Gulf Coast US) Mites, hemispherical scale and mealybugs.
— J. Eich

(Holland) Hardly any.
— a major commercial grower

(California Coast US) In the order of damage inflicted: Humans, mites, aphids, et al.
— H. Freed

(Maui Hawaii US) Mealybugs, red spider, and thrips.
— R. Fukamura

(Central Atlantic Coast US) Scale and thrips.
— R. Griesbach

(Atlantic Coast US) Number one pest is hard scale.
— K. Griffith

(Gulf Coast US) Brown scale is my worst pest.
— J. Grimes

(Northeastern US) Mainly hemispherical (brown) scale. Mites are seldom a problem due to strong and frequent spritzing of plants nearly every day, along with good air movement which keeps every part of each plant in high humidity. Also bush snails.
— D. Grove

(Florida Atlantic Coast US) Roaches.
— C&L Hagan

(Southeastern US) Mealybugs are the worst, followed in order by spider mites and pill bugs (on the greenhouse floor).
— T. Harper

(Indian Coast South Africa) Mealybugs and snails.
— A. Harris

(Southern California US) Phalaenopsis mites, slugs, snails and various types of scale.
— E. Hetherington

(Southern California US) Red spider mites, scale and slugs.
— D. Hirsch

(Midlands of England) Soft, brown scale and Phalaenopsis spider mites, neither of which is indigenous to this country.
— P. Hirst

(Arizona Desert US) Mealybugs, scale, and crickets.
— J&G Johnson

(Florida Caribbean US) Primarily mealybugs.
— W. Kelly

(Southeastern Australia) Mealybugs are our prime worry. Field mice and migrating rats can call in at any time, especially in the winter.
— J. Kilgannon

(Southern California US) Thrips, scale and mealybugs.
— T. Koike

(Holland) Scale and mites.
— H. Kronenberg

(France) We have never any pests from our plants when they are grown normally, but pests may come from the trees on the outside and from the plants coming back from our clients or from shows.
— Marcel LeCoufle

(Central California US) I've had problems with brown scale, but have it under control now and haven't seen any for 2 years. Mealybugs surfaced in 1986 and has been a problem since.
— B. Livingston

(Florida Caribbean US) Generally, the most severe pests are scale, mealybugs and mites.
— L. Lodyga

(Queensland Coast Australia) The main pests are Phalaenopsis mite and the small snails that live in the potting mix. (Bush snails?)
— J. Mackinney

(Southern California US) Mealybugs and slugs.
— M. McCooey

(Puerto Rico US) Spider mites.
— R. Melendez

(Luzon Philippines) Slugs, snails, caterpillars and flower bud borers. (There are other minor ones, but I'm away from my source of information. Sorry.)
— D. Mendoza

(Southeastern Australia) Phalaenopsis mites.
— A. Merriman

(Queensland Coast Australia) No apparent pests affecting the plants. Roaches and small grasshoppers attack flowers, but we find that a piece of rosemary herb keeps the flowers immune.
— R. Merritt

(Southern California US) Mealybugs and scale; occasionally mites, bush snails, millipedes and sow bugs.
— J. Miller and others

(California Coast US) Scale, spider mites, snails, and what I think are orchid wasps.
— M&J Nedderman

(Indian Coast South Africa ...and caterpillar.
— G. Paris

(Northcentral US) I've been very lucky. I have had trouble with only mites in all my years of growing phals.
— A. Roberts

(Florida Gulf Coast US) ...and turtle-back scale.
— J&M Roberts

(California Coast US) Scale (hard shell), spider mites and bush snails.
— F. Robinson.

(Queensland Coast Australia) False and red spider mites.
— R. Robinson

(Puerto Rico US) Spider mites, thrips, and snails.
— R. Rodriguez

(Central Atlantic Coast US) Scale, slugs and chewing insects are our primary problems.
— E. Rutkowski

(Southcentral US) Mostly brown scale and spider mites.
— P. Scholz

*(Northcentral US) Under artificial lighting...Scale mainly, and some mealybugs.
— W. Schumann

(South of England) Slugs and mealybugs.
— P. Seaton

(North of England) Bush snails, mealybugs, mites, moss fly, scale, snails, slugs and weevils.
— D. Shuker

*(Central Atlantic Coast US) Under artificial lighting...The main pests that have been problems are mites, scale and mealybugs. We have had only three infestations of mites in 15 years.
— K&M Smeltz

*(Northeastern US) Under artificial lighting...Mostly pest-free. Occasional mite problem.
— D&D Strack

(Oahu Hawaii US) The are at least three major insects that infest phals: Mealybugs, soft brown scale, and spider mites.
— R. Takase

(Midlands of England) This year I had my first encounter with mealybugs.
— H. Taylor

*(Northeastern US) Under artificial lighting...Red spider mites, white flies, and centipedes.
— J. Vella

(California Coast US) Mealybugs, scale, slugs and snails, sow bugs, and ants.
— J. Watkins

(Texas Gulf Coast US) Scale and spider mites.
— C&J Wilson

Bob Shuker's weevil trap made of a 4-inch disc of double-wall greenhouse roofing material, painted black on the bottom.

False spider mite damage on a rhynochostylis leaf that could be mistaken for microfungus damage. Note that this damage is black; microfungus damage is tan or light brown in color.

QUESTION 6(b) WHAT PESTICIDES DO YOU USE AND IN WHAT STRENGTH DO YOU USE THEM?

(Indian Coast South Africa)

CONTROL PROGRAM   I will only use poisons if there is no other way out. I prefer a natural prevention program. In nature, things balance themselves out. This is not the case now, but there are still a fair number of predators left. For scale, there is the Ladybird species (Chiloehores Nigritus), a small black beetle which works like an army. From a research station, I get the beetle eggs which I lay on cotton wool pads of 4x6 cm and I fix the pad to the affected area of the affected plant. The eggs hatch in about 5 days, but it is still some time before the grub develops into the beetle that does the controlling. It takes time to build up a population in the greenhouse. I also catch beetles outside the greenhouse and shoo them in to join the crowd. Local breeding in the greenhouse does take place.

Red/green ladybirds, praying mantis and geckos will all make short work of aphids. Mealybugs are a more difficult problem as the predators don't appear to like them (I empathize with the predators. ed.), but research is going on with a wasp not yet available locally. The best way to get rid of them is with a concentrated jet of water or with a brush dipped in a solution of 50% water and 50% spirits. Ants I destroy with poison. Many of the jumping spiders are eaten by the geckos and I squash any of the remainder I can catch.
— A. Adriaanse

(California Coast US)

SCALE   Cygon 2E, 2 tsp/gal.

SNAILS/SLUGS   Metaldehyde granules. (Not the pellet-form. It molds. Try to keep the granules out of the leaf axils. Promotes crown rot.)
— L. Batchman

(Southeastern Australia)

SCALE   One application of Disyston 5, US equivalent is Di-Syston 51% G. (Note: not for use in greenhouse), active ingredient Disulfoton 50g/kg, and I have had NO scale for 5 years or more. (Note: Di-Syston is a restricted material in California. JN[1])

---

[1] JN = John Niedhamer, a southern California entymologist. I asked John to review these responses and offer constructive comments.

MEALYBUGS A severe infestation of mealybugs was wiped out for 4 years by a spray over the foliage with Lebaycid, active ingredient Fenthion, 550g/l, sprayed at a dilution of 10ml/10 litres, with one followup spray 14 days later. With a preventive spraying occasionally, I never see mealybugs. A couple of drops of wetting agent helps spread the good news. Withhold watering for 24 hours to allow absorption.

— M. Black

*(Mid-Atlantic Coast US) Under artificial lighting...

MEALYBUGS Safers Ag Soap is the only thing I use inside as a shotgun approach and I use that mostly as a preventive measure. The Ag Soap will work on mealybugs if used persistently...at least once weekly until the mealies have gone. It will also work on mites...used twice weekly for 3 consecutive weeks.

— M. Bowell and others

(Central California US)

SLUGS   I use Deadline around the base of all bench supports. Also, I check my plants every night when I inspect the greenhouse before going to bed.

MEALYBUGS I use Malathion, sparingly, when required or about 2 or 3 times each year. A few drops of household dishwash detergent is a cheap and effective spreader-sticker. (Detergent is also occasionally damaging to the chemical structure of pesticides. Be careful with Agrimycin! JN)

— R. Buchter

(California Coast US)

CONTROL PROGRAM   I use Temik 10G twice a year. The dry powder is broadcast by hand and watered in. Rubber gloves, breathing apparatus and complete protective suit is used. (Temik 10G is a restricted, highly toxic compound which, in the state of California, can only be dispensed by licensed/trained technicians.)

— E. Carlson

(Central Atlantic Coast US)

COCKROACHES/MEALYBUGS We seem to have good luck controlling both problems with Orthene aerosol. For the cockroach problem, we release the Orthene in the greenhouse after dark.

— L. Clouser

*(Northeastern US) Under artificial lighting...

BROWN SCALE   Cygon 2E.

CONTROL PROGRAM   I always have No-Pest strips in the plant room. They seem to keep everything under control. (Some contain DDVP which can be hazardous to people, but not plants.JN)

— I. Cohen

(Indian Coast South Africa)

SLUGS   We use Mesurol to deal with the slugs and we use it in the salt form rather than the pellets. We lay it on once every 3 months. I also use Dipholi-tane in a one in ten percent solution and spray that on about once every second month.

— C&I Coll

(Southern California US)

MEALYBUGS   I do not spray for them on any routine schedule; rather, I have small spray bottles on every bench in the greenhouse and hit any bug with the recommended dosage of Cygon 2E and Sevin. I see no flower damage from the Cygon...which I've used for 10 years.

MITES I have Shell Vendex on hand for use on mites, but have only rare occasion to use it.

— W. Cousineau

(Southern California US)

SNAILS AND SLUGS   Metaldehyde and Mesurol

SCALE   Cygon 2E

APHIDS   Cygon 2E

SPIDER MITES   Pentac, Vendex

— D&R Cowden

(South of England)

NO INSECT PESTS   No pesticides are specifically used for phals as these seem to be very pest-free when grown in rockwool. Other orchids seem to be subject to aphids and spider mites, so greenhouses are smoked with various commercial pesticide smokes and sprayed with acaricides (mite-getters).

— R. Dadd

(South Australia)

MEALYBUGS   Kelthane as directed. (That's right, Kelthane. Works fine, but is now off the market in the US due to DDT contamination. Some was up to 10% DDT and it was the DDT that worked on the mealybugs. JN)

CONTROL PROGRAM   Control by using washing up detergent, 1 teaspoon per pint of water, in a spray. Use only during the non-flowering season as this solution opens buds prematurely...causing furling of the petals and sepals.
— M. Dennis

(Central Atlantic Coast US)

OYSTER MITES   I use Orthene or Isotox at the recommended application rate. I only spray when I detect a problem.
— R. Drejka

(Florida Gulf Coast US)

MITES   Pentac, 1 tablespoon per gallon.

HEMISPHERICAL SCALE/MEALYBUGS   Malathion and Sevin, 1 tablespoon of each per gallon.

CONTROL PROGRAM   We use the above sprays on sight or every 8 weeks if none are seen.
— J. Eich

(Rome Italy)

MEALYBUGS   I use Malatox (250 to 300 grams per 100 litres of water) with White Oil (1 kilogram per 100 litres of water) and a spreader-sticker. Use two irrigations, 20 days apart. Caution: this mix damages flowers and buds.
— A. Fanfani

(Holland)

NO INSECT PROBLEMS   If your environment is right, you have no insect problems.

CONTROL PROGRAM   None.
— a major commercial grower

(California Coast US)

HUMANS, MITES AND APHIDS How to get rid of them? I knew, but I forgot. (Hugo was 90 when this was written in August of 1987, but his sense of humor doesn't know it yet. ed.)
— H. Freed

(Maui Hawaii US)

MEALYBUGS, RED SPIDER AND THRIPS Cygon 2E and Kelthane according to directions. No prevention program.
— R. Fukamura

(South Australia)

MEALYBUGS I eliminated the pest by using C.I.G. Insectigas, which fumigates the whole glasshouse over a 24-hour period.
— D&J Gallagher

(Central Atlantic Coast US)

SCALE Avid (1/8 teaspoon per gallon) + Diazinon (1 teaspoon per gallon) + Malathion (1 teaspoon per gallon). [Avid is only so-so on scale, but is a good miticide. JN]

THRIPS Dithio smoke bombs.
— R. Griesbach

(Atlantic Coast US)

HARD SCALE We use Orthene 75SP or Cygon 2E (2 teaspoons per gallon of water). We normally use this twice in the spring and twice in the fall and do not normally have to spray at any other time of the year.
— K. Griffith

(Gulf Coast US)

BROWN SCALE The most effective pesticide for brown scale is Cygon 2E, but it is very toxic and, if used while the plant is in spike, will cause deformed blooms. Does not injure the plant if used after blooming. Presently, I've switched to insecticidal soap and hard work.

SPIDER MITES Kelthane.

SLUGS Quebane.
— J. Grimes

(Northeastern US)

HEMISPHERICAL (BROWN) SCALE   I don't like using Cygon because of some reports of phyto-toxicity, but nothing works nearly so well for me in eradicating scale once it becomes entrenched in my collection, a thing that can happen easily. I use 2 teaspoons of the Cygon per gallon of water and apply it twice, 2 weeks apart. (Should wait 30 days for reapplication. It is systemic and builds up in the plant tissues. Reapplying it too soon will almost certainly result in a burn. JN)

I do this early in the morning and only on gray days when the temperature is not expected to rise above 75°F. . .and when the temperature is at least 65°F at the start. Also, I see to it that the plants are not dry; this generally means a thorough watering the day before and, weather conditions permitting, a light misting the middle of the afternoon before. (Dr Grove's careful timing of application of Cygon is good practice. Plants are not stressed. JN)

I think these precautions help prevent phytotoxic reactions. In any case, I am unaware of having had any great problem. If I have only a small infestation, I try manual eradication and, if that doesn't do the job, I will set aside the infested plants and spray them with Malathion WP a couple of times. I hate general spraying and do it only in desperation, a couple of times a year.
— D. Grove

(Florida Atlantic Coast US)

ROACHES   When the roaches build up beyond hand control, I spray the greenhouse with liquid chlordane. (Chlordane is no longer registered in the US as a plant spray. JN)
— C&L Hagan

(Southeastern US)

MEALYBUGS   Control by liquid Sevin, 1 tablespoon per gallon, and Orthene, 1 teaspoon per gallon. [Caution: liquid Orthene is not recommended for use in a greenhouse. . .extensive damage can result. Use only the wettable powder indoors. ed.] I also use Diazinon and Malathion at the recommended rates.

SLUGS   Slug control by Que-Bane distributed freely about the greenhouse in pots, on benches and floors three or four times per year.

CONTROL PROGRAM   Pest control program consists of spraying when needed with a three-gallon sprayer. I'm in the process of examining electric sprayers for purchase. (I have a 5-gallon battery-operated spray unit and think it is great. ed.) However, from May until October, I fog the houses every month with an atomizer of Orthene or Diazinon and Pentac.
— T. Harper

(Indian Coast South Africa)

MEALYBUGS   Pestox Systemic insecticide at the rate of 1ml/litre. Where immediate action is necessary, I apply Malathion contact in the same concentration.

CONTROL PROGRAM   Applied every 3 to 4 months.
— A. Harris

(Midlands of England)

PHALAENOPSIS SPIDER MITE   Childion (Tetradifon and Dicofol) which controls all active stages of spider mite and is very effective. Applied at manufacturer's recommendations. Applied only when necessary.
— P. Hirst

(Arizona Desert US)

SCALE/MEALYBUGS   We use Orthene 75 twice a year to control scale and mealybugs. Alcohol spray for spot control of mealybugs.

CRICKETS   Spraying the floor of the greenhouse with malathion seems to take care of the problem.
— J&G Johnson

(Florida Caribbean US)

MEALYBUGS   We use Vydate at 1.5 pints per 100 gallons or Metasystox-R at the same rate. (Metasystox-R is no longer registered as a spray. Causes deformed seedlings. JN)

CONTROL PROGRAM   We find very few pests except during the late part of our blooming season. Usually a good spraying in April and another one in September keeps the insect population under control.
— W. Kelly

(Southeastern Australia)

MEALYBUGS   Mealybugs seem to be controlled by meta-systox or Supracide. The latter does not harm the flowers if it becomes necessary to spray the blooms.

SLUGS   Baygon pellets will attend to any stray slug.

GRASSHOPPERS   A sudden lunge will usually put an end to the green grasshopper or, failing that, Supracide.
— J. Kilgannon

(Southern California US)

THRIPS/SCALE/MEALYBUGS   Cygon 2E at 10 ounces per 50 gallons. Also Vapona fog.

CONTROL PROGRAM We normally clean up with a systemic such as Cygon during the non-blooming season.
— T. Koike

(Indonesia)

ALL PESTS   I use Supracide every week in the concentration prescribed.
— A. Kolopaking

(Holland)

SCALE   Undeen; 1 gram per litre. Repeat after 10 days.

MITES   Kelthane; 1 gram per litre. Repeat after 10 days.
— H. Kronenberg

(France)

CONTROL PROGRAM   We do not treat in prevention, but only when we detect some insect. The insecticides are similar to the ones used in the US. Concentrations are as prescribed. Orchids are hard to injure.
— Marcel LeCoufle

(Central California US)

MEALYBUGS   I use Sevin 50WP and Malathion 25WP combined, a tablespoon of each in a gallon of water. (Sevin 50WP will disappear from the American market in 1988. The Sevin XLR [extra long residual] that will replace it will be restricted...and will come in 10 quart jugs. JN)

CONTROL PROGRAM   Once a year I use Cygon 2E, a systemic insecticide, at 2 teaspoons per gallon. It is tough to spray when flowers are in bloom. That's when we spot spray when we see the critters.
— B. Livingston

(Florida Caribbean US)

SCALE/MEALYBUGS   We use several different types of pesticide to keep them from becoming immune to any one. Cygon 2E, two teaspoons per gallon; Orthenex, two tablespoons per gallon; Malathion 50, two teaspoons per gallon.

MITES Pentac Aquaflow, one teaspoon per gallon. In most cases, a wetting agent is used to increase coverage.
— L. Lodyga and others

(Northern California US)

SCALE   One heaping tablespoon of Diazinon 50W plust 2 tablespoons of Cygon 2E in 3 gallons of water.

SLUGS AND SNAILS   Cookes Slug and Snail spray (50% metaldehyde). One tablespoon to the gallon and spray over the plants and under the benches. Kills them when they crawl over it.
— W. Loescher

(Queensland Coast Australia)

PHALAENOPSIS MITE   We use Temik once a year or more often, if needed.

SMALL SNAILS   Controlled with a mixed spray of metaldehyde and Mesurol together with a general purpose fungicide which is used throughout the nursery about every 4 to 6 weeks.

CONTROL PROGRAMME   We carry out a regular spraying programme once every 4 to 6 weeks with Diazinon for general pests.
— J. Mackinney

(Texas Gulf Coast US)

SOME BUGS   We spot spray with insecticidal soap.
— J. Margolis

(Puerto Rico US)

SPIDER MITES   Kelthane.

CONTROL PROGRAM   Spray with Orthene every 3 months; 1 teaspoon per gallon.
— R. Melendez

(Luzon Philippines)

SNAILS   Metaldehyde in rice bran for slugs and snails.

CATERPILLARS AND FLOWER BUD BORER   Monocrotophos alternated with methyl parathion. Used in accordance with manufacturer's directions.
— D. Mendoza

*(Mid-Atlantic Coast US) Under artificial lighting...

MEALYBUGS/SOFT SCALE   I use a spray bottle of rubbing alcohol or Safer's Insecticidal Soap (basically a lye soap). Two cautions: (1) be sure to use isopropyl alcohol...ethyl alcohol destroys plant tissues; and (2) the lye in Safer's Soap is caustic, so be careful. The alcohol and soap dissolve the insect's protective shell and drown the buggers.

In the event the problem is serious and is not responding to soap and alcohol, I spray or dip with Diazinon with a wetting agent. I only resort to this when the family and I will be out of the house for a day or two, because the stuff really stinks.

I have used petroleum-based pesticides in the past and have really caused some horrible damage to new leaf tissue, so I discourage its use on phals.

SPRINGTAILS/FUNGUS GNATS   Another group of pests, those that do not necessarily damage the plants, are insects such as Springtails and Fungus Gnats. These guys infest the potting mix itself and get particularly vulgar indoors when their populations make them conspicuous. Wives, especially, do not appreciate having little black gnats flitting about the house, so a drenching of the potting mix with Diazinon every 6 months keeps these insects in check.
— E. Merkle

John Niedhamer advises some ornamental plant nurseries have developed a resident Diazinon-resistant fungus gnat after lengthy use of the Diazinon. For them he is recommending the use of Knox Out 2 FM in place of the Diazinon and getting excellent control. The puzzling part is that Knox Out 2 FM is micro-encapsulated Diazinon. Maybe the slow-release quality of the micro-encapsulation accounts for the control. No point in looking a gift-horse in the mouth, though.

Phals potted in New Zealand sphagnum moss are more likely to attract the fungus gnat. The young feed on the inevitable algae that forms on the moss. Ed Merkle's control program should be of interest to the NZ moss users. (Laid-Back Publications expects to publish John's new book on orchid pest controls in 1988. Help is on the way. ed.)

(Southeastern Australia)

   PHALAENOPSIS MITES   I use Neoron and Metasystox to control them.
                                 — A. Merriman

(Southern California US)

   MEALYBUGS/SCALE   Mealybugs are thoroughly controlled with methaprine (Orthene) 75%WP, 1 teaspoon per gallon. Methaprine is effective against all sucking insects and I find the greenhouse stays 'clean' for months after one application. However, all sprays should be rotated after three applications because I think it is important not to 'marry a spray' as immunities develop rapidly. This being the case, we switch off occasionally to Cygon 2E and Volck Supreme Oil for scale.

   MITES   We rotate Diazinon with Kelthane (Dicofol) every 10 days of use as the hatching eggs will be immune to the last spray used. We have not had a mite infestation for years.

   SOW BUGS/MILLIPEDES/BUSH SNAILS   We scatter carbaryl-metaldehyde granules on the benches and walks.
                                 — J. Miller

(California Coast US)

   CONTROL PROGRAM   No prophylactic use; only use pesticides as needed.
                                 — N. Nash

(California Coast US)

   SCALE   Malathion 25WP, Diazinon WP, and Cygon 2E.

   MITES   Pentac WP.

   CONTROL PROGRAM   I always use wettable powders as the oil carriers in liquid pesticides will, more often than not, cause damage to the leaves of my plants. I spray for spider mites; many times before seeing any actual damage, especially at the warmer and drier times of the year. (Wettable powders leave an unsightly residue, so if appearance is a consideration, look into the new, flowable [water-based] formulations. Mavrik AQ and Pentac AQ are good examples. More will be coming out in the next few years. JN)

Other pests are usually treated at the first signs of damage or actual pests. Thereafter, preventive treatments may be continued for several months after initial outbreak and treatments. The reason for this is in a crowded greenhouse filled with phals, it is impossible to spray all the surfaces of the plants. Malathion and Diazinon are generally alternated to prevent resident strains, and Cygon use as a last resort. . .as it may damage some plants.

                                 — M&J Nedderman

(Central Atlantic Coast US)

SLUGS   Mesurol.

COCKROACHES   PT-1300 (Orthene) aerosol bomb.

CONTROL PROGRAM   None.
— M. Owen

(Indian Coast South Africa)

CATERPILLARS   Diazinon, one gram per litre with a wetting agent.
— G. Paris

(Southeastern US)

ANTS   Rx with Terro (arsenic).   [Note: all arsenical baits and poisons are now banned in the US. JN]

SCALE/MEALYBUGS   If lots of plants have scale or mealybugs, I use Fertilome Absorbable Insecticide.

MITES   For mites I spray with wiltproof anti-transpirant or Pentac WP, 2 teaspoons per gallon with spreader-sticker added.

CONTROL PROGRAM   No formal program.
— S. Pridgen

(Western Australia)

MEALYBUGS AND BROWN SCALE   A light sprinkle 2 or 3 times a year with Thimet, a granular systemic.
— K. Rex

(Northcentral US)

MITES   I use Morestan 25WP to control mites at 1 teaspoon per gallon. Once or twice a year I use Kelthane, 2 teaspoons per gallon. I use wetting agents with both. (Wetting agents are not recommended for use with Morestan. Vastly increases the chances of plant injury. JN)
— A. Roberts

(Florida Gulf Coast US)

TURTLE-BACK SCALE   Orthene 75SP, 1 teaspoon per gallon.
— J&M Roberts

(California Coast US)

SCALE   Malathion, 1 tablespoon per gallon. Additionally, I use Cygon 2E as a drench every 6 months.

MITES   Kelthane; three treatments at 1-week intervals...every 3 months between March and October.

SNAILS   Cookes Slug-N-Snail granular snail bait, every 2 months. (Best snail bait I've run across. ed.)
— F. Robinson

(Queensland Coast Australia)

MITES   Torque (US equiv Vendex) at recommended strength.
— R. Robinson

(Central Atlantic Coast US)

SLUGS   I use Slugit once or twice a year, as needed.

SCALE/CHEWING INSECTS   I rely on systemics such as metasystox-R, Cygon, Orthene and Temik as needed. Concentrations as recommended. To prevent leaf damage (in winter), I use hot water from the tap to mix insecticides (also evaporates solvents quicker) and spray only on bright, sunny days. [This type of application contradicts manufacturer's instructions and while probably increasing control efficiency, would also increase the likelihood of plant damage. JN]
— E. Rutkowski

(Southcentral US)

BROWN SCALE/SPIDER MITES   Liquid Cygon or Orthene; both at 1 tablespoon per gallon.

CONTROL PROGRAM Only when necessary, twice in the spring and twice in the fall before closing up the greenhouse for the cool weather. Spray early or late in the day in very hot weather.

SPECIAL NOTE 1: The day before I spray the greenhouse with either an insecticide or fungicide, I water the plants thoroughly. This prevents any spray damage to the plants.

SPECIAL NOTE 2: I prefer to use liquids instead of powders. A powder spray spots the leaves and blocks light from reaching leaves.
— P. Scholz

SPECIAL NOTE FROM EDITOR: Read the label of every pesticide before use, of course, but particularly that of liquid Orthene. It is <u>not</u> intended for use in a greenhouse and the manufacturer rejects liability for any damage done by the product if used indoors. A friend used it on his cattleyas and <u>lost 1,000 mature plants</u> from the damage done and that many more suffered genetic damage. I understand it isn't the product that does the damage; it's the hydrocarbon carrier. As Marty Nedderman and others have pointed out above, <u>that</u> is the reason for using wettable powders instead of the liquid forms.

(South of England)

SLUGS   Good greenhouse hygiene, clear concrete path around the greenhouse, rock salt on that path, slug pellets when I spot any problem (metaldehyde), fingers and a boot.

MEALYBUGS   A sharp stick and winkle them out. (I just copy it like I see it. ed.)

COMMENTARY: Quality of observation is most important, prevention being better than cure. I disapprove most strongly of the use of pesticides unless absolutely necessary on the following grounds: they are expensive, often unnecessary, lead to the buildup of resistant forms of the pest, and pose a toxic hazard to the operator (and his children and pets). They should, therefore, be used judiciously. I occasionally use malathion as a 'spot' spray on plants which have escaped attention, although having said that, I have found it unnecessary for the past two years. There is no substitute for looking at your plants.
— P. Seaton...and others

(North of England)

SLUGS AND SNAILS   Since we put two baby frogs which we caught on the moor into our greenhouse, we haven't seen a slug or a snail...but we've seen four more frogs along with the original two.

WEEVILS   Five years ago I started seeing half-moon-like indentations on some of my phal flowers and was told they were caused by weevils. I made a 5-inch disc of double-walled plastic material used to double-glaze greenhouses, painted the top of it black, and placed it on the bench with a phal flower on it as an offering. Nailed 'em. If there are weevils, they will be found in the reeded section of the plastic <u>during daytime.</u> (For weevils, try Orthene. The black vine weevil is moving into southern California, so watch for these symptoms. When spraying, soak pots and spray under benches. Weevils feed at night, so evening sprays are best. JN)

(Might work for other pests as well. In the same line of simple, but elegant solutions: Years ago, I read in the Orchid Review, I believe, of a man in Britain who allowed a child's pet goose, Peter, to wander freely in his orchid greenhouse...and his slug-snail problem went away. Gourmet Goose. I had a rat in my backyard who caused a very abrupt end to my slug-snail population. He topped them off with avocado...a little off each one on my tree. Now, that's a mixed blessing. ed.)

CONTROL PROGRAM Morestan-Childion-Dicofil once every six weeks, alternating. Malathion-Sybol.2-Liquid Slugit once every 8 weeks approximately, alternating, in every pot. This is done in a watering session. All water used for pesticide mixing is adjusted to a pH of about 7.0 with 17% hydrochloric acid.
— D. Shuker

*(Central Atlantic Coast US) Under artificial lighting...

COMMENTARY: In all cases when we use pesticides, we carry the plants to be treated OUTSIDE. PESTICIDES ARE NOT USED IN THE HOUSE. Furthermore, heavy rubber gloves and other protective equipment are used during application with the air blowing the spray away from the applicator. We do not believe in preventive spraying or application of pesticides and only use them when absolutely necessary. These chemicals are designed to attack cells and nerves in pests. Human cells and nerves are not that much different from those of pests. Be aware of the hazard! (Dr Smeltz is a retired chemical engineer.)

MITES We used Kelthane early on and Pentac more recently and believe the Pentac did a better job. (This is a surprise. Most of the local flower growers complain that Pentac is less and less use to them. Besides, it doesn't kill eggs. JN)

SCALE/MEALYBUGS I used Cygon 2E at one time, but have discontinued its use because of the toxicity and its systemic nature. Presently, we are using Diazinon WP or Malathion WP.
— K&M Smeltz

(Northeastern US)

*CONTROL PROGRAM Under artificial lighting...I use Kelthane for mites, but for overall health of plants, washing with Ivory soap removes pests as well as dust and dirt. Ivory seems to do the best. Frequent inspection helps. (Note: see Mick Dennis' comments above in this section regarding the use of detergents.)
— D&D Strack

(Oahu Hawaii US)

MEALYBUGS   Diazinon at 1 tablespoon per gallon.

SCALE   Sevin at 1 tablespoon per gallon.

MITES   Vendex at 1 tablespoon per gallon.
— R. Takase

(Midlands of England)

CONTROL PROGRAMME   The insecticides I use are mixed with horticultural soft soap, which acts as an insecticide and a spreader-sticker. Every plant is washed in the spring with meths (alcohol) and in the winter with a stronger solution, horticultural soft soap. The soft soap is available with a nicotine base.
— H. Taylor

*(Northeastern US) Under artificial lighting...

RED SPIDER MITES/WHITE FLIES   I use predatory insects for control; in this case, praying mantis.

CENTIPEDES   I spray all the benches at least once a month with a mix of a half-tablespoon of sulfur with a quarter-tablespoon of Kelthane.
— J. Vella

SECTION 6.3

COMMON OR TRADE NAMES OF INSECTICIDES/FUNGICIDES USED WITH PHALAENOPSIS

AGRISTREP...Streptomycin.

AVID...Abamectin.

BANROT...a mixture of ethazole and thiophanate-methhyl, a BENLATE relative.

BAYLETON...Triadimefon, Amiral.

BENLATE...Benomyl, Tersan 1991.

BORDEAUX MIXTURE...Universally available.

CAPTAN...Orthocide, Merpan.

COOKES SYSTEMIC...Contains Metasystox-R.

CYGON 2E...De-fend, Dimethoate.

DEADLINE (snailbait) Contains metaldehyde, but the sticky bait is the key. Also, it lasts better under wet conditions.

DIAZINON...Diazatol, Diazide, Gardentox, Spectracide.

DIFOLATAN...Captafol, Sanspor, Pillartan, Micodifol, Merpafol.

DI-SYSTON...Disulfoton.

DITHANE M45...Fore, Mancozeb.

DURSBAN...Chlorpyrifos, Lorsban.

FERBAM...Carbamate, Fermate.

FORE...Widely available under this name.

GENTAMICIN...See your doctor.

ISOTOX...Kelthane and Orthene combined.

KELTHANE...Dicofol, Acarin.

KOCIDE 101...Hydroxide of copper.

MALATHION...Cythion.

MESUROL...Methiocarb metmercapturon.

METASYSTOX-R...Oxydemeton-methyl, Bay 21097.

METHOXYCHLOR...Marlate, Chemform.

MORESTAN...Oxythioquinox, Bay 36205.

NATRIPHENE...Sodium salt of O-hydroxy-phenyl.

ORTHENE...Acephate, Ortran, Tornada.

PARATHION...8E-Parathion.

PENNCAP M...Methyl Parathion.

PENTAC...Dienochlor.

PHYSAN...Consan, Morpan.

PLICTRAN...Cyhexatin, Dowco 213.

PT1300...Aerosol Orthene.

SEVIN...Cabaryl.

SLUG-N-SNAIL...Contains metaldehyde and Carbaryl.

SUBDUE...Ridomil, Metalaxyl.

TEMIK...Aldicarb.

TERRAMYCIN...Talk to your doctor...or farm supply.

TRIFORINE...Funginex, Saprol, Cela W524.

TRUBAN...Ethazole.

VENDEX...Fenbutatin-oxide, Torque.

X CLUDE...Diazinon.

SECTION SEVEN
DISEASE CONTROL

(a) If you have a disease prevention program, what bactericide/fungicides do you use, in what concentration and when do you use them? (b) What and how do you use controls to stop diseases which are affecting some plants? (c) Do you have any 'special' techniques for saving otherwise doomed plants?

SECTION 7.1   DISEASE CONTROL
CONSENSUS AND OPINION

Q 7(a) IF YOU HAVE A DISEASE PREVENTION PROGRAM, WHAT BACTERICIDE/FUNGICIDES DO YOU USE, IN WHAT CONCENTRATION AND WHEN DO YOU USE THEM?

Cleanliness of the growing area, the plants, the tools, the air and anything else that might impinge on the plant's space...is the overriding message of the respondents.

BROAD SPECTRUM ANTISEPTICS: Kocide 101, a copper hydroxide, manufactured by the Kocide Chemical Corporation has consistent support from the respondents as a fungicide/bactericide with residual action. Its low cost and high degree of effectiveness make it a good bet for use with phals, but it is also a very strong agent. I would caution starting with a concentration of a half-tablespoon per gallon; use of no more often than monthly in the winter; ceasing its use when spikes break; use in a slightly alkaline solution of pH of 7.2 or above; and not mixing it with other pesticides. It is one of a number of antiseptics that are alkaline in nature. If combined with an acidic agent, the action of one or the other is likely to be impaired.

Physan was used as a broad-spectrum antiseptic by growers at all levels, but was de-certified by the Environmental Protection Agency in June, 1987. Several commercial growers were using it regularly in watering programs. (I use it in my swimming pool, a fountain, and in evaporative coolers to prevent algae formation).

But, at least one respondent had problems with its toxicity. See Bob Dadd's comments. (I have found a similar product, R.D.-20, to be a suitable substitute and it is certified for use with orchids. Note, however, that neither Physan nor R.D.-20 has any residual action. One watering and the antiseptic action is gone.)

The broad-spectrum agents seem to have a leg up on bacteria- or fungi-specific agents for general usage and are more popular with the respondents. Maybe because they, like most of us, can't tell a bacterial infection from a fungal infection and the antiseptics can handle both.

I believe the lack of understanding of the difference between the two problems and what kind of an agent is needed to correct either or both...is responsible in large measure for so many new growers turning away from phals after only a short experience with them. It doesn't take much imagination to see the frustration new growers experience when they try a series of fungicides (and sometimes, insecticides) to correct a bacterial problem...and, predictably, none of them work...and out go the phals.

New growers should be encouraged to keep antiseptics such as Physan (or Listerine) on hand to head off the inevitable crisis. (Steve Pridgen advises that household vinegar works, too.) They may not have to have fertilizer during that first year, but they sure as hell are going to need Physan or something like it. Plant vendors can look on this as a repeat-customer insurance policy. Little 2-ounce bottles would do the trick. Imagine how many more people would be growing phals now if they hadn't run into the Pseudomonas problem in the first winter after buying their plants?

And it isn't only beginners that are stumped by the Pseudomonas boogeyman. Every society has their cattleya stalwarts who got tired of losing their phals to Pseudomonas and switched to a kind of orchid that could be hit with a stick and wouldn't die. Boilerplate orchids. No more ego-bruising losses of finicky phals. "I got three more of them suckers that ain't died yet. You want 'em?"...Broad spectrum antiseptics.

MICROFUNGUS: Ernie Campuzano's experience with what may be the first major outbreak of a microfungus infection is worth noting. It is unreasonable to think that any collection that has regular additions is going to escape. The therapy program that Don Baker came up with after consultation with John Miller is one of those things that should go into the card file of every serious phal grower. It is detailed under John Miller's comments in this section and again at the end.

The key words in coping with the problem are 'systemic fungus'. I know this sounds stupid, but it takes a systemic fungicide to correct the problem. Don't waste time and money throwing topical agents at it; they won't help. That is what has been so damned frustrating about this fungus; none of the conventional measures worked.

AIR MOVEMENT: One case does not make a trend, but you might consider Walt Cousineau's experience with complete disappearance of bacterial and fungal problems when he went to his open-wall system of ventilation. His plants get quite dry, no doubt about that, and few growers will be able to open their greenhouse walls to the passing breezes as he has, but the point is that AIR EXCHANGE APPEARS TO HAVE ELIMINATED HIS PROBLEM OF BACTERIAL/FUNGAL INFECTION. What he has done is to have duplicated nature. Back to basics again.

KOCIDE: Ken Griffith's comments on a side benefit of the use of Kocide or Difolitan is interesting: no slugs or snails. I don't know about the Difolatan, but Kocide is a copper compound and molluscs don't like copper. There may be a connection there.

I haven't had any slugs or garden snails since using Kocide, either, but I still have some bush snails. Maybe because I only use the Kocide in the winter and repot with fresh medium (and bush snails?) in the summer. Maybe I see the bush snails in the interval between repotting and the first application of Kocide. Maybe. (I envy people who remember precisely when they saw or did something. Ever since I passed 40, I've had trouble remembering things...I think it was 40.)

IF YOU DON'T GET ANYTHING ELSE OUT OF THIS SECTION, NOTE THE POINT MADE BY DAVID GROVE AND MIKE OWEN IN THIS REGARD...WHY DID THE DISEASE PROBLEM ARISE IN THE FIRST PLACE?

A good management problem-solving technique: first, relieve the symptoms;

second, eliminate the cause; and third, prevent it from happening again. In this application, look for a cultural practice that needs to be changed and stay changed.

In the 'All is not well in paradise' department', I note that Dorotheo Mendoza and Liem Khe Wie (A. Kolopaking) in the Philippines and Indonesia, respectively, have to use fungicides as <u>often as twice a week</u> in the rainy season. You think <u>you</u> have fungal problems.

Note, too, they both use the 'natural' method for stopping a plant disease: stop watering; and move the plant to a drier, brighter, better ventilated place. (I do that too, but after I get it where it is going, I spray it with Kocide and Dithane M-45.)

Q 7(b) WHAT AND HOW DO YOU USE CONTROLS TO STOP DISEASES WHICH ARE AFFECTING SOME PLANTS?

Most of the hygiene practices narrated in this section are worthy of consideration. Each has its place.

The use of Benlate and Banrot is widespread.

You may notice that Mick Dennis is very big on washing-up detergent. He apparently gets a lot of mileage out of soap as you will note his numerous references to its use. The idea goes back a long way and is a very sound one, but note John Niedhamer's caution. The lye-based soaps are in vogue now and serve a very useful purpose: like what to use for mealybugs when you have new flower spikes emerging...that might be damaged by a chemical insecticide.

I wiped out <u>500</u> flower spikes one spring by spraying them with Diazinon to control some mealybugs.

Stop the watering, increase the light and air circulation... many advised. If you are looking for a nontoxic method of controlling disease, this may be it. Be prepared for a slow response, though.

Q 7(c) DO YOU HAVE ANY SPECIAL TECHNIQUES FOR SAVING OTHERWISE DOOMED PLANTS?

Some excellent comments; very useful.

You have <u>got</u> to read Arthur Harris' method of handling sick plants. (I worked for a boss years ago who had a similar flair for getting the message across. He announced one morning that he was going to hold a contest for all his employees...and the winner would get to keep his job. Believe it or not, there was one bozo there who thought the boss was kidding.)

Again, in this section as in the last, John Niedhamer's comments on the responses are indicated by the initials 'JN'.

— editor

SECTION 7.2 DISEASE CONTROL
SELECTED RESPONSES

QUESTION 7(a) IF YOU HAVE A DISEASE PREVENTION PROGRAM, WHAT BACTERICIDE/FUNGICIDES DO YOU USE, IN WHAT CONCENTRATION, AND WHEN DO YOU USE THEM?

(Indian Coast South Africa) To prevent orchid diseases, one must be absolutely clean. Up to now I have used very few poisons, preferring to use Jeyes Fluid, a carbolic acid compound, 3 tablespoons per 5 litres. There is a wide selection of similar cleaning compounds. Spray the floors, benches, etc., every month. Permanganate of potash, 1ml to 60 litres of water for overall applications including your plants. If you wish to use it for walls, floors and benches, try 10-20 ml per 60 litres, but do not let it come into contact with the plants.
— A. Adriaanse

(Central California US) Natriphene is my bactericide/fungicide of choice. I spray all phal roots with a dilute Natriphene solution when repotting. I use Kocide during the winter to prevent crown rot (Pseudomonas cattleyae) from dripping overhead structures.
— R. Buchter

(Southern California US) A few years ago, I had a serious problem with microfungus infection in my greenhouses. I used the therapy recommended by John Miller (see below) and the problem went away. I use the same therapy program every 6 months now as a preventive measure.
— E. Campuzano

(California Coast US) December through March, Physan and/or Truban and Banrot are used once a month as a preventive measure.
— E. Carlson

(Western Australia) The only time I have a problem is when a few frogs may come visiting. They hop across the tops of the plants and, sometimes, crack a leaf or a crown. If I don't notice the damage, Brown Rot sets in. If it is in a leaf, no problem; I just cut the leaf off and dust the wound with sulfur powder. If the rot happens in the crown, I cut the damaged part out and cover the wound with keiki paste. This way, I may lose the plant, but am assured of a keiki or two.
— K. Clarke

(Mid-Atlantic Coast US) We spot spray or drench with Banrot or Natriphene only when we have a problem. Again, we feel air circulation and watering early in the day help prevent spread of disease.
— L. Clouser

(Southern California US) Since developing an 'open air movement' (fully-open greenhouse sidewalls which are closed by inflating plastic tubes) I do not have crown rot or fungus. I use no bactericide/fungicide on seedlings, compots or mature plants. I rely on the drying effect of air movement to dry leaves and crowns by nightfall.

W. Cousineau

(South of England) Until recently I have used Physan at 1/2 ml per litre in all water which has prevented crown rot. I have stopped doing this as I have found it caused tissue cell damage in the roots, allowing phenolics to escape, oxidise, blacken the damage area and be reabsorbed as a mild poison to the plants.

— R. Dadd

(Florida Atlantic Coast US) I practice sterile technique. Using a 10% solution of household bleach, I sterilize benches, floor, used pots, and potting bench tools. I sterilize the potting bench every time I use it. I soak pruning tools in a saturated solution of trisodium phosphate. If I've been working on a diseased plant, I dip the tools in a bleach solution, then leave them to soak in the TSP.

I spray the plants with a solution of 1 tablespoon of Benlate and 2 drops of Subdue to a gallon of water during the summer from one to three times or at 6-week intervals. I never spray with a systemic while the plants are in spike or in bloom. I spray monthly with Dithane M-45 during the rainy season at a rate of one and one half tablespoons per gallon.

— D. Davis

(South Australia) Sick plants are repotted in sphagnum moss after being washed and soaked in washing suds.

— M. Dennis

(Mid-Atlantic Coast US) I apply Benlate in the spring. In the winter I use a dusting of bordeaux mixture to head off problems arising from the effects of cold water.

— R. Drejka

(California Coast US) I paint dark spots on plants with Difolitan. I use a toothpick to scratch spots, then apply the Difolitan.

— W. Eckberg

(Florida Gulf Coast US) Subdue 2E, 2.5ml/gal, 3 times per year. Physan, 2 teaspoons per gallon, every 6 weeks.

— J. Eich

(Southern California US) A light spray of Physan from a handsprayer after watering controls disease and water spot deposits.

— R. Engel

(Holland) No program.

— a major commercial grower

(Maui Hawaii US) For mature plants, I spray twice a month with a solution of Physan.
— R. Fukamura

(Southern California US) I think it is important to recognize that the most prevalent and damaging disease affecting phals is Pseudomonas cattleyae, A BACTERIAL PROBLEM. It does little good to try to prevent Pseudomonas or cure it with a fungicide...but I find people doing just that over and over again...then complaining "...these damned weeds; I can't grow them."

Prevention, of course, is the preferred method of coping with Pseudomonas problems but, if that isn't feasible (like when you have 2-3,000 plants and a job) a good bactericide is in order. I like Kocide 101, a copper hydroxide, an upgraded bordeaux mixture, as a prophylactic measure. Use bordeaux if you can't get Kocide. Use at a rate of one and one-half <u>teaspoons</u> per gallon and apply at 6-week intervals starting with the short days in the autumn and stopping when flower spikes begin to break. Copper can damage new tissue.

Kocide is a slow-release agent in an alkaline solution and will have residual action for 6 weeks or so when water used is about pH 7.5 to 7.8. However, in an acidic solution it becomes a fast release agent and can cause copper poisoning. I've never lost a plant to copper poisoning, but I have lost some flowers, so don't use it after spikes emerge. DO NOT ACIDIFY WATER USED TO MIX THE PESTICIDE SOLUTION OR APPLY FERTILIZERS...for reasons I've just mentioned. If your water is naturally acidic, raise the pH to 7.0 or above before using Kocide.

A cautious approach to using Kocide or any other copper compound would be to alternate its use with an antibiotic such as Terramycin or Agri-Strep, particularly if growth and flowering appear to be less than you expect. There have been reports of harmful effects stemming from long-term, heavy doses of copper-based compounds.

Another reason to use Kocide; it's cheap.
— editor

(Mid-Atlantic Coast US) Once a month spray a solution of:
>   one tablespoon Benlate 50WP
>   one teaspoon Physan
>   one teaspoon Truban 30WP
>   five drops of Subdue
>   one gallon of Water
>   (Known on the east coast of the US as "The Blitz" or "Griesbach's Cocktail". Strong stuff. ed.)
— R. Griesbach

187

(Atlantic Coast US) Our major disease problem is Pseudomonas and it is a constant battle. We use clean sanitation, plenty of air movement and regular spraying with a bactericide during the spring and through the fall months. We use Difolitan at a rate of 1 tablespoon per gallon for normal spraying and at times drop this down to half that. We alternate the Difolitan with Kocide 101 at the same rate. Both chemicals can be disastrous to plants if they are overused and Difolatan can cause allergic reactions in some people.

These are the only two preparations we've found that work. Physan and tetracycline have been totally ineffective. With the two mentioned products, we need no other fungicide or even slug bait or spray.

— K. Griffith

(Northeastern US) Truban-Benlate mixture (one tablespoon of each per gallon). I also use Subdue (10 drops per gallon). I use these only when necessary. Generally, a need for bactericides and fungicides indicates something needs adjusting in cultural practices.

— D. Grove

(Indian Coast South Africa) Every 3 to 4 months I apply Physan 20 fungicide, 1ml per litre.

— A. Harris

(Southeastern US) From November to March, I add two tablespoons of Physan to five gallons of water through a Hozon (syphon proportioner) to water the plants. This allows water to drain better off the plants and provides some disease control. I do not have a regular disease control prevention program.

— T. Harper

(Arizona Desert US) Kocide 101 applied during the cooler nights will take care of the problem. I apply it usually on the first of December and the first of February.

— J&G Johnson

(Florida Caribbean US) Our injector is programmed to inject Physan for a 2-minute cycle. This keeps things pretty clean.

— W. Kelly

(Southeastern Australia) This is a vexing problem; as we all know the world around us is rich in spore-forming organisms and dust-borne bacteria...all of which are just waiting for the right conditions to allow them to get on with their dirty work. The conditions that phals require are fairly good for most of these little beasts, so at the first sign of a problem, one must be ready to act.

I have used a host of fungicides. None give miracle cures, but require continued applications at the recommended strength and frequency.

The greatest problem from a grower's point of view is to identify the organism. (Underlining mine. ed.) Failing outside help, a number of alternatives can be used but, if the wrong diagnosis is made, the problem may go untreated. We are limited here by government regulations to what is gazetted (labeled or published) for use on orchids. Probably the first line of defence is to maintain good hygiene throughout your glasshouse and surrounding area. This, coupled with good culture, cannot help but lead to strong and healthy plants.
— J. Kilgannon

(Southern California US) Kocide, 6 ounces per 50 gallons; Agri-Strep, 4 ounces per 50 gallons; Benlate, 4 ounces per 50 gallons...beginning in the fall.
— T. Koike

(Indonesia) Fungicide is used mostly once a week and twice a week in the rainy season. I use Antracol.
— A. Kolopaking

(France) No prevention, normally. However, we use a fungicide now and then. If a plant from a client has got some rot, we treat it with concentrated fungicide. We use pure fungicide on the spot, without any dilution.
— Marcel LeCoufle

(Central California US) We use Kocide and Dithane M-45 together for a fungicide. One tablespoon of each per gallon. We use the mix when we see the beginning of a problem.
— B. Livingston

(Florida Caribbean US) Plants are sprayed routinely with:

Captan	3 teaspoons per gallon
Benlate	2 teaspoons per gallon
Kocide 101	1 teaspoon per gallon
Banrot	1/2 teaspoon per gallon
Subdue	1/8 teaspoon per gallon

— L. Lodyga

(Queensland Coast Australia) Botrytis is best handled by raising the temperature and increasing air movement.
— J. Mackinney

(Puerto Rico US) I spray liquid copper every month, 1 tablespoon per gallon.
— R. Melendez

(Luzon Philippines) I use Captan and Mancozeb every 10 days during the rainy season at manufacturer's direction.
— D. Mendoza

(Southeastern Australia) I spray monthly in the summer with Dithane M-45. If, by chance, there is Botrytis spotting, I use Benlate. If leaf spotting occurs, I use Wescodyne.

— A. Merriman

(Southern California US) On the basis of 'never marry a spray', for contact sprays we rotate from Dithane 78 to Difolitan. However, sometimes a condition prevails that is caused by a **systemic infection of microfungi.** As there are literally hundreds of these, the symptoms vary from plant to plant.

Some of the more common are a spotty, ill-defined chlorosis; a streaky chlorosis beginning at the edge of the leaf where it looks as if the leaf edge had been burned with a match or candle; a red-brown coloration appearing at the apical third of half of the lower leaves followed by a dehydrated and senescent (old) appearance and also mesophyll tissue collapse where deep pitting becomes apparent on the surface of the leaves. This latter condition can also be caused by cold water and by virus infections. However, in the latter instance, the pitting is usually dark-brown to black in appearance rather than the white to light-fawn as caused by fungi. Treatment is as follows:

Day One;
* Ridomil 2E (A bit cheaper than Subdue, but only Subdue is legal for ornamental plants. JN), one teaspoon per five gallons of water and in the same spray mix,

* Bayleton 25% WP four teaspoons per five gallons.

(Spray until it runs down off the leaves. It goes without saying that you should wear breathing mask, gloves and protective clothing for any spraying job.)

Day Two;

* Triforine (Funginex), two teaspoons per gallon

Thirty days later;

* repeat the process.

The reason for the 30-day separation is that Bayleton, if used too strongly or too often, can cause shortening of the flower spikes. (Watch the rate of application. Too high a rate of Bayleton is the same as respraying too soon. JN)

I have used this combination three times for microfungus with good results. The affected leaves will continue to die and improvement will be seen in the new growths. This treatment was developed by my good friend, Don Baker.

In my experience, crown rot begins outside the crown at the junction of the lower leaves and works its way in...often aided by small sow bugs. I can usually control this with a direct application of undiluted Difolitan. Years ago, while many growers in Hawaii were having problems with growing phals, Oscar Kirsch had none. He grew his phals hung on A-frames and chicken wire racks.

In nature, phals grow pendently or with their leaves down. Water does not accumulate in the crowns and rainwater flushes fungus spores and bacteria out. In culture we force them to grow in an upright position so the leaves form a cup and water accumulates in the center...along with the fungus and bacteria ...with disastrous results.

I've experimented with cutting away the top inch or so of 5- and 6-inch round pots in an arc of 80 to 90°. I've used these for phal plants whose foliage tends to lie flat on the surface of the medium such as the violaceas and amboinenses. The cutout allows the crown to lay tilted open and only slightly above the level of the medium. Looks like the idea may have merit.

Maybe Phalaenopsis greenhouses should be built with rows of vertical chicken wire to hang plants on. (Dan Ellis in Phoenix, Arizona grows his phals that way. Step benches help, too. ed.)
— J. Miller

(I've tried some of the modified pots John suggests and they work just fine. Hanging the pot by its side will tilt the crown, too. This cutout John Miller is suggesting allows that same tilt to be used in a pot which is sitting flat on a bench. Same benefit as hanging the pot the way Oscar Kirsch did. You could also fill an unmodified pot up the rim with medium and achieve the same effect, but would likely wash medium out of the pot during watering. ed.)

(California Coast US) In winter and overcast periods, such as May and June, I try to spray at least once a month. I use Subdue at a half-teaspoon per gallon, Agri-Strep at one tablespoon per gallon, and Benlate at the recommended dosage. I always use two of these products as a combined spray. On subsequent sprayings, the components are alternated by at least one type to prevent resistant strains from developing.
— M&J Nedderman

(Mid-West US) I use Physan 20 right after repotting to protect from bacterial rot from any cracked leaves or root damage. Also as a wetting agent on the new bark. I use one of the following in the spring and fall when plants do not completely dry off by nightfall:
   * Truban 30WP, one and one-half teaspoons per gallon
   * Benlate 50WP, one tablespoon per gallon
   * Banrot, one tablespoon per gallon (adjust pH to 6.0)
   * Kocide, two or three teaspoons per gallon; adjust pH if necessary to 7.5 to 8.0.
— R. Pallister

(Queensland Coast Australia) For fungus prevention, we use Physan or Daconil 2787 at recommended rates. For bacteria, we use Terramycin antibiotic powder at one-half teaspoon per litre of water. We find we normally only need to use these measures in the winter.

— D&E Penningh

*(Northcentral US) Under artificial lighting...I spray all plants every other month to control fungal and bacterial problems. I use the following mixture:

Physan	1 teaspoon
Truban	1 teaspoon
Benlate	2 teaspoons
Subdue	1/4 teaspoon

— A. Roberts

(California Coast US) Physan used in watering program twice each month. I use Kocide if I see evidence of bacterial problems.

— F. Robinson

(Queensland Coast Australia) We have used Physan with not excellent results. We will use Kocide in the future.

— R. Robinson

(Mid-Atlantic Coast US) Main problem is bacterial rot. This can be controlled without chemicals by giving the plants fresh air and sunshine. I tried a variety of products without much luck. Bacterial rot has been essentially a non-problem, though, since I started using Kocide about 6 years ago. I use it at 1- to 3-month intervals and mix it with insecticides.

— E. Rutkowski

(Southcentral US) I always include a fungicide with the pesticide when I spray. I generally use Funginex, 1 tablespoon per gallon.

— P. Scholz

*(Northcentral US) Under artificial lighting...I use Truban, Banrot, Physan, Subdue, Captan, and Natriphene. Unfortunately, I usually use them after the damage has been done.

— W. Schumann

(South of England) Good hygiene.

— P. Seaton

(North of England) I spray my plants and pots with Natriphene three times each year. I water-in Physan to the plants every 8 weeks with the exception of November and December when I use Physan in both months. I apply Green Sulphur in paste form whenever I cut a flower spike or part of a leaf or root. (In the third case, try using Physan, 1 teaspoon per gallon, as a spray mix. Simpler and easier and has never failed. ed.)

— D. Shuker

*(Mid-Atlantic Coast US) Under artificial lighting...Our disease prevention program consists mainly of lots of air movement and watering or feeding only in the mornings, about 7-9AM. When we spray in the afternoon, we allow from 5 to 6 hours of drying time before we shut off the lights.

— K&M Smeltz

(Oahu Hawaii US) Thiram is sprayed at 2 tablespoons per gallon after and before flowering. For control of bacterial rot, I use Tribasic copper sulfate at a quarter teaspoon per gallon only on plants that show symptoms of bacterial problems.

— R. Takase

*(Northeastern US) Under artificial lighting...As a strict regimen, I spray all plants with a solution of (1) Physan and ammonium nitrate at a rate of half a tablespoon per gallon, or (2) Benomyl 50 and/or Truban 75... mixed with two drops of motor oil, about grade 10W, with a spreader-sticker in 5 gallons of rainwater. Blend further in a hydrosonic mixer.

— J. Vella

(Mid-Atlantic Coast US) We have had problems with crown rot in Phalaenopsis in the past and treated them with Truban and Benlate as a preventive. (Note that Truban and Benlate are fungicides and crown rot [Pseudomonas cattleyae] is a bacterial problem. ed.) We found we had problems with malformed flowers, so we abandoned the fungicide approach. We've adjusted the pH of our water to 5.0-5.5 and find our disease problems are no more.

— C. Williamson

(California Coast US) Copper sulfate when problems arise; 10 ounces in 5 gallons of water.

— J. Wilson

(Mid-West US) Because I am allergic to molds, I drench with Physan every 2 weeks...on advice of an allergist. Much to my surprise, the plants are doing much better.

— M. Zimmer

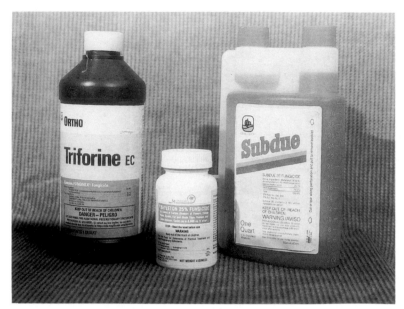

Microfungus combat kit: Triforine (Fungenex),
Bayleton, and Subdue. See text.

194

QUESTION 7(b) WHAT AND HOW DO YOU USE CONTROLS TO STOP DISEASES WHICH ARE AFFECTING SOME PLANTS?

(Indian Coast South Africa (1) Read the directions fully on any chemicals you use on your plants and (2), follow them.
— A. Adriaanse

(Southeastern Australia) The only disease problem I have experienced was a most disastrous bacterial infection, at which I threw everything I could get hold of. Unfortunately, there are very few bactericides available and my guess is, probably, bordeaux mixture finally stopped the rot. (Good guess. JN)
— M. Black

(Central California US) I use Kocide in the winter and have not had a serious disease problem in 12 years.
— R. Buchter

(California Coast US) If my monthly treatments with Physan and/or Truban and Banrot don't work, I dump the plants. (Sanitation is an excellent disease control technique. JN)
— E. Carlson

*(Northeastern US) Under artificial lighting...Isolate and use appropriate chemicals. Increase temperature and air movement, if necessary.
— I. Cohen

(South of England) While not exactly control of a disease, when a plant of mine suffers total root loss I do the following:

1. Prop up the leaves and, with cotton wool, paint the leaves with normal food solution to which has been added two tablespoons of sucrose per litre of water.

2. Repeat every 3 days.

3. Spray with plain water to rewet leaves twice per day and keep the humidity high.

For the first two applications add 1 ppm of naphthalene acetic acid (NAA) and 1 ppm vitamin B1. The leaves will stiffen in the propped position and new roots will appear within 2 to 3 weeks. (That one goes in my try-it-next-time notebook. ed.)
— R. Dadd

(Florida Atlantic Coast US) For root rot: Using a solution of 1 tablespoon of Benlate and 3 drops of Subdue in a gallon of water, I soak the plant for 10 minutes after all the diseased roots have been removed. Then I leave the plant to dry without media for 2 to 3 days.

Then I partially repot in bark, leaving the crown free of media. When new roots appear, I add media up to the base of the crown.

— D. Davis and others

(South Australia) Kelthane for pests and Fongacid for fungi and bacteria at 7-day intervals in the months of January, February, and March. A little white oil is also used.

— M. Dennis

(Florida Gulf Coast US) Direct application of either Benlate or Banrot in paste form to the diseased area. Keep water off the foliage.

— J. Eich

(Holland) Again, if your culture is all right, you will have no problems with bacteria and fungi. Only if your culture is wrong will you get these problems.

— a major commercial grower

(California Coast US) Crown rot is usually caused by too much humidity, poor air circulation and too little heat. It is highly contagious and spreads easily to other plants, mainly by splashing of water.

We had a major infestation at one time and lost hundreds of plants in a short period of time. We finally found a cure with Agrimycin, which is a combination of streptomycin and terramycin. However, when the next crop of flowers opened we found a lot of crippling, not only in the plants, but also in the flowers. The villain was streptomycin and this was corrected by substituting another -mycin (I can't remember the name) for the strepto. Fortunately, there was no crippling in the following crop.

But, every cloud has a silver lining: after we had almost eliminated the crown rot, I discovered three plants next to one other that were badly infected with crown rot. I carried them out and put them on a bench in the potting shed where the windows were open and the cold night air circulated throughout the shed. I asked Amado to dump the plants the next day...and he forgot...for 30 days. When I noticed the plants still on the bench, the crown rot had stopped and a new growth was just starting. It returned to perfect health. Conclusion? Maybe crown rot can't take temperatures of 50°F or less.

— H. Freed

(Southern California US) I have 24 pairs of cutters I use with my phals and I sterilize them with a propane torch before each use. I use each cutter once, then resterilize it. Because I use the torch a lot during our annual repotting cycle, I have a 20-pound propane bottle, a flexible hose and a piezo-electric igniter. For short interval use, such as when I work in the laminar hood, doing tissue culture or seed sowing, I have a propane torch with one trigger which operates both gas and ignition. Very handy for short bursts of use.

— editor

(Gulf Coast US) Sterilize cutting tools.
— J. Grimes

(Northeastern US) Move diseased plants to a position with better light and air movement and adequate space around. Cut off the diseased portions at once. Spot treat any other spots with a paste of bactericide and fungicide powders which have been mixed with a little dilute Physan. Or, use an antibiotic such as Agri-strep or Terramycin in paste form. Subdue can also be used. There are many possibilities. Sear or treat the remaining cut edges after having cut off the diseased portions.
— D. Grove

(Florida Atlantic Coast US) I cut away diseased tissue and use Physan or a bactericide to stop the problem.
— C&L Hagan

(Southeastern US) Disease in a plant can be controlled by combinations of the following:
   1. Isolate from other plants.
   2. For soft rot, lightly score the wound area with a razor blade.
   3. Dry off and move the plant to a bright, dry location.
   4. Spray with Ridomil/Subdue, five drops per gallon. (Phytophthera fungus only. JN)
   5. Remove infected tissue.
— T. Harper

(Arizona Desert US) We have saved 90% of our plants which have been infected by crown rot with a product called Stoprot (Bordeaux in lanolin) purchased from Dr James D. Brasch (Box 354, McMaster University, Hamilton, ONT, L8S 1C0, CANADA). See a current AOS Bulletin for an ad.
— J&G Johnson

(Florida Caribbean US) Should a plant have a problem, it is usually painted with a heavy concentration of Kocide.
— W. Kelly

(Indonesia) A control I use to stop diseases is to stop watering for 7 to 10 days.
— A. Kolopaking

(Florida Caribbean US) Infected parts of a diseased plant are cut off to avoid reinfection, making sure to cut only into green, healthy tissue. Keep leaves dry and well-ventilated.
— L. Lodyga

(Queensland Coast US) I remove infected leaves and apply a paste of Captan to the cut edge.
— J. Mackinney

(Southern California US) I use a propane torch to sterilize cutting tools.
— M. McCooey

(Luzon Philippines) Simply pull them out of your collection and apply treatment (surgery). Put the diseased plant in a drier, brighter and better-ventilated place until it is either cured or dead.
— D. Mendoza

(Southern California US) Throw the plant away. (Hard to argue with this technique. I love it. JN)
— H. Moye

(California Coast US) Once plants become infected, I'm not sure if they can be totally cured, but the best chance is to remove the infected area and a good deal of 'normal' tissue along with it. Any plants of marginal quality are discarded. If you have a good plant with crown rot, get it to keiki or stem (prop) it. Then discard the mother plant to prevent spread of the disease to other plants.
— M&J Nedderman

(Northcentral US) I cut off any affected areas and swab the cut portion with Providine Topical Solution. It stops further spread of the disease. If caught early, PTS also stops crown rot.
— A. Roberts

(California Coast US) Infected plants are (1) isolated and (2) treated, in that order.
— F. Robinson and others

(South of England) If bacterial rots do occur, they are cut out and the cut edges are treated with flowers of sulfur. After watering, any water that lodges in the crown of the plants is removed with kitchen roll (absorbent paper or paper towels).
— P. Seaton

(North of England) I isolate all new plants coming into my greenhouse until I'm sure they are healthy and completely free from pests and disease. Before allowing new plants to join the others, I unpot each and soak the plant in Natriphene for half an hour and wipe each leaf with a solution of Morestan.
— D. Shuker

*(Mid-Atlantic Coast US) Under artificial lighting. . .We have, on occasion, used with success Neosporin ointment, a first aid antibiotic. We smear this on the affected area, both top- and bottom-sides of the leaf. (As long as you're in the medicine cabinet, Ken, get out the Listerine mouthwash, too. It will do just fine in a pinch as a broad spectrum antiseptic. Lysol disinfectant, used at 1/3rd the recommended dosage, also works well as a broad spectrum bactericide/fungicide and does not harm phals. It is labeled (gazetted) for Pseudomonas. ed.)
— K&M Smeltz

(California Coast US) For bacterial rots, I use oxytetracycline purchased from pet shops (used to stop fin rot in tropical fish). Sometimes I mix the compound with water and use as a drench or, at other times, open the capsule and spread the powder directly on the affected area.
— J. Watkins

Pruning roots: a mature plant before pruning.

Pruning roots: a mature plant after pruning.

QUESTION 7(c) DO YOU HAVE ANY SPECIAL TECHNIQUES FOR SAVING OTHERWISE DOOMED PLANTS?

(California Coast US) I remove the plant from its pot and leave it out in the air, misting occasionally. I've never had any success in curing a sick plant by putting it in a plastic bag. (Me neither. ed.)

— W. Adams

(Indian Coast South Africa)If the plants are infected to an advanced state, I remove and destroy them. These doctored plants seldom recover completely anyway.

— A. Adriaanse

(Mid-Atlantic Coast US) I've had more problems of disease with p. stuartiana (and its hybrids), violacea hybrids, and yellow phals than any others, but have had success with them using the following: Paint their crowns with Banrot and spray regularly (weekly) with alternate fungicide/bactericide solutions.

— M. Bowell

(Central California US) When a leaf develops a 'wet' (Pseudomonas cattleyae) spot, I immediately remove the affected leaf area, cutting with a sterile, flamed blade one-half to three-quarters of an inch into the healthy tissue. I then reheat the blade and cauterize the cut section. The searing seals the leaf tissue to further infection from the outside.

— R. Buchter

(California Coast US) No, I can't waste time nursing plants back to health when doing this for a living.

— E. Carlson

(California Bay Area US) I give them to an amateur who usually saves them and never lets me forget it.

— W. Cecil

*(Northeastern US) Under artificial lighting...If you lose the crown of a phal, you can sometimes save the plant by cutting watering frequency in half...this may induce keikis.

— I. Cohen

(Mid-Atlantic Coast US) The doomed plant will sometimes send up a bloom spike even though the plant itself is dying. If it is a valuable plant, I will attempt to make stem propagations from it.

— R. Drejka

(Southern California US) Straight Listerine mouthwash spray.

— R. Engel

(Holland) No.
— a major commercial grower

(Gulf Coast US) I have salvaged all but dead plants by putting them in enclosed terrariums made from plastic soda pop bottles or clear plastic shirtwaist (sweater) boxes. I use sterile sphagnum sprayed with Banrot.
— J. Grimes

(Florida Atlantic Coast US) I remove a diseased plant from the pot, wash it with a solution of Physan, dip a plastic bag in the Physan, put the plant in the plastic bag, tie the bag closed and hang it under the bench. (until it does something, one way or the other. ed.)
— C&L Hagan

(Southeastern US) If the plant is doomed and it has been given all the other treatments except the last rites, scoop away the bark from the base of the plants and place it in a bright, dry place; do not water; be patient and the plant will usually throw a keiki from the base.
— T. Harper

(Indian Coast South Africa No special techniques, but I remove any plant which appears beyond saving from the greenhouse. . .and nail it to a tree in the garden some distance from the greenhouse. Very often, some survive! (I think we know who the boss of that greenhouse is! Yessir! How much and what color? ed.)
— A. Harris

(Southern California US) Segregate or throw out all plants which have a condition.
— E. Hetherington

(Florida Caribbean US) Cut out the top and paint with Kocide and it will usually keiki.
— W. Kelly

(Southern California US) If it is a special plant, I will make a stem propagation of it, if possible.
— T. Koike

(Central California US) We have no special technique for saving doomed plants other than putting them to one side and reducing watering to a nil. If they kick a side growth, they stay. Otherwise, they go in the dumper. The only plants that get this treatment are selected or awarded plants. We don't have room for a sick bay.
— B. Livingston

(Southern California US) When a plant gets crown rot, I have saved some by putting dry Benlate powder in the crown of the plants and not watering for at least 2 weeks.
— M. McCooey

(Mid-Atlantic Coast US) Plants that suffer crown rot have pretty much had it. I try to dig out the infected tissue, treat the plant with a strong 'Blitz' solution and hope that a dormant eye will sprout a keiki. If a keiki is not produced right away and the plant is valuable, I treat a dormant eye with keiki paste.

— E. Merkle

(Mid-Atlantic Coast US) Bite the bullet and pay more attention to what caused the plant to get sick in the first place.

— M. Owen

(Florida Gulf Coast US) Sometimes repotting will help; but before repotting we soak the plant in a solution of SuperThrive, 25 drops per gallon. (SuperThrive is a mix of hormones and vitamins.)

— J&M Roberts

(Southcentral US) Full-strength Ivory soap applied directly to the affected area and left on the plant seems to solve most problems. Do not leave the soap covering the whole plant during hot weather, just the diseased area, and wash it off there, too, after an hour.

— P. Scholz

(Northcentral US) Under artificial lighting...Smear the whole base of the plant with keiki paste and put it in a plastic bag.

— W. Schumann

(South of England) Don't dispose of any sick plant until it is well and truly dead! Repot and mist carefully; they often shoot from the base.

— P. Seaton

(North of England) If a plant has a problem and seems to be on the way out, I'm afraid I give it a helping hand to the dustbin. Fortunately, I've lost very few good plants. Those that I did lose convinced me to be most careful when watering, making sure that if any water get into the leaf axils, that I remove it with paper handkerchiefs at once. (Mr. Shuker made and uses a watering wand with a 20-22" long, quarter-inch diameter plastic tube with a slight downward bend in the end...for precise water placement.) (If I didn't have 3,000 plants to water, Don, I'd copy your idea. ed.)

— D. Shuker

(Mid-Atlantic Coast US) To arrest crown rot, cut off the affected part of the leaf and set the plant in a stream of moving air for 48 hours.

— M. Steen

(Midlands of England) Stick them under the bench where it is cool and humid, say a Hail Mary, and let nature take its course.

— H. Taylor

(California Coast US) Patience and time will do it usually.

— J. Watkins

(California Coast US) Let plant dry out almost completely.
— J. Wilson

SECTION EIGHT
VIRUSES

(a) What means do you have for detecting viruses in plants? (b) How do you cope with or control virused plants? (c) Do you hybridize with them?

SECTION 8.1
CONSENSUS AND OPINION

There is perhaps more confusion and misunderstanding in this area of phal culture than any other. I thought I was the only one who didn't have a good grip on the issue, but I have lots of company. Fortunately, there has been some useful guidance in the literature recently. Some of it is cited below.

Murphy's Law operates here, though. Every discovery of a new cure for an old problem is accompanied by two new problems...neither of which has any known cure. Read the bad news about 'bacteriophage virus' in Ed Merkle's comments under Q 9(b).

The answer to the virus problem in orchids will not be found in this section. It may not be found in our lifetimes, probably because a solution offers too small an economic incentive to draw the focus of current technology. So, we're going to have to live with it and do the things in our power to limit its spread.

Many virused plants show no outward sign of the disease. Some do and, in the hands of some growers, these plants would be tested by one of the various reliable indicators for the presence of the virus pathogens.

Most growers say they would dispose of plants that were known to be virused. Some would isolate and possibly breed with the better ones as pod parents only, a practice which appears to be quite safe if the capsules are allowed to go to full term and the seed shaken out rather than green-podded. An alternative was demonstrated by Bryan Carder MD, a Glendale, Arizona dermatolgist, who showed that sterile green-podding might be possible using an electro-scalpel which cuts with an electric arc. The electrical current to the scalpel can be varied to accommodate differing thicknesses of the capsule wall...and no physical contact is made between the green pod and the seeds. However, some pathogens might be blown into the seed cavity by the force of the arc.

BUT THE OBVIOUS QUESTION GOES UNANSWERED. If virused plants can go undetected, how can you tell the condition of your collection at any given time? At present there is no way (short of an obsessive pre-occupation with virus-avoidance) of establishing and maintaining a virus-free collection. I have several thousand plants and little motivation to begin testing all of them. Until we have something like a little pop-up indicator or a button that turns blue when the plant is infected with CyMV or red when infected with ORSV, we just won't have a convenient way of knowing. BUT THERE ARE MEASURES WE CAN TAKE TO LIMIT THE SPREAD OF THE DISEASES.

Personally, I find it useful to presume that every plant I handle is virused and act accordingly. That way, if I DO have diseased ones, they are likely to keep their condition to themselves. (I test all the plants I breed with and those I stem.)

Until someone advertises that pop-up indicator or color indicating button for sale, about all we can do is test when the visual clues are there, watch sanitation measures very closely and control aphids, if they are a local problem. (See below.) What a dismal prospect!

READ THIS CAREFULLY! An article of considerable interest on the subject of viruses and their means of transmission appeared in the October 1987 issue of the American Orchid Society <u>Bulletin</u> and is excerpted here:

* "Cymbidium mosaic virus and odontoglossum ringspot virus, the most common viruses in orchids, are **not transmitted by insects,** but rather by contaminated pruning tools.

* Decontaminating tools will not only stop CyMV and ORSV, but also the other 20-some viruses that have been identified with orchids.

* ...While transmission studies with orchid viruses <u>per se</u> have been limited, at least six have been shown to have aphid carriers.

* Aphids are either proven or highly suspect vectors of many orchid viruses and pose a threat even when they are not causing obvious damage to plants through their feeding. It may be many years before the transmission relationships of all orchid viruses are fully resolved, but until then, a careful aphid control program is advised. Controlling aphids and routinely sterilizing pruning tools (household bleach is recommended. ed.) when dividing plants or cutting flowers are likely to be very helpful in

minimizing the spread of most viruses in greenhouse-grown orchids.

It would seem to be prudent to take preventive measures to keep aphids away from your plants if they are a local pest. Sooty molds are an indication of their presence. Orthene 75S at 1 teaspoon per gallon is a good control. If you prefer a nontoxic control, Safer Soap is labelled for aphids.

Meanwhile, Woody Carlson and Mick Dennis point out that some spider mite damage looks much like the popular mental image of virus symptoms. A magnifying glass can clear up any confusion quickly. If the damage is stippled, you're off the hook. By all means, read Woody's comments in section 8(a).

Q 8(a) WHAT MEANS DO YOU HAVE FOR DETECTING VIRUSES IN PLANTS?

Answers included home test kits, lab analysis, electro-microscopy, indicator plants, (all of which are fairly reliable); and the eye ball technique, (which is not). The trouble with visual appraisal is that you only see the worst cases.

Many of the respondents point out that they have no virused plants ... but, neither have they a means of detecting virus.

Home test kits, such as those produced by Orchis Laboratories of Burdett, NY, appear to be a realistic means of virus control which starts with identification. The use Orchis' gel-diffusion technique was recommended by the three research scientist noted above in endnote #2.

Q 8(b) HOW DO YOU COPE WITH OR CONTROL VIRUSED PLANTS?

Another article in the AOS Bulletin, this time in 1986, detailed some common questions and misconceptions concerning orchid viruses...which are of concern to most serious phal growers. I've lifted some of those points here:

* **"Although cymbidium mosaic virus (CyMV) and odontoglossum ringspot virus (ORSV) infect most orchids, they rarely — if ever — are transmitted through seed**.

* ....it is strongly recommended that orchids to be meristemmed be tested for virus first and only those which are virus-free be processed for tissue culture.

* Will I transmit virus to my orchids if I smoke cigarettes? No...because tobacco mosaic virus (TMV) does not infect orchids readily. Nevertheless, since TMV does have an exceptionally wide host range, it is advisable for growers who smoke to wash their hands thoroughly (including scrubbing fingernails) or to wear plastic gloves before handling any ornamental plants such as gesneriads, which are very susceptible to TMV.

* What is effective in sterilizing tools and pots between use? ...Unlike fungal or bacterial organisms which can move in air currents and splashing water, viruses must be moved in leaf sap or plant residue by the grower... Disposable razor blades or several knives/shears which have been soaking in either a 10% household bleach solution, a saturated solution of trisodium phosphate

(available in drug stores) or a solution of 2% NaOH (sodium hydroxide) plus 2% formaldehyde are all acceptable.

If a grower has a series of tools to be used, excess plant residue should be wiped off before placing in the solution. Position the tools such that the last tool used gets reused last.

Heat can also be used to disinfect tools and/or pots. Tools can be dipped in alcohol (I use the cheapest vodka I can buy. ed.) and flamed, preferably with a propane torch, for several seconds. A simple alcohol dip and short flaming with a match or candle may not create enough heat to inactivate the virus.

(Brush contaminated cutting tools with a stiff-bristled brush thoroughly before flaming. There are almost <u>always</u> bits of tissue left on cutting tools after use and these can shade a spot from the cleansing action of the flame. Paint the torch flame over the cutting edge, both sides, for 1 or 2 seconds or until the 'sweat' disappears. I have 24 pairs of cutters for this task, so I'm not constantly stopping to sterilize tools. ed.)

* Although virus particles have been observed in pollinia of virus-infected orchids, unless the receptor plant is actually wounded, there is little chance of infecting it. ...<u>Our studies of seedlings which had been green-podded from one or both infected parents showed that no infected seedlings were produced.</u> Although the chances of transmission are very low, if the mother tissue (placenta) is infected, and wounding

of the seedling occurs with transfer of sap from the mother tissue to the seedling, it is possible that transmission could occur, but this appears to be extremely rare.

* Once any plant is infected with a virus, it and all of its propagative parts are likely to be permanently infected.

* Should I destroy all my infected plants? As long as an infected orchid continues to bloom, it does not necessarily have to be discarded... If healthy and virus-infected plants are maintained in close proximity, it is recommended that one never work with the infected plants and then move to the healthy ones. It would be wise to not even work with infected orchids the same day as the healthy... If healthy and diseased plants are kept together, special care should be taken to control aphid colonies, which sometimes appear on the inflorescences, in order to control viruses known to be aphid-borne, such as cucumber mosaic virus (CMV).

* What is the recommended strategy for control of orchid viruses?... The most important consideration is an awareness and demand for a quality product by the orchid grower.

....strict sanitation procedures should be used as follows: (1) never work with infected plants before the healthy ones; (2) use sterile tools and pots; (3) wash hands thoroughly or use plastic gloves that can be disinfected with a 10% bleach dip; (4) whenever new orchids are purchased, be suspicious of them and have them tested before you add them to your healthy group.

....As long as infected orchids produce enjoyable blooms, they can be maintained, but certainly they should be separated from the healthy ones."[2]

* These few paragraphs summarize the virus problem better than anything I've seen to date. It is not a hopeless situation...it can be controlled...and we can enjoy them, warts and all. As orchid growers, I think we all owe a debt of gratitude to the five researchers who did this work and these two articles...and also to the AOS Bulletin for publishing it.

Q 8(c) DO YOU HYBRIDIZE WITH VIRUSED PLANTS?

There is mounting evidence to support the idea that pollen from an unvirused plant may be used on a virused plant without harm to the pod parent. If pollen from a virused plant is used on an un-virused plant, there appears to be only a rare possibility of infecting the pod parent. Most authorities agree that through dry-podding, the progeny of a virused cross can be protected from the virus because the virus does not bridge the placental fuzz to the seed.

In dry-podding, the seed capsule is allowed to ripen fully and the seed is poured out into a vessel for sterilizing before sowing. If a cross is desirable enough, the extra effort would seem justified; but, many growers point out that they'd rather use a different, un-virused plant and forget the whole virus problem.

— editor

SECTION 8.2
SELECTED RESPONSES

QUESTION 8(a) WHAT MEANS DO YOU HAVE FOR DETECTING VIRUSES IN PLANTS?

(Indian Coast South Africa) I have no device to detect unseen viruses, but if the effects can be seen as is the case with mosaic virus, I destroy the plant. For plants that I suspect have virus, but cannot tell, I send a sample off to a testing laboratory.
— A. Adriaanse

(California Coast US) Virus is detected by a serological technique such as the home kit offered by Orchis Labs.
— L. Batchman

(Southeastern Australia) I have had no detectable virus problem to date, so I just keep my fingers crossed.
— M. Black

(Central California US) No means other than 'eyeballing' plants and flowers regularly.
— R. Buchter

(California Coast US) Constant observation. It is important to note that there are two types of injury to Phalaenopsis plants that cause dark brown, pitted and sunken areas on the leaves that **resemble virus.** One of these is injury caused by the false spider mite, Tenuipalpus pacificus, and is usually found <u>on the upper leaf surface.</u> Included in this group are injuries caused by the various specimens of the mite Brevipalpus and these are generally found on the <u>underside</u> of the leaves. The dark, brown, dead sunken areas caused by these latter mites can be horrendous.

The second type of injury that closely resembles virus is the severe spotting and pitting of the upper and lower leaf surfaces caused by the collapse of the mesophyll cells due to severe chill injury. This injury usually occurs during the winter months due to low temperatures in 40-45°F range. Most injury of this type, however, occurs when plants in a warm greenhouse (70-80°F/20-20°C) are watered with ice-cold tap water or water from wells, ponds, etc.

During the 35 years I've grown them, I've seen very few Phalaenopsis plants that were actually virused. The majority of virused-appearing plants I've hauled home, when treated with miticides and/or given warmer water and environmental conditions, have outgrown, in time, all the symptoms of virus and remained so for years after. I wonder how many thousands and thousands of plants I and others have tossed in the trash bin thinking they were virused when, in reality, they were only suffering from the effects of little mites and cold water or temperatures.

As a remote, but distinct, possibility: A deficiency in magnesium robs a plant of the ability to produce chlorophyll and this causes a yellow mottling of the leaves and a condition similar to chlorosis. Chlorosis, caused by an iron deficiency, can resemble virus symptoms. Iron salt is the only universal constituent of the chlorophyll molecule. Magnesium sulfate (Epsom salts) is to orchids what iron is to humans.

— E. Carlson

*(Northeastern US) Under artificial lighting...Send a tissue sample to a lab for testing.

— I. Cohen and others.

(Mid-Atlantic Coast US) In the past we have used a bioassay method involving Cassia Occidentalis as an indicator plant. If a plant shows symptoms of virus which detracts from its appearance, we discard it.

— L. Clouser

(Indian Coast South Africa) To this point at least, we have been very lucky. We've had no virused plants...that is, as far as we can tell from clinical (observable) impressions. In the past when we've thought we had a virused plant, we sectioned a leaf and put it under an electron microscope ...but each such test has proven negative. Virus has not been a problem here.

— C&I Coll

(Southern California) Observation is the key factor in control. Any suspect plant is discarded. Valuable or stud plants that are suspect have a leaf removed and sent for lab testing. Infected plants are discarded.

— W. Cousineau

(South of England) Visual.

— R. Dadd and others.

(South Australia) I would suspect any irregular markings not related to pests. False spider mites make markings similar to virus, but is controlled by Kelthane.

— M. Dennis

(Florida Gulf Coast US) Observation. I watch for pigmented or yellow streaks up and down flower spikes; twisted or bent flower spikes; irregular streaking or circular pattern in the foliage.

— J. Eich

(Mid-Atlantic Coast US) Electron microscope. Note: a new bacilliform virus has been identified in phals (identified by Lesemann in Germany.) It is very serious and widespread. The symptoms are similar to cold water or false spider mite damage. Symptoms are sunken, yellow spots which eventually turn black.

At present, there is no reliable means available to the general public for detection...and no means of coping with it. Bottom line: a virus-free reading from a commercial testing lab does <u>not</u> indicate your plant is free of this disease. Maybe a means will be found to detect this new form in the coming years.
— R. Griesbach

(Gulf Coast US) I'm an ostrich. I try not to think about virus.
— J. Grimes

(Northeastern US) To the best of my knowledge, I've had no problems with virus in my phal collection. I have only a few meristems and stem propagations from other sources.
— D. Grove

(Southeastern US) No means of detecting virus. However, plants that are suspicious, i.e. leaves with brown streaking, pitting, crippled flowers or overall poor health, are isolated. Most of these will be eventually discarded and <u>all</u> of these with real, identified problems will be canned.
— T. Harper

(Southern California We watch for necrosis of the leaves. However, on valuable plants, we will send a leaf to the state department of agriculture for a virus check.
— E. Hetherington

(Florida Caribbean US) Viruses are checked by the Florida Department of Agriculture under electron microscope...at no charge.
— W. Kelly

(Southeastern Australia) An interesting paper was read at the 12th World Orchid Conference in Tokyo in March of 1987 outlining procedures for rapid identification of orchid-hosted viruses...by F.W. Zettler, and others.
— J. Kilgannon

(France) We use the ELISA test for our mother plants from which we get the multiplications and the plants in this case are tested every 9 months or at least once each year.
— Marcel LeCoufle

(Florida Caribbean US) Suspected plants are indexed for virus.
— L. Lodyga

(California Coast US) We (Rod McLellan Co) are currently testing for the presence of CyMV and TMVO by serological techniques. All plants of all genera which are mericloned are tested for the presence of virus at each tissue cutting. If the test for virus is positive, the plants are not mericloned, but may be held for hybridizing in a quarantine area and used for production of dry seed. These precautions may not be necessary.

We are currently starting a program of virus testing all of the plants in our Phalaenopsis breeding stock. Considering today's low cost of serological testing, this procedure may be feasible for hobbyists' collection also.

Unlike certain other genera, Phalaenopsis frequently do not show symptoms of viral infection until quite old. We hope that you might warn your readers that virus may be much more widespread in a phal collection than one may realize and we have found that many growers are currently selling stem propagations of virused plants. (It can only be hoped that all conscientious vendors of propagated phals take the same precautions as does Rod McLellan Co. We laud the practice. ed.)
— S. Hawkins

(Queensland Coast Australia) When we suspect a plant of being virused, we send a leaf sample to the Department of Primary Industries to have it examined under an electron microscope.
— J. Mackinney

(Luzon Philippines) There are symptoms for this class of ailment and we normally consult with virologists at the University (of the Philippines, Los Banos, Laguna).
— D. Mendoza

(Queensland Coast Australia) If virus is suspected, the plant is destroyed.
— R. Merritt

(California Coast US) Visual.
— N. Nash and others.

(California Coast US) I plan to start testing.
— M&J Nedderman

(Indian Coast South Africa) Radial diffusion test.
— G. Paris

(California Coast US) Tissue test.
— F. Robinson

(Puerto Rico US) I look for color breaks, depressions in the leaves, poor growing habit and flower deformities. I destroy these plants.
— R. Rodriguez

(Mid-Atlantic Coast US) We don't attempt to detect viruses in the greenhouse. We tear off a specimen leaf and send it out for testing.
— E. Rutkowski

(Southcentral US) Observation and experience.

— P. Scholz

*(Northcentral US) Under artificial lighting...United States Department of Agriculture testing.

— W. Schumann

(South of England) None. I considered using (and offering) an antiserum test which does not seem to be available in this country.

— P. Seaton

(Oahu Hawaii US) Suspected plants are sent to the University of Hawaii, Tropical Agriculture, for testing.

— R. Takase

*(Northeastern US) Under artificial lighting...By extracting some juice from the suspected plant and sending it to a virus testing lab.

— J. Vella

QUESTION 8(b) HOW DO YOU COPE WITH OR CONTROL VIRUSED PLANTS?

(California Coast US) Generally, a virused plant is discarded unless it is a valuable breeding stud plant.
— L. Batchman

(Central California US) I bloom all plants at least twice before weeding out inferior plants. If any color irregularities appear in subsequent flowerings, I trash the plant...regardless of desirability or value.
— R. Buchter

(California Coast US) Deep-six them right into the garbage can.
— E. Carlson

(Mid-Atlantic Coast US) We use only sterile shears and knives, disposable gloves, and clean pots.
— L. Clouser

*(Northeastern US) Under artificial lighting...Throw them out.
— I. Cohen

(Southern California US) To the trash can it goes.
— D&R Cowden

(South of England) Segregation. If the condition is worse after 3 months, I destroy the plant.
— R. Dadd

(South Australia) I don't have any; but if I did, they'd be burned.
— M. Dennis

(Florida Gulf Coast US) Suspect plants are isolated for confirmation. If positive, they are destroyed.
— J. Eich

(Holland) First, we start with virus-free plants. If we see virused plants, we throw them away.
— a major commercial grower

(California Coast US) Badly virused ones are dumped.
— H. Freed

(Maui Hawaii US) If I suspect virus, I get rid of them. I don't see too much virus with phals.
— R. Fukamura

(Mid-Atlantic Coast US) Destroy them.
— R. Griesbach and others.

(Atlantic Coast US) Never had a virused phal that I know of. The real problem with virus is with cattleyas.
— K. Griffith

(Northeastern US) I use only sterilized or new pots and cut flower spikes only with new razor blades.
— D. Grove

(Southern California) If we know it has a virus, we either isolate it or throw it out.
— E. Hetherington

(Southern California) I don't cope with virused plants. I trash them.
— D. Hirsch

(Midlands of England) If a plant is obviously virused, it would be destroyed.
— P. Hirst

(Florida Caribbean US) Usually discard it.
— W. Kelly

(Southeastern Australia) Incinerate.
— J. Kilgannon

(Southern California US) Dispose of obviously virused plants and only hand pick the flowers of those not obvious. (cut flower grower.)
— T. Koike

(Queensland Coast Australia) With good culture, some plants carry viruses with no outward indication. Any we find to be virused are incinerated unless the plant is one we wish to breed with.
— J. Mackinney

(Mid-Atlantic Coast US) Some of my plants have recently fallen victim to what appears to be a new form of virus. It takes the form of an 'incurable' bacterial infection which first causes yellow spotting and then mesophyll collapse...which turns brown, slowly spreading across leaf surfaces, trunk and flower stems. Flowers don't seem to be affected. The tissue damage starts out looking like the pitting caused by false spider mite, but quickly collapses the mesophyll tissue similar to the thermal shock of cold water on warm, new phal tissue. It affects older tissue first, then spreads to new.

Dr Rob Griesbach of the US) Department of Agriculture (and a Phalaenopsis grower) called it a 'bacteriophage virus' ("...any of various specific viruses normally present in sewage and in body products") and described it as very contagious...spread by mere contact with other plants or water splashing from plant to plant. It does not seem to be deterred by bactericides or fungicides. I destroyed the affected plants at Dr Griesbach's suggestion. Since it takes about 6 months for the symptoms to begin to show, I'm watching several other plants which may have been compromised. (Damn, just when I thought I had things under control. ed.)
— E. Merkle

(California Coast US) Dump.

— N. Nash

(California Coast US) Any plant that has symptoms is trashed except the awarded ones. If, when tested, they show positive, they are trashed, too.

— M&J Nedderman

(Mid-Atlantic Coast US) Remove all vectors and discard diseased plants. We then sterilize all cutting tools, surfaces, and containers using heat, sodium hydroxide, bleach, etc.

— M. Owen

(Mid-west US) I destroy any plant that does not grow or shows the usual signs of virus on the leaves or flowers.

— R. Pallister

(Northcentral US) If an awarded plant has virus I keep it away from others. I destroy unawarded, virused plants.

— A. Roberts

(California Coast US) I flame tools and stakes and soak used pots overnight in a solution of trisodium phosphate.

— F. Robinson

(Mid-Atlantic Coast US) I have a number of stainless steel kitchen knives which have been sharpened to a keen edge. These are sterilized by soaking in a Physan (or generic) solution.

— E. Rutkowski

(South of England) Plants which perform badly are incinerated. (I'm glad Phil Seaton is not my employer. ed.)

— P. Seaton

(North of England) If any plant develops streaky leaves or distorted leaves in any way, I destroy it straight away. That is a ruthless practice, but I have far too much invested in my collection to take chances on ruining it with a diseased plant.

— D. Shuker

(California Coast US) I sterilize cutting tools with a propane torch. Any plant that looks unusual (mutated flowers or leaves) gets dumped.

— J. Watkins

QUESTION 8(c) DO YOU HYBRIDIZE WITH VIRUSED PLANTS?

(Indian Coast South Africa) Certainly not. I think this is a criminal offence. It is not difficult to suppress the (viral) appearance, but I think this also is an offence.

— A. Adriaanse

(California Coast US) Virused plants may be used as a pod parent with the seed harvested from dry, open pod and sterilized with calcium- or sodium-hypochlorite.

— L. Batchman and others.

(Central California US) Never! As a physiologist, I am not convinced yet that transfer of virus can be avoided in hybridizing. Why take a chance? (With the value of my collection, you bet I'm conservative).

— R. Buchter

(California Coast US) No.

— E. Carlson

*(Northeastern US) Under artificial lighting...God, no!

— I. Cohen

(South of England) No reason why not.

— R. Dadd

(Holland) No.

— a major commercial grower and others.

(California Coast US) Yes, virus does not affect progeny.

— H. Freed

(Mid-Atlantic Coast US) No. There is evidence that virus-infected pollen can infect the pod parent.

— R. Griesbach

(Southeastern US) Only as pod parents, but most often, not at all. The threat to the rest of my collection is not worth the chance. There are better and more healthy plants available.

— T. Harper

(Southern California Yes, we hybridize with them; however, the pods are permitted to go full term with the seeds shaken out.

— E. Hetherington

(Midlands of England) According to information given in the AOS Bulletin, there is little danger of transmitting viral diseases in the hybridising process and I accept this view.

— P. Hirst

(Florida Caribbean US) Yes, I will use the pollen if I have to.
— W. Kelly

(Southeastern Australia) No, but evidence was submitted at the 12th WOC in Tokyo that indicated seed does not transmit a plant's virus.
— J. Kilgannon

(France) We have got seedlings without any trouble coming out from parents which have viruses, but, of course, we try to use plants which have been tested as free from any illness.
— Marcel LeCoufle

(Central California US) We do not knowingly hybridize with virused plants.
— B. Livingston

(Queensland Coast Australia) If the plant is one we wish to breed with, then we keep it isolated and use the virused plant only as the pod parent and sow only dry seed.
— J. Mackinney

(Luzon Philippines) Certainly not with green-pod culture of the seeds. A scalpel passing through the infected green pod can pass the virus on to seeds that it comes in contact with.
— D. Mendoza

(California Coast US) On occasion.
— N. Nash

(Mid-west US) I will not hybridize with a virused plant.
— R. Pallister and others.

(California Coast US) Not if I know they are virused.
— F. Robinson

*(Northcentral US) Under artificial lighting...Sometimes.
— W. Schumann

(North of England) I have not, but, theoretically, there is no reason not to if the virus does not enter seed as reported.
— P. Seaton

*(Northeastern US) Under artificial lighting...Suspected plants, e.g. Golden Sands "Canary", are used only as a pod parent.
— D&D Strack

Endnotes:

1. Zettler, F., G. Wisler, M. Elliot and N. Ko, 1987; Some New, Potentially Significant Viruses of Orchids and Their Probable Means of Transmission; Amer. Orchid Bull. 56: 1045-1051

2. Wisler, G., F. Zettler, and T. Sheehan, 1986; Common Questions and Misconceptions Concerning Orchid Viruses; Amer. Orchid Soc. Bull. 55:472-479

Virus control kit: Piezo-electric torch, grain alcohol for flaming, brush to remove bits of tissue, and a second type of piezo-electric ignitor torch with a flex hose to a 20-pound propane bottle for production work. I use 24 pairs of shears to avoid interuption of the potting process.

Table 1. Probable taxonomic affinities and natural means of transmission of 23 orchid viruses.		
Virus	Group*	Natural vector
Bean yellow mosaic	potyvirus	aphids
Brazilian bacilliform	(rhabdovirus)	(aphids)
Clover yellow vein	potyvirus	aphids
Cucumber mosaic	cucumovirus	aphids
Cymbidium mild mosaic	(rhabdovirus)	(aphids)
Cymbidium mosaic	potexvirus	unknown
Dendrobium rhabdovirus	rhabdovirus	(aphilds)
Dendrobium mosaic	potyvirus	aphids
Dendrobium vein necrosis	(closterovirus)	(aphids)
Filamentous cypripedium	(potyvirus)	(aphids)
Filamentous orchid	unknown	unknown
Grammatophyllum bacilliform	(rhabdovirus)	(aphids)
Isometric masdevallia	unknown	unknown
Laelia red leafspot	rhabdovirus	(aphids)
Long orchid rhabdovirus	(rhabdovirus)	(aphids)
Odontoglossum ringspot	tobamovirus	unknown
Orchid fleck	rhabdovirus	(aphids)
Phalacnopsis chlorotic spot	rhabdovirus	(aphids)
Short orchid rhabdovirus	(rhabdovirus)	(aphids)
Tobacco rattle	tobravirus	nematodes
Tomato ringspot	nepovirus	nemotodes
Turnip mosaic	potyvirus	aphids
Vanilla potyvirus	(potyvirus)	aphids
*Groups in parentheses are tentative and not officially acknowledged by the International Committee for the Taxonomy of Viruses (Matthews, 1982). Vectors in parentheses also are tentative and not yet established conclusively.		

(Source: American Orchid Society Bulletin) 56:1046

Table 1. Incidence of cymbidium mosaic and odontoglossum ringspot viruses detected by G.C. Wisler in individual collections of cultivated orchids since 1980.

Genus	Number of Plants Tested	
	Infected/Total	Total %
Angraecum	2/51	4
Asocenda	14/84	17
Brassocattleya, Brassolaeliocattleya	147/487	30
Cattleya	123/496	25
Cymbidium	100/204	49
Dendrobium	51/194	26
Epidendrum	19/161	12
Laelia	9/69	13
Laelicattleya	151/431	35
Miltonia	2/30	7
Odontoglossum	3/25	12
Oncidium	12/147	8
Paphiopedilum	6/168	4
Phaius	3/6	50
Phalaenopsis	74/267	28
Potinara	23/54	43
Sophrolaeliocattleya	37/151	25
Vanda	30/151	20
Miscellaneous	59/363	16

(Source: American Orchid Society Bulletin 55:473)

Table 2. Incidence of cymbidium mosaic and odontoglossum ringspot viruses among various orchid genera sampled by G.C. Wisler in 1980.

Collection No.	CyMV	ORSV	Both Viruses	Total Tested	% Infected
1	29	0	2	57	54
2	5	0	1	33	18
3	127	6	6	426	33
4	105	2	3	630	17
5	8	0	0	36	22
6	58	6	2	177	37
7	18	6	3	153	18
8	19	2	5	167	16
9	90	0	8	253	39
10	10	0	0	21	48
11	34	4	6	194	22
12	1	1	0	22	9
13	48	15	18	130	62
14	6	0	9	16	93
15	39	5	9	114	46
16	24	2	1	208	13
17	19	6	0	96	26
18	9	1	0	136	7
19	21	8	5	430	8
20	27	18	12	268	21
21	1	0	8	20	45

(Source: *American Orchid Society Bulletin* 55:473)

SECTION NINE
FLOWER INDUCTION

(a) What special steps do you take to induce flowering? (b) How far in advance of desired date of blooming?

Note: Many of the answers to these questions are listed under Section 2, HEAT, but the following are a more precise delineation of recommended procedures...and, as such, deserve separate handling.

SECTION 9.1 FLOWER INDUCTION CONSENSUS AND OPINION

Q 9(a) WHAT SPECIAL STEPS DO YOU TAKE TO INDUCE FLOWERING?

I don't think I can improve on E. (Woody) Carlson's response to this question. Please read it before proceeding with this section. There is 35 years of astute phal watching summarized in those few paragraphs.

When you get done with that, read what Hugo Freed has to say on the subject. More words of wisdom.

Most growers make no deliberate attempt to control flowering. There is a lot to be said for not tinkering with nature, but knowing how is a handy tool.

Items from the menu for inducing flowering intentionally; (1) lower the night minimum temperature; (2) raise the light; (3) lower the humidity and reduce watering; (4) feed Epsom salts (magnesium sulfate); (5) feed high phosphorus; (6) feed less or no nitrogen; (7) increase air circulation; (8) under artificial lighting, shorten the day; or (9) do nothing.

I'm a little puzzled by the commentary of Bob Dadd and other British growers who say their problem is not getting phals to spike, but is in keeping them from spiking year-round. Their greenhouse temperature ranges appear to be the same as elsewhere; their daylengths vary more than the warmer latitudes ranging from longer summer days to shorter winter days...no clues there; maybe it's the water. Ideas, anyone? (Maybe the phals don't dare disappoint their owners; the Brits have got to be the flower-lovingest people on earth...as I found in the 3 years I lived there in the early '50s. I think that's where my affection for flowers came from.)

Note under (8) above on the menu of items inducing flower spiking that the artificial light growers shorten the plant's day to induce spiking. That sounds like a statement that the phals under lights are photoperiodic or that they respond to an artificial autumn by spiking. I've heard several reliable sources say that, but I've never seen evidence to support the idea.

Could it be that phals grown under artificial lights respond to a different seasonal signal? Maybe the primitive forms from which the phals sprang were indigenous to more temperate latitudes where greater daylength swings signaled the changes of season and of flowering times at a time when more ultraviolet light was reaching the earth...and the phals under lights 'remember'?

Or are they responsive to a reduced total daily exposure to ultraviolet radiation to which they may have become accustomed under artificial lighting?

Can flowering be chemically-induced? Empirical wisdon ways to feed phosphorous heavily in the fall (during the flower induction period) for best flower production. Is it possible that the phos is helping to <u>induce</u> the flower spikes? How does magnesium figure into all this? Experience, again, says apply Epsom salts in the fall. It doesn't hurt and probably helps . . . at least it seems that way and the stuff is cheap so, what the hell, we'll use it.

It occurs to me that a lot of this conjecture could be cleared away if we could interest the University of Hawaii or the University of Florida in looking into some of these questions. If a commercial crop is involved, they will, but. . . **It would be nice, too, if we get some graduate students to do a study of the ideal chemical norms for species Phalaenopsis tissue.**

Studies that tell what chemical levels are present in a plant don't do a lot of good if we don't know what the plant <u>should</u> have. Most lab analyses I've seen were based on projections or extrapolations from other known crop standards. Considering the limited application and the cost involved, it isn't likely to happen soon. (Now, if we could only interest the United States Department of Defense. . .)

Information regarding these questions would be of considerable interest to phal growers in the temperate zones and would be welcomed for inclusion in future revisions of this book. . .or, I'm sure, publication in any of the orchid periodicals with worldwide distribution.

Q 9(b) HOW FAR IN ADVANCE OF THE DESIRED BLOOMING DATE DO YOU TAKE THESE SPECIAL STEPS?

Consensus is 90 to 125 days. Woody Carlson's program offers a means of adjusting the interval within these general limits.

— editor

SECTION 9.2 FLOWER INDUCTION SELECTED RESPONSES

QUESTION 9(a) WHAT SPECIAL STEPS DO YOU TAKE TO INDUCE FLOWERING?

(Indian Coast South Africa) Since I'm feeding with a balanced fertiliser, the plants follow the seasonal way of flowering with good success. However, if my self-contained house is ready, I'd like to experiment.

— A. Adriaanse

*(Mid-Atlantic Coast US) Under artificial lighting...I summer plants outside...leave them out until temps regularly go down into the low 50's at night. At this time, I provide more light and less water.

— M. Bowell

(Central California US) In addition to cooling the plants, I 'dose' the reluctant spikers with Epsom salts for 3 weeks. I have used this technique for years (Herb Hager suggested it).

— R. Buchter

(California Coast US) During the months of October and November, I lower my night temperature to 55°F for a period of 2 to 3 weeks to help accelerate the initiation of flower spikes.

Relative humidity is lowered to 30-40% during this period and plants are watered less often.

Also, note that during this time light intensity is very important. With a light intensity of 1,500 footcandles and over, initiation of flower spikes is decreased. Decreased light intensity of under 1,200 footcandles increases the initiation of new flower spikes.

In addition, it is important that the plants have an ample supply of magnesium in the form of Epsom salts available to them during this time. This is a very important part of the successful flowering of the Phalaenopsis plants as a low level of magnesium sulfate at this time correlates to poor flower production and the number of flowers per stem. Epsom salts may be applied at a rate of one level teaspoon per gallon of water every 2 weeks.

Within 85/95 days thereafter on the average, the first flower on the secondary spike will open. These flowers are sometimes smaller than normal as is the case with primary spikes which are allowed to carry too many laterals. Cropping is usually only done once on a spike because, with each additional cropping, the blooms tend to get smaller.

CROPPING (SECOND SPIKES) Mature Phalaenopsis plants can be flowered once or twice a year, the blooms lasting up to 3 months or longer. When the last of these blooms starts to wilt, the flower spike can be cut back to about an inch above the 3rd or 4th node up from the base of the spike. When this is done, one of the lower nodes will initiate a secondary spike within 2 to 3 weeks.

FLOWER CONTROL If flowers are needed at a later date than is likely to occur on a new spike, the top of the spike may be pinched off. This action will force the spike to initiate a secondary. As is the case with older spikes that have been cut, the pinched spike will initiate a new one in 2 to 3 weeks and will produce blooms off the secondary spike in 85/95 days on the average.

Although this interval is an average time for the first blooms to open when cropping, temperature control is the key to exact timing. When spikes are either cut or pinched and warm night temperatures over 70°F and day temperatures of 85/90°F are maintained, the initiation of secondary spikes will be delayed. Under these conditions it will take 95/120 days for the secondary spike to develop and produce the first bloom.

Cool temperatures, however, will accelerate the initiation of secondary spikes from a cut or pinch. Night temperatures of 60/62°F and day temperatures of 70/80°F will cause the secondary spike to initiate faster and produce the first blooms in 85/95 days. Of course, along with the correct temperatures, a light intensity of 900/1,200 footcandles is desirable; good air movement is a must; and a well-balanced feeding and watering program must be maintained.

— E. Carlson

(California Bay Area US) Coconut incense, Mozart and Bach arias, Vivaldi oboe concertos. (...? ed.)

— W. Cecil

(Western Australia) With our summers being so hot, this is a hard one. I have tried nearly everthing except the freezer. The only way I can do this is to open the doors, vents and everything else on the house, and leave all the fans and coolers going round the clock. I do this in January and carly February for flowering for our winter shows in June and July and say a good prayer.

— K. Clarke

(Mid-Atlantic Coast US) We drop the minimum night temperature from 70° to 60°F during September to early October.

— L. Clouser

*(Northeastern US) Under artificial lighting...Lower temperature at night below 60°F for about 4 weeks.

— I. Cohen

(Indian Coast South Africa) We have not worried about flower induction. We used to allow a chilling period, but have not been very impressed with this.

— C&I Coll

(Southern California US) None.

— W. Cousineau and others

(South of England) Normally no special steps are needed in England. Plants spike the year-round. The problem on mature plants is often to maintain balance between growth and excessive spiking.

— R. Dadd

(South Australia) I delay heating at the onset of the cooler nights for 3 weeks in the autumn (March). Flower spikes will show in April and plants will bloom in July through September, according to light factors.

— M. Dennis

(Mid-Atlantic Coast US) I let the plants chill slightly in late September without the use of greenhouse heat at night. This will induce spiking in early types. Not all the white Phalaenopsis hybrids will respond to this culture.

— R. Drejka

(California Coast US) I talk to the phals; they love it. Also, I have a radio on with soft music.

— W. Eckberg

(Florida Gulf Coast US) Lower night temperature to 55-60°F; shorten day-length to 10 hours or less.

— J. Eich

(Holland) From mid-May and for 6 weeks, we keep night temperature at 18°C (64°F). This will not hurt the plants or flowers which are still on the plants. Plants will flower in August through October. The second spikes come in February and March.

— a major commercial grower

(California Coast US) We were able to control flowering season of Phalaenopsis by cutting the heat at night down to 50°F for around 5 weeks in July and restoring it to a 60-62°F minimum by day. This, coupled with raising the phosphate and potassium levels in the fertilizer and lowering the nitrogen will cause the flowering to begin around the middle of November, slowly at first for Thanksgiving (about November 25), and the balance flowering heavily through December and all the way through to Easter.

As any Phalaenopsis grower knows, a new flowering spike can be produced by cutting of the old spike (when through flowering) above the second plump node. I found that on an average a new spike would appear from one of the nodes in 3 to 4 weeks. It would grow rapidly and the first bud would appear in about 30 days and the first flower about 40 days after that. The balance of the flowers would open one at a time about every 4 days. The new spike would carry only about three-quarters as many flowers as the original one.

We would cut off the old spike around the end of March at which time most or all of the original crop would be through flowering. The new crop gave us loads of flowers from early June through heavy August and September wedding seasons as well as for the June weddings.

However, let me give you a few words of caution: We were located in Malibu only one mile from the ocean with a moderate climate throughout the year. We were favored by cool ocean breezes, so that we experience no extremes of temperature. I suggest that those growing in greatly different areas experiment with a few plants in order to adapt to your own climatic conditions.
— H. Freed

(Atlantic Coast US) Dropping greenhouse temperature in the fall plus cutting the original stem back early enough to induce another spike for later flowering. Keiki paste will also induce flowering.
— K. Griffith

(Southeastern US) I like to get the temperature down to the low 50's as early in the fall as possible for 10 to 14 days. Also, I switch to 10-30-20 fertilizer when spikes begin to appear.
— J. Grimes

(Northeastern US) None. I get enough temperature drop naturally in the summertime.
— D. Grove

(Indian Coast South Africa) No specific steps taken. Spiking commences in autumn (April/May) with late spiking starting about July. Flowering starts about July/August and ends about February.
— A. Harris

(Southern California US) 55°F for 3 weeks.
— E. Hetherington

(Midlands of England) By lowering minimum temperature to the 55/60°F range for around 2 weeks.
— P. Hirst

(Florida Caribbean US) Temperatures are dropped by leaving the cool-pad system on longer starting September first. This gives us a heavy crop for Christmas.
— W. Kelly

(Southern California US) Heaters are shut off in the fall for a month, but the effectiveness of this practice is questionable, because of the variance of weather conditions. Nature controls blooming more than heating or cooling systems.
— T. Koike

(Indonesia) By using Vitabloom instead of Gandasill.
— A. Kolopaking

(Holland) Temperature and daylength both influence flowering time. Main flowering time is May-June with flower induction during the low temperatures of March with shortened days. Second flowering time is November with flower induction August-September, again, with shortened days.
— H. Kronenberg

(France) A drop in temperature to under 13°C (55°F) each night during 3 weeks.
— Marcel LeCoufle

(North of England) I never need to induce flowering. My problem, if it is one, is flower prevention (emphasis mine. ed.).
— P. Lindsay

(Central California US) A drop in night temperature to 50/55°F (10/12°C) for several weeks works rather well. Day temperatures should be 78 to 85°F (24/26°C) to be effective in setting spikes. Two waterings with straight Epsom salts (6 pounds per 100 gallons) followed by a clear water flushing. Resume normal feeding program after this.
— B. Livingston

(Florida Caribbean US) Reducing the night temperature and fertilizing with Bloom Booster (10-30-20). Low temps are not encountered until late fall or early winter here in Miami. Fans are used all night to help in dropping the temperature.
— L. Lodyga

(Luzon Philippines) Our technique is low night temperature which we get under natural environment at high elevation (800 metres) above sea level. Another technique we employ is to kick mature plants to flower at high elevation and finish them up at lower elevation.
— D. Mendoza

(Southern California US) I give them lots of tender, loving care and let them bloom when they want to.
— H. Moye

(California Coast US) In November, I change to a low nitrogen fertilizer, quarter- to half-strength. I don't drop the temperature as this seems to promote rot and the temperature drops naturally in my greenhouse in December, anyway. I like to bloom phals late in the season, i.e. March through May.
— M&J Nedderman

(Mid-Atlantic Coast US) Cool September nights and 10-30-20 Blossom Booster.
— M. Owen

(Mid-west US) I do not drop temperatures to induce flowering for a special flowering time. After normal flowering, I let the strength go back into the plant. Also, I do not let flower spikes branch or cut spikes back to induce re-spiking.
— R. Pallister

(Indian Coast South Africa) We installed a cool room to alter temps to induce earlier spiking, but did not find it a great success. Outside plants spiked just as well at the same period without any artificial influence. It was a costly and inconclusive programme.
— G. Paris

(Southeastern US) Stop fertilizing.
— S. Pridgen

*(Northcentral US) Under artificial lighting...I drastically reduce light and lower temperatures.
— A. Roberts

(Florida Gulf Coast US) Cool nights and warm days.
— J&R Roberts

(California Coast US) I remove shade cloth from October through April, for more light; I also change fertilizers to a 15-30-20 mix.
— F. Robinson

(Queensland Coast Australia) Leave it to nature.
— R. Robinson

(Puerto Rico US) During the October through December, we use 10-30-20 Peters Special fertilizer.
— R. Rodriguez

(Mid-Atlantic Coast US) I have tried several controlled experiments of day-length and temperature combinations using a variety of genetic ancestry. Contrary to other reports, I was not able to get any consistent or predictable results. I presume that if one uses a narrow lineage, then some sort of predictable results may be possible.
— E. Rutkowski

(Southcentral US) Switch to 10-30-20 fertilizer in the fall and I allow a natural cool period of 10 days below 60°F.
— P. Scholz

(South of England) None. My nighttime temperature dips to 55°F occasionally and this possibly induces flowering. Certainly mature plants bloom two or three times a year and I always have a lot of flowers with peak blooming from December through April.
— P. Seaton

(North of England) I leave well enough alone and keep my fingers crossed each year. Not much need, though. Everything flowers.
— D. Shuker

*(Pacific Northwest US) Under artificial lighting. . .Reduce daylength.
— S. Skoien

*(Mid-Atlantic Coast US) Under artificial lighting. . .We cool the basement of our house off by ventilation as described in Question #2. This means having to wait for cool nights as nature sees fit. Attempts to use ice-cooled water on their roots did not result in any observable success. However, I have shown that the phal's roots should be wet or damp during the night cooling period. One season I carefully watered only the roots of 50 phals in 6 to 10'' pots each evening for 2 weeks during the cool-down period. After an additional week, 49 of them had initiated flower spikes.
— K&M Smeltz

(Midlands of England) Lower temperatures to 55°F.
— F. Smith

*(Northeastern US) Under artificial lighting. . .Nothing except to shorten day-length.
— D&D Strack

(Mid-Atlantic Coast US) We usually keep our cooling system operating at night in late summer (August) when the weather is unseasonably cool. This frequently results in early spiking.
— C. Williamson

(Texas Gulf Coast US) Cold nights and high phosphorus fertilizer (9-59-8).
— C&J Wilson

QUESTION 9(b) HOW FAR IN ADVANCE OF THE DESIRED DATE OF BLOOMING DO YOU TAKE THE SPECIAL STEPS?

(Central California US) I do not intentionally regulate spike induction. Rather, I 'dose' only plants which have not begun to spike after others have already established spikes as expected on time. I consistently have 95% plus spikes well in advance of our society's annual spring show in March each year.

— R. Buchter

(California Coast US) If all factors I mentioned in Q-9(a) above are in place and on time, the plants should start initiating their spikes 15 to 30 days after the cooling-off period and the first flowers should start opening 90 to 100 days thereafter.

— E. Carlson

*(Northeastern US) Under artificial lighting...My plants bloom when they feel like it. I've tried putting them outside in April or May to get them to bloom in the fall for our show, but it doesn't work very well.

— I. Cohen

(Mid-Atlantic Coast US) We use a 10-30-20 fertilizer in late summer to early fall.

— L. Clouser

(South of England) If plants are required for a show date, I drop the temperature at night to 50°F for 3 weeks...four to four and one-half months earlier.

— R. Dadd

(Florida Gulf Coast US) For us, 3 months starting in mid-September.

— J. Eich

(Holland) For flowering in November/December, the cooling period of 18°C at night and daytime temperature of 21°C for 6 weeks should be finished by July. The second spike will come on this way for Mother's Day in the following year.

— a major commercial grower

(Florida Atlantic Coast US) Three to four months.

— C&L Hagan

(Southeastern US) We give a 3-month lead time, but weather plays a major part in spike development. Our crop can vary as much as a month early or late, depending on weather conditions.

— T. Harper

(Southern California US) Three months in advance of desired flowering.

— E. Hetherington

(Midlands of England) Three calendar months.
— P. Hirst

(Florida Caribbean US) 115 days.
— W. Kelly

(Holland) The time between flower induction and flowering is about 90 days.
— H. Kronenberg

(France) At least 4 months in advance before the season we desire. Impossible to manage in the hot months of the summer season in normal greenhouses on account of too hot nights.
— Marcel LeCoufle

(Central California US) I chill nights and use Epsom salts about 4 to 5 months before desired flowering. Time of year and the weather are taken into account.
— B. Livingston

(Luzon Philippines) About 3 to 4 months ahead of natural flowering in common growing areas.
— D. Mendoza

(Mid-Atlantic Coast US) 10 weeks.
— M. Owen

(California Coast US) High phosphorus fertilizer is used in December and January.
— F. Robinson

(Oahu Hawaii US) I make no attempt to control flowering time.
— R. Takase

SECTION TEN
SHOW PREPARATION

(a) What steps, if any, do you take to prepare a plant for showing judging?...and when do you take them?

SECTION 10.1 SHOW PREPARATION CONSENSUS AND OPINION

Q 10(a) WHAT STEPS, IF ANY, DO YOU TAKE TO PREPARE A PLANT FOR SHOWING OR JUDGING?...AND WHEN DO YOU TAKE THEM?

Again, this section is a menu of things that can be done, but there are trends.

Many respondents said their preparations went on throughout the year and were not concentrated in the days before the showing. While this practice might not be economically feasible for commercial growers, it certainly makes sense for the hobbyists.

Those who grow under lights will want to read Ed Merkle's interesting ideas on how to prep plants for showing. Some neat ideas.

— editor

SECTION 10.2 SHOW PREPARATION SELECTED RESPONSES

QUESTION 10(a) WHAT STEPS, IF ANY, DO YOU TAKE TO PREPARE A PLANT FOR SHOWING/JUDGING?..AND WHEN DO YOU TAKE THEM?

(Indian Coast South Africa) The preparatory steps are an on-going process rather than a last-minute effort. The pots should be clean, the medium healthy, and the plant should be of good culture. Since the Phalaenopsis is one of the most graceful plants, the spike should be trained in a gentle arch along a well-constructed stay which must be solid and not move around. Tying must start as soon as the spike is 15 cm (6'') long and must continue all along. This way, the buds will place themselves in the right position for best display.
— A. Adriaanse

(California Coast US) The only show or judging preparation I take is to orient the plant and spike to the light to get the best spike habit and flower presentation. The spike should also be staked early if it is going to need staking at all.
— L. Batchman

(Southeastern Australia) A plant in good health needs only support of the flowering cane till it 'sets' and then only staked to the first bud, allowing the spike to arch naturally. With my diffused light, there is no single source to draw blooms in a particular direction, so flowers arrange themselves quite naturally.
— M. Black

(Central California US) Our water is quite alkaline, so I remove the inevitable spots with milk and a piece of old panty hose and some elbow grease. I stake spikes as soon as they show and tie as they develop. Once in spike, not bud, I don't move the plant. I recheck all plant labels for condition of the label, completeness of the entries and new registered hybrids. I do this 1 to 2 weeks before show time.
— R. Buchter

(Southern California US) I clean the plant with a solution of one teaspoon of mayonnaise mixed into a half cup (4 oz) of regular, full-fatted cow's milk. Wash/scrub the plant with it. Cut off old leaves, secure the spike with a wire stake which has a one-inch 'U' bend. Put a strip of clear plastic tape across the 'bottom' of the U, slide the U over the stem, and place another strip of tape across the'top' of the U, holding the stem in a shock-absorbing retainer.
If a plant is not in full bloom, don't waste your time and the judges'. Bring it in for judging when it is.
— E. Campuzano

(California Coast US) I stake them early and make sure young buds are facing south from the start to final opening. Also, I make sure the plant itself looks presentable, as well. Two months ahead.

— E. Carlson

(Mid-Atlantic Coast US) All of our plants are used for display. (Larry Clouser and Michael Owen, quoted herein, are the keepers of the DuPont orchid collection at Longwood Gardens in Kennett Square, Pennsylvania, USA, one of the world's great estate gardens. The estate, a sensory overload, gives new dimension to the word 'magnificent'. ed.) We try to keep foliage attractive and stake flower spikes for a pleasing presentation.

— L. Clouser

*(Northeastern US) Under artificial lighting...Make sure it is repotted on time; cut the stubs of old inflorescences; orient so buds grow toward the light; take care with watering and feeding; and stake when buds are enlarging. It is an on-going process most of the year.

— I. Cohen

(Southern California US) Clean any calcium, water-spotting residue from the leaves by wiping with cotton balls soaked in milk a few days in advance of the show. Flower stems are staked from about 9" growth on.

— W. Cousineau

(Southern California US) All year long I try to keep the plants growing in good health and keep them clean. At showtime, it does not take long to get them ready to go.

— D&R Cowden

(South of England) The only step I take is in training spikes as they develop to give a near-vertical rise followed by a gentle arching over and/or cascade for multi-branching spikes. Some doritaenopsis are prone to brittle spikes and should either be tied fully vertical or wired in an arch.

— R. Dadd

(South Australia) Stake spikes early to control the spike habit, usually before the buds start to open. Clean the leaves and the pot the day before exhibiting. Check the label for accuracy and the blooms for spots or blemishes. Clean blooms with a small art brush soaked in a little washing up solution.

— M. Dennis

(Mid-Atlantic Coast US) A plant which is to be displayed or shown for judging, should be left in the same position once the spike begins to elongate. Otherwise, the flowers will not be displayed in a proper order and angle on the spike. I don't worry about show time, because we have an AOS judging every month and the flowers last longer than that.

— R. Drejka

(Florida Gulf Coast US) Nothing really. We groom our phals throughout the year, so the only last-minute preparation is to clean the leaves with clear, warm water followed by gentle wiping.

— J. Eich

(California Coast US) Groom the plant for best possible presentation. Put it in a warmer place if it is not quite ready for showing...to speed up the flowering process. Put it in a cooler place to slow it down.

If the flower spike has been cut and is a little limp, plunge the whole spike into cool water for a few hours or even overnight. This will quite often refresh the flowers and restore them to their natural substance.

— H. Freed

(Maui Hawaii US) No steps; just leave them as they are.

— R. Fukamura

(Southern California US) When the flower spikes are about half their mature height (late January in Southern California), I stake them gently at a point where the stem has started to harden. I move the tie up slightly during the next few weeks, but allow the increasing weight of the spike and flowers to determine the arch of the spike...as is the case in nature.

For the classic whites and pinks, the object is to have the bottom flower on the spike at the highest point on the arch. Does that make sense? I always think of the breathtaking photos of Hugo Freed's and Lewis Vaughn's greenhouses in full bloom in this regard.

At this point, too, I switch over from a program of inducing the flowers to one of preparing them for showing. This latter process is like 'babying' them...or more specifically, treating them like seedlings. Lower the light level; lower the max temperature and raise the minimum; keep the plants a bit wetter by watering a little more often; switch to a high nitrogen fertilizer; give them a little more air movement to cope with the increased water; and, finally, increase the humidity somewhat. These conditions are the same as those in the natural setting at flowering season. Nature's plan.

— editor

(Atlantic Coast US) Make sure the new spikes are tied when they are about 10-12'' long. Keep the sprays off the buds or blossoms. Same for fertilizer.

— K. Griffith

(Southeastern US) Any plant one would consider worthy of 'showing' should be earmarked for care from the moment inflorescences begin to form. Spikes should be carefully staked as soon as practicable and maintained in that position until showtime. Good grooming and a bath with insecticidal soap from time to time will keep the foliage beautiful.

— J. Grimes

(Northeastern US) None, but I should. Certainly, judges are favorably impressed by a well-prepared and groomed plant.
— D. Grove

[Editor's note: a number of respondents said they grew phals for their own pleasure and not for other's...and for that reason would love their plants, warts and all, without any artificial attempt to improve their beauty. When I get my courage up, I think I'm going to adopt that philosophy...when I get my courage up...]

(Southeastern US) Clean leaves thoroughly, usually with milk to give them a clean, shiny look. Stake the spike to best display the flowers and to withstand the trip to the judging site. Last, but certainly not least, check for bugs and diseases. After plants initiate inflorescences, I stake them as they grow. This is no easy task when I make each stake by hand for the hundreds that are spiking.

During the week of the show I select the plants for flower quality and display look, restake if necessary, and secure the flower spike firmly to the stake for the journey to the show. Plants are thoroughly watered before departure. (Sounds like getting the kids ready to go somewhere, doesn't it? Decide who's going, clean them up, water them, fasten their seat belts and go. ed.)
— T. Harper

(Southern California US) No particular preparation of plants in advance of shows except, a few days before, we pick from what are in their prime and properly stake for transportation and display.
— E. Hetherington

(Midlands of England) Early securing of flowering spikes. Maintenance of the plant's orientation to the sun to ensure eventual uniform display of opened flowers. Cleaning off the leaves any residual fungicides, etc. Start all this about 2 months before the show.
— P. Hirst

(Arizona Desert US) Show preparation starts the day after the last show. The grooming takes place all year long. The plant goes in that special area in the greenhouse and is treated with special care the rest of the year.
— J&G Johnson

(Florida Caribbean US) We stake and adjust plants during their maturity. All leaves are wiped clean with a 50/50 solution of evaporated milk and water. Pots are blasted with a high pressure sprayer of Physan to clean them of salt deposits. Two to three weeks ahead.
— W. Kelly

(Southeastern Australia) We no longer show on the bench, but if good culture is carried out and flowers well looked after, little should be required apart from the cleaning of wettable

powder fungicide residue fromthe leaves. Be careful not to damage roots in removing plants from the bench as this is where infection will start and the loss of roots will set the plant back.
— J. Kilgannon

(France) No special preparation at all; we pick up the plants in flower just as they are.
— Marcel LeCoufle

(Florida Caribbean US) Plants are staked as soon as the spikes are high enough that they can be tied. As the spike lengthens, the tie is raised up the stake. Plants are not moved as the buds are developing so that the alignment is not impaired.
— L. Lodyga

(Luzon Philippines) I would say a very good plant needs at least a year of proper care for showing/judging.
— D. Mendoza

*(Mid-Atlantic Coast US) Under artificial lighting. . .The most important aspect of showing a plant is to ensure a healthy, nicely-formed flower spike. It can sometimes be difficult to get good-looking spikes under fluorescent lights, so when spikes are less than 1 inch high, I place the plant in a position near the outside of the shelf with the fan of leaves pointed towards the middle of the light shelf. The spike will grow in the direction of the brightest light, which is above the middle of the shelf. When spikes reach a length of 1 foot or so, I watch them carefully because they can grow nearly an inch a day and, if they get too hot from getting near or actually touching the light tubes, the spike tips will die.

Most novelty phal hybrids and others with short spikes can be accommodated very easily under the light shelves all through blooming. However, plants that throw tall spikes can be a real problem. If you keep them under the lights, the stems will not grow into the beautiful arch Phalaenopsis are loved for. The desired effect is to let the stem grow unhampered. To do this, I treat the plants to the only sunlight they ever get.

When I know that a particular plant's spike is going to be too tall to keep under the lights, I move the plant to a position near the large east-facing picture windows in our apartment. I am very careful when doing this to make sure the plant is positioned in such a manner that the spike will continue to grow in the same direction, towards the light; otherwise, I get an imperfect, twisted spike. I get some very beautiful arching spikes using this method. Although plants in an east window get the mid-morning sun, I am careful to make sure that they don't get the strong light after 11:00 AM because they have been under lights and burn easily when exposed to the hot sun.

Another precaution I take with the flowers is to protect them from damage by pests. Before flower buds begin forming, I take a large cotton ball soaked in alcohol and clean the stem to rid it of any scale or mealybug insects.

Particular attention must be given to the bracts along the stem where the tiny, young insects can easily hide. The young are almost invisible, so it pays to go over the whole stem. Then I take another cotton ball and stretch it out long enough to where it can be wrapped around the flower stem and tied in a knot to hold it in place. Scale and mealybugs as well as snails and slugs do not crawl over or under a well-snugged cotton 'ring'. Two rings may give added protection. This prevents the pests from damaging the forming buds.

The night before showing the plant I clean the leaves and then wipe them with a dilute powdered milk solution. The proteins and fats in the dilute milk give a natural, healthy shine to the leaves.
— E. Merkle

(California Coast US) First, hope for the best! Second, allow the entire spray of flowers to open before showing it for judging. I feel that makes the difference of 3 to 5 points on the American judging scale...and the difference between an HCC and an AM in many cases. Waiting also gives the grower...and the judges...a better feel for the real worth of the plant.
— N. Nash

(California Coast US) Show preparation begins with good culture. Generally, if a phal has award potential, I try to repot on schedule and give it a microenvironment that it likes in the greenhouse...and baby <u>hell</u> out of it I start with the first blooming if it appears to have award potential.
— M&J Nedderman

(Mid-west US) Keep water and fertilizer off the flowers. Keep humidity high as more moist air will increase flower size and substance.
— R. Pallister

(Queensland Coast Australia) Lower the light level.
— R. Robinson

(Mid-Atlantic Coast US) Spikes are staked as they develop. Final grooming is done in the week prior to showing.
— E. Rutkowski and others

(Southcentral US) Repot twice a year as needed; keep foliage clean; and take special care of spike orientation and staking. All my special plants get continuous care.
— P. Scholz

(North of England) When a spike appears on a plant, I firstly put a white dot on the pot which enables me to know how to position it when I return it to the bench, should I have to lift it for any reason. When the spike is 4 inches high, I insert a sterilized stake into the medium and secure the spike to it. I adjust the tie daily until the spike flowers and try for the gentle arch which shows off a Phalaenopsis plant so well. Leaves are cleaned with

milk just prior to the show and any unsightly roots are removed with a sterile razor.
— D. Shuker

*(Northeastern US) Under artificial lighting...Make sure the plant is free of insects and diseases...and make sure the blooms are all or almost all open. I start special steps 3/4 weeks before the show or judging.
— J. Vella

(California Coast US) If necessary, I train the spike for proper flower presentation; I stake the spikes so the blooms will all face one direction...the judge's; I twist flower stems so the blooms line up; and finally, I wash the leaves with a little Green Glo (a commercial plant leaf cleaner and polish. ed.)
— J. Watkins

SECTION ELEVEN
CULTURE TRICKS

What special things do you do to improve your plants/flowers that you are pleased with and that others may not know of?

SECTION 11.1 CULTURE TRICKS CONSENSUS AND OPINION

My choice of terms in titling this section may not have inspired people to dig deeply and I think I made a mistake in using it, because the term implies that there is some gimmickry involved in growing phals well. That's not the case as several respondents pointed out, but there is some good, solid advice here worthy of note.

SECTION 11.2 CULTURE TRICKS
THE RESPONSES

QUESTION 11: WHAT SPECIAL THINGS DO YOU DO TO IMPROVE YOUR PLANTS/FLOWERS THAT YOU ARE PLEASED WITH AND THAT OTHERS MAY NOT KNOW OF?

(Indian Coast South Africa) Outside of proper care, make sure that you turn the plant in the right position, i.e. to the strongest light. That way your spike will be in the middle of the plant and not sideways over the leaves. During spike development, feed well and make sure that the humidity is constant and not under 70%RH. This way the buds will open without stagnation and it also prevents the reshaping of the petals and sepals.
— A. Adriaanse

(Southeastern Australia) Once, I had a spike of 12 blooms, four and a quarter-inch pinks, that I showed for 7 months. This was with overhead automatic mist spraying of water. As an experiment, I lowered the spray to just above the plants, but below the flowers. This resulted in a dramatic reduction in the longevity of blooms. Restoration of the overhead system corrected that situation.

During the period when blooms were not watered, by the time the fifth bud was opening, the first was collapsing. I could not get a complete spike open, but as soon as I reverted to overhead watering, full spiking returned.

Conclusion: blooms really like a lot of water.
— M. Black

(Central California US)

(1) Quarantine all new plants for 7-10 days before putting them on the bench, regardless of the source.

(2) Repot every new plant to determine condition of the roots and the medium.

(3) When repotting, prune dead or weak roots and spray with Natriphene.

(4) Pot out new seedlings from flask into 3-inch pots in New Zealand moss. I haven't lost a single seedling to date. Root development is great, filling the pot in just 8-10 months. Caution: do no pack moss too tight or roots will rot. Potting in New Zealand moss also allows me to periodically knock the moss/root ball out of the pot to check root development. Plants are usually ready for medium bark and 4-inch pots after 1 year out of the flask.
— R. Buchter

(Southern California US)

(1) Don't leave flowers on a plant any longer than you have to or 2 weeks at most...if you plan on showing it in the next year. Leaving the flowers on stresses the plant.

(2) Allow show plants enough bench space so they don't come in contact with any other plants.

(3) Put phals in a house by themselves, if you can.

(4) Good housekeeping is absolutely essential. Keep it clean!

(5) Balance of cultural controls...when you change one, look at which of the others has to be changed to keep the balance.

(6) Do a lot of visiting with other growers. You'll be able to see what to do and what not to do. (Hear, hear! ed.)

(7) Keep a journal of what you do and try. The idea is to keep from making the same mistakes again.

— E. Campuzano

(California Coast US) I grow them to the best of my ability using the techniques I've listed and let nature do the rest; but, here's one you may find handy:

> STUMP PROPAGATION At the time of repotting all dead roots should be cut off and the old stump below the new roots may be cut off. However, mature plants can be divided by cutting off the top portion of the plant just above the surface of the potting medium, one to one and a half inches, provided the top portion has an adequate number of roots to sustain itself when potted separately. Seal the cut on both the top and bottom portions with Tree Seal (asphalt) or dust with sulfur.

> Pot the top portion in the normal fashion, but do not disturb the stump. Within a month or two, one or more plantlets will sprout from the stump. (Several years ago, I topped my Golden Sands "Canary" and the stump has since produced seven plantlets for me.) When the plantlets have reached sufficient size and have roots 2 to 3 inches in length, remove them from the stump and pot them normally like any seedling.

> As the subject of powdered sulfur just crossed my mind, I'd like to mention that for the past thirty-plus years I've always had a cup of sulfur nearby. Every leaf I cut or broke, every stump I cut and every diseased area I found...was dusted with sulfur. It dries and heals these open and exposed areas better than anything I know of without fear of hurting the plant. Sulfur is also good for certain types

of rot, mildew and pests like red spider and leafhoppers. It's also an essential factor in neutralizing alkaline soils.

— E. Carlson

*(Northeastern US) Under artificial lighting...I think keeping the phals' 'feet' warm while adjusting room temperature for other genera is a big help. Also, it is important to give them that 'big chill' to make them flower.

Additionally, I have poor tap water. I collect rainwater and water plants with the condensate from the dehumidifier. It seems to help. Always (if possible) let water stand before using on houseplants, especially orchids. Regulates the temperature, lowers pH, and eliminates chlorine.

— I. Cohen

(South of England)

(1) <u>No more often than once every 2 months</u>, include in the watering/feeding drench 1PPM of napthalene acetic acid and 1 PPM of Vitamin B1. This promotes considerable additional root starts and side-branching root starts.

(2) Beware of strong feeding when spikes are starting to open buds. Best flower size and form come with good osmosis, allowing high water rise in the plant for good flower expansion.

— R. Dadd

(South Australia) Reflex the petals to make the flower appear flat. Press the dorsal in the centre to make it hood forward.

— M. Dennis

(Mid-Atlantic Coast US) Sometimes an application of MagAmp (7-40-6, slow-release) will encourage a plant to flower almost continuously from the main spike on through a secondary spike. After the last flower dies, I remove the flower spike from below the first flower scar. This seems to encourage a secondary flower spike.

— R. Drejka

Editor's Note. Regarding the use of MagAmp, any high phos fertilizer or phosphoric acid to lower the pH of water used for feeding your phals:

"The unusually high level of phosphorus in MagAmp can result in the reduced availability of iron, manganese, copper, and zinc in the root media. Careful attention should be paid to the micronutrient fertilizer program as a result. This fertilizer also contains 12% magnesium (Mg) which is high enough to antagonize the uptake of calcium in some plants and result in serious nutritional problems. Special care should be exercised to maintain calcium at a moderately high level in the root media to avert a deficiency. This problem is particularly important in areas where the water

supply has a low calcium content. MagAmp at one-third the normally recommended rate supplemented with periodic liquid fertilizer is suggested in New England)."
— (Nelson, 1981)

(The PureGro company of West Sacramento, California makes a supplement to compensate for the problem Mr Nelson refers to above; Leaf Life Complexed [11%] Copper-Iron-Manganese-Zinc. ed)

(Southern California US) (1) Spraying Physan on plants after watering reduces disease, cleans water spots, discourages algae, and helps control snails. (2) Styrofoam cubes in potting mix has virtually eliminated any type of root disease and extended the life of the medium.
— R. Engel

(Rome Italy) I love my plants and there is not a day goes by that I do not observe them all very attentively.
— A. Fanfani

(California Coast US) I have never had trade secrets. I have always shared what little I know with others, even competitors.
— H. Freed

(Mid-Atlantic Coast US) I've found that phals can be tricked into growing in a direction other than toward the light source. . .by putting a highly reflective surface where I want the spike to grow.
— M. Frier

(Maui Hawaii US) No secrets.
— R. Fukamura and others

(Atlantic Coast US) Water in the mornings in the winter before it gets too hot in the greenhouse. . .to avoid mesophyll collapse. Plants will streak yellow when watered with cold water, too. Some greenhouses have to watch this in the winter if the city water is too cold.
— K. Griffith

(Southeastern US) A small, inverted pot in the bottom of a larger pot slows medium breakdown. Seedling growth can be accelerated by growing them in a terrarium with sphagnum moss. (Phal stem propagations can be done the same way as Jack has pointed out in his article in the April, 1987 issue of the American Orchid Society Bulletin. ed.)
— J. Grimes

(Northeastern US) I don't think there are any 'tricks' and looking for them distracts one from concentrating on the careful and constant observation of each plant's condition and needs.

THE BEST GROWERS I HAVE KNOWN ANTICIPATE NEEDS for more or less light, more or less frequent watering, fertilizing and air movement; they are very attentive to any need for repotting or for spraying with insecticides, bactericides or fungicides (and they use the right ones...not fungicides when bactericides are needed, for example). The difference between the best growers and the rest of us is that they <u>anticipate</u> plants' needs instead of waiting until there is a problem which really threatens it.

— D. Grove

(Northeastern US) My New England greenhouse has a west-northwest exposure, <u>lousy</u> light. I have four 1 kw metal halide fixtures which are on auto timers from 6:00 AM to 11:00 AM and from 5:00 PM to 9:00 PM. This has given me fast, vigorous, hard growth and larger flowers over previous years in the same plants.

— L. Guida

(Southeastern US) I love the term 'culture tricks', but I really have none. After growing phallies for 17 years, I have found that <u>daily</u> inspection and care are essential to the general health and maintenance of the plants and flowers. Because I have a 'regular', 8:00 to 4:30 job, the orchids must receive their attention at other times. Therefore, my schedule is other than normal.

To explain...I awake at 5:00AM from Monday through Friday and by 6:00 I'm in the greenhouse. Spot watering, spraying, light repotting, controls adjustment for the day are done by the time I leave at 7:00. At 5:30PM when I return from earning a living, it's off with the tie and on with the jeans. A quick inspection before dinner gives me a status report on how the plants are doing. After dinner, it's back to the greenhouse for hybridizing, staking, major repotting and so forth. Weekends are magnified weeknights frequently involving all day Saturday and Sunday. Of course, this is when I'm not involved in exhibiting and judging at orchid shows. Isn't orchid growing a fun and relaxing pastime?

— T. Harper and others

(Southern California US) The larger and healthier it is without being disturbed and the better the culture is...these are the secrets of top quality production in a given plant. It may sound over-simplified, but there are not a lot of tricks. Basic good culture comes first.

— E. Hetherington

(England) Foliar feeding, when good drying conditions permit, is done as a light misting during the morning.

— P. Hirst

(Florida Caribbean US) All benches should run east and west. All spikes flow south naturally. Daily inspection and removal of old, dry leaves. Keep a very clean atmosphere in the greenhouse.

— W. Kelly

(Southern California US) Breed with only the best stock.

— T. Koike

(France) In the coloured flowers, more shade induces darker shades or colours than bright light. The spikes coming out from plants underneath the benches (mostly in the pink ones) are more coloured than those on the top of the bench.
— Marcel LeCoufle

*(North of England) Under artificial lighting. . . If a plant looks a bit off colour, then I don't let it flower; I bung it under the 40W lights for a new leaf and root stimulation.
— P. Lindsay

(Central California US) I talk to my plants. I praise them and tell them they're going to be beautiful or they are beautiful. I also tell them either shape up or be shipped out.
— B. Livingston

(Florida Caribbean Coast US) Plants seem to respond to frequent repotting. Small plants and sluggish ones appear to take off when repotted. (I wish I'd said that first. ed.)
— L. Lodyga

(Northeastern US) We occasionally wash the leaves of all the plants with a sponge and water. Otherwise, all the water is aimed directly into the pots or baskets.
— B&C Loechel

(Southern California US) In the winter, I use lukewarm water when watering the plants.
— M. McCooey

(Puerto Rico US) Good culture and healthy well-growing plants will improve flower quality tremendously.
— R. Melendez

(Luzon Philippines) Growers should know the environmental conditions that are favorable to good phal growth. You can get these from studying the natural habitat in the wild of the plant. With this knowledge, modify the new environment where you wish to put them.
— D. Mendoza

(Mid-Atlantic Coast US) A beautiful Phalaenopsis is one that has large leaves devoid of disease or sunburn spots and damage from cuts or breaks. Special attention should be given to growing a beautiful plant. Treat your plants with kindness and thoughtfulness and you'll get as many 'Ooooos and Ahhhhs' over your plants' leaves as you will over its blooms. Growing your phals under lights is the best thing you can do for them.
— E. Merkle

(California Coast US) We let them grow; not get them to grow.
— N. Nash

(California Coast US) I repot my plants with a mixture of fir bark and sponge rok that has been soaked in a solution of chelated iron, 20-20-20 fertilizer, and a small amount of Joy liquid detergent (washing-up liquid) as a wetting agent. I soak this mixture for a minimum of 3 to 7 days, depending on what the weather conditions are; longer for hot dry summers, and shorter for early spring and the late fall. This has prevented repotting shock and plants seem to really appreciate it. They grow like crazy. Oh, by the way, plants are potted wet using plastic gloves as this mixture stains your hands. The resins from the fir bark seem to be the cause of the stains.

— M&J Nedderman

(Indian Coast South Africa) Minute quantities of plant food at each spraying. The plants look very good since this changeover.

— G. Paris

(Southeastern US) With plants that stall or stubbornly refuse to grow, I apply a few drops of a solution of gibberellic (1:1500) to the crown of the plant...and repeat a second time a few days later. (It works! ed.)

— S. Pridgen

*(Northcentral US) Under artificial lighting...I use a reverse osmosis unit to clean the water I use on my phals and find growth rate and flower size show a significant increase.

— Randy Robinson

(Queensland Coast Australia) If plants look 'off', we repot...at any time of the year.

— R. Robinson

(Southcentral US) Keep a calendar-diary of what you have done so that you can make logical changes if necessary.

— P. Scholz

*(Northcentral US) Under artificial lighting...Apply keiki paste around the base of a plant that has lost its crown.

— W. Schumann

(England) I had an odd experiment that has been successful for me, i.e. finding the 'right' place in the greenhouse for a plant that is growing well, but will not flower. I move it until it finds a place it likes. I also repot plants that do not bloom on schedule and have had some success in repotting plants that seem to be going downhill...with compost from a well-growing plant. Some of these latter have recovered dramatically.

— D. Shuker

(British Columbia Coast Canada) Talk to other growers. Works every time.

— L. Slade

*(Mid-Atlantic Coast US) Under artificial lighting...

(1) Since we've switched from chopped gumballs to all charcoal as the potting medium, we have gotten better roots and therefore better flower production. The charcoal tends to dry out more evenly on our water-spray-feed schedule.

(2) For the past 12 years we have used terraria containing live sphagnum moss for seedling and rootless plant culture, especially for phals and paphs. We use clear, plastic shoe- and sweater-boxes with about an inch of clean pea-sized gravel on the bottom. Over that we put a layer of long-needled, white pine needles. We collect them within a day or so of their having dropped from the trees. The needles are sprayed with de-chlorinated water until wet. A layer of cleaned, live sphagnum moss is then added on top of the pine needles. The moss should be arranged loosely enough to permit some air spaces between clumps. The water in the moss is not removed by squeezing. Rain-, spring-, well-, or dechlorinated tap-water is then added to the box to about three-quarters of the weight of the gravel. The box is then placed under fluorescent lights or in shaded, sunlit area. The lid of the box is kept slightly ajar. The moss should not be allowed to get hot or be watered with chlorinated tap water.

Collected live sphagnum moss usually contains hard-shelled bush snails. After the moss has been picked through to remove dead leaves, weeds, sticks, etc., it should be soaked, at least overnight, in a plastic tub of de-chlorinated tap-water. The snails will climb the sides of the tub since they can't seem to stand that much water. To get rid of them we smash them on the side of the tub.

A word of caution when working with live sphagnum moss. I've heard that some moss, especially that found in Wisconsin (in the central northern tier of the US) may contain the fungus Sporotrichumschenckii. This can cause sporotrichosis, a lymphatic disease in humans. Infection occurs when spores of the fungus are introduced through a small abrasion or scratch in the skin. It is, therefore, not advisable to work with this moss with open sores on the skin unless rubber or plastic gloves are worn.

The terraria can be used with success in place of a replating flask, to grow roots back on jungle-collected rootless plants, and to grow roots on stubborn phals and rootless pieces of paphs. We also use these to make phal stem propagations. (For further information on this subject, see Jack Grimes' article on p. 369 of the April 1987 issue of the AOS Bulletin.)
— K&M Smeltz

(Mid-Atlantic Coast US) If you are potting with sphagnum, it is important to use clay pots.
— M. Steen

(Gulf Coast US) Like good cooks, don't fool with the dough too much.
— B. Steiner

(Mid-West US) (1) The use of bottom heat makes a significant improvement in Phal culture in cool country. (2) After repotting, add a tablespoon of Q.E. Bane mixed with a little Sevin dust to control bush snails, slugs and sow bugs. Add a little more when the plant is in bloom.
— W. Stern

*(Northeastern US) Under artificial lighting...Our water supply is high in calcium and magnesium...and we're sure that explains our extremely strong and usually-upright spikes.
— D&D Strack

(Oahu Hawaii US) None whatsoever.
— R. Takase

(Midlands of England) Dirty, grimy leaves will throw off the most careful calculation of light allowances for phals...so I keep my plants very clean by washing and scrubbing when necessary, especially when a plant is newly-acquired from the trade.
— H. Taylor

(Southern California US) POTTING PHAL SEEDLINGS IN NEW ZEALAND MOSS. Lay out dampened moss in a pad, 2 to 4 inches wide and 6 to 12 inches long (for 2 to 4 inch pots). Arrange seedlings with the roots on the moss and the foliage above the top level. Starting at one end, roll up the seedlings and moss just as though you were making a jelly roll. Making sure the roots are all surrounded by moss and evenly spaced, stuff the "jelly roll" into the pot. Slick.
— D. Vander Tuin

*(Northeastern US) Under artificial lighting... Propagate good plants for the future of Phalaenopsis growing.
— J. Vella

(California Coast US) Once I'm sure of flower quality, I sometimes prevent a plant from blooming, by cutting off flower spikes, until it is mature. Blooming really slows some plants down if the flowers are left on for 3-4 months. Once the plants have buds, I sometimes keep the light intensity down so the flowers don't fade.
— J. Watkins

(Hawaii US) "THE HAWAIIAN MOON SYSTEM" (of making hybrids) I have good results when making Phalaenopsis seed pods by using the Hawaiian Moon System. I pollinate flowers 2 days before the first quarter of the moon, 2 days after the first quarter, on the full moon, 1 day before the last quarter...and when the tide is coming in high. I leave the pollen on the seed flower and check after 5 days. If it took, I take the pollen off the seeded flower. I believe the late Mr WGG Moir also used this system.
— R. Yohiro

(Mid-West US) Grown under lights, long spikes can be a problem. A graceful arch can be achieved by using S-hooks and weights. Often a phal bloom can be improved with the fingers. Just fix the petals and dorsal so the cupping is to the back, not front. It is amazing how many reflexed flowers we see at shows.

— M. Zimmer

SECTION TWELVE
MOST IMPORTANT CULTURE FACTOR

(a) If you consider one factor of cultivation of phals to be more important than the others, what is that factor and why do you think it is more important...and what special steps do you take on the matter?

SECTION 12.1   MOST IMPORTANT FACTOR CONSENSUS AND OPINION

This section is worth the price of admission because it is the essence of a lot of years of experience, sometimes painful and expensive.

This was kind of a sneaky question that was intended to make the respondents dig deep for one more answer. The object is to identify that factor of cultivation that needs more attention than the others. For each of us there is one aspect of growing phals that demands more of our time than the others, one problem more persistent than the others, and one area more fraught with possibility for disaster.

I reasoned that the answers would be from those areas where the respondents had enjoyed his or her best success...and it appears to have come out just that way.

It's interesting to note that the answers got pretty short in this section...probably because of the 1 to 3 hours respondents spent answering the preceding 11.

Regarding John Watkins' comment on the need for balance: While it is probably true that some culture controls are more critical to a plant's immediate well-being than others, there is a great deal of merit in what John Watkins...and others... have to say about balance and I agree.

I think the key to successful culture of phals (or any other plant for that matter) is balance; balance between enough and too little/much water; enough and too little/much fertilizer or light; medium that is too old or too new; air circulation that is stagnated or that which damages the plants by drying them out too quickly.

A plant integrates all the environmental factors of its habitat. Its being and growth are a fundamental response to controlling conditions...which must be held within the plant's envelope of health...and that is a balance of conditions. All things in harmony; not anything in excess. This is the essence of Yin and Yang that the Chinese have used for centuries to guide their lives.

To carry John Watkins' example a step further: if you raise the amount of light a phal plant is getting, you'll need to increase the air circulation to keep the leaf surfaces cool; you'll need to increase the fertilizer to permit the plant to grow faster; you'll need to increase the cooling to carry away the extra heat in the greenhouse; and increase the watering because the plant will need more to compensate for losses caused by increased evaporation. Better raise the humidity, too. The cultural controls are all interrelated and a change of one may necessitate a change in one or more of the others...to balance the equation.

THE POINT: ANY TIME YOU CHANGE A CULTURE CONTROL, LOOK AROUND AND SEE WHAT ELSE IS GOING TO BE AFFECTED. Increase an element in the fertilizer diet and you'd better look at the possibility of an antagonism. Increase air circulation and you'd better start watering more. Increase the heat and you'd better match that with increased light or get soft growth.

A healthy plant is one that has stabilized in its environment. Change anything and you may destabilize the plant. Don't hesitate to make changes, but when you do, consider the consequences... and, when necessary, balance the cultural equation again. This is what the Yin and Yang philosophy in Section 1 is all about.

SECTION 12.2   MOST IMPORTANT FACTOR SELECTED RESPONSES

QUESTION 12(a) IF YOU CONSIDER ONE FACTOR OF CULTIVATION OF PHALS TO BE MORE IMPORTANT THAN THE OTHERS, WHAT IS THAT FACTOR AND WHY DO YOU THINK IT IS MORE IMPORTANT. . . AND WHAT SPECIAL STEPS DO YOU TAKE ON THIS MATTER?

(Indian Coast South Africa) The most important factor is to know the history of the Phalaenopsis. Investigate to find the sources of the plants and the environment they had there through the changing seasons. Try to copy this as near as possible.

— A. Adriaanse

(California Coast US) Temperature seems to be the most important single factor in producing the optimum Phalaenopsis bloom provided, of course, the plant has had adequate light, water and fertilizer.

— L. Batchman

(Southeastern Australia) Mitigation of extremes of temperature and humidity to relieve stresses on the plants. Temperatures over 90°F are to be avoided.

— M. Black

*(Mid-Atlantic Coast US) Under artificial lighting. . . Repot annually (change the mix and loosen it) at the time of most active growth; July here. Plants never show ill effects of 'moving' and I rarely have dead roots to remove.

— M. Bowell

(Central California US)

(1) Know your plants intimately and keep records.

(2) Keep the benches and the greenhouse scrupulously clean. Trash containers belong outside.

(3) Get rid of mediocre plants. Don't perpetuate mediocrity.

(4) Update your collection. Read and keep abreast of current hybridizing and what's going on in the phal world.

— R. Buchter

(California Coast US) The quality of water used is the most important factor for me, because our well water is horrendous and has a pH of 8.5. (I keep a blank mind and make believe the problem isn't there...and hope the other factors in good culture will compensate.)
— E. Carlson

(Mid-Atlantic Coast US) Keeping temperature, light and watering in a good balance.
— L. Clouser

*(Northeastern US) Under artificial lighting...Humidity. I see a lot of growers who are doing everything else right, but their phals do poorly and I believe their humidity is too low. A way to cope when you're growing under lights is to enclose the growing room and use a humidifier...set to 70/75% RH. Use a little lower setting in December and January.
— I. Cohen

(Indian Coast South Africa) Give your plants sensible feeding (not overdone), adequate light, allow them to face the northeast (southern hemisphere); all this on a sloping frame. Don't pack your plants too closely; leave plenty of space between the pots. Good air flow, ventilation, and humidity all the time between 70/85% RH, and keep the temperature between 68 and 85°F all the time. They will respond admirably to this.
— C&I Coll

(Southern California Good air movement; natural, if possible with the sides of the greenhouse open whenever temperatures permit.
— W. Cousineau

(Southern California US) Air movement.
— D&R Cowden

(South of England) A high air-to-water ratio in the potting medium. I recommend the use of water-repellent rockwool and perlite. Wet only the outer surfaces of the 'lumps' of rockwool and perlite. Rockwool lumps are 95% air by volume!
— R. Dadd

(South Australia) Water and humidity. This is an individual technique that has to be felt. When entering the phal house, is the atmosphere right? Is more water required? It's a personal feeling that develops with experience over the years. It should feel tropical and moist at all times of the year.
— M. Dennis

(Florida Gulf Coast US) Good air; warm (70°F+), humid (50/80% RH), and well-circulated. On air circulation, I have four 48-inch and two 30-inch fans with one to four always in operation.
— J. Eich

(Holland) Never lower nighttime temperatures below a normal of 20°C (68°F). When grown in bark, the plants should be fed with every watering; they like nitrogen. Never grow them dry.

Keep the light level somewhere between 12,000-15,000 lux. (1,100-1,400 footcandles)
— a major commercial grower

(California Coast US) Observation and a love of plants. Visit orchid shows and other ranges and really observe.
— H. Freed

(Maui Hawaii US) My area is not suitable for Phals. Too dry, too windy, too near the ocean, and too hot during the day. No way to control growing conditions. If I have good plants, I take them to my friend who lives at about 1,300 feet above sea level to grow properly and flower nicely. If you have a good greenhouse and can control growing conditions, it doesn't matter where you live. (All is not well in Paradise. Anybody else as surprised as I am? ed.)
— R. Fukamura

(Mid-Atlantic Coast US) Constant feeding and preventive control of the known fungi and bacteria which infect phals.
— R. Griesbach

(Atlantic Coast US) Adjust the pH of the water to 5.5 to 6.0. It helps with Pseudomonas.
— K. Griffith

(Gulf Coast US) The most important single culture factor for me was finding the right potting medium. It turned out to be charcoal. I started off with bark and Off-mix. Maybe all I got was bad or poisoned bark, but roots rotted and plants died...especially the expensive ones. I also tried Oasis, expanded clay, coconut husk fiber, sphagnum, cork, walnut hull and Pro-mix. Charcoal is so much better for me and my growing conditions that there is no real comparison. I have yet to hear anyone say it did not work for them.
— J. Grimes

(Northeastern US) Frequent repotting, because no other practice can succeed if a plant is in deteriorated potting medium. I'm referring to deterioration at the bottom of the pot, something that can happen when there is no evidence of it at the top.
— D. Grove

*(Northeastern US) Under artificial lighting...Switching from bark to New Zealand moss was the best cultural move I've made. The plants can be kept constantly moist without rot. This has given me incredible root growth and great top growth.
— L. Guida

(Florida Atlantic Coast US) Tipping the pots so water runs out of the crowns.
— C&L Hagan

(Southeastern US) Temperature. Phals show their resentment to sudden changes in temperature by dropping buds. They show their resentment to low temps by producing smaller flowers... and plants will not develop their plump foliage. Light follows next in importance.

Having the right automated equipment to control the greenhouse environment is essential. The consistency of temperature and humidity allows the plants to grow at their maximum efficiency and to bloom at their best.
— T. Harper

(Southern California US) Phalaenopsis, as fine as or better than any grown anywhere in the world, can be grown in the Marine Belt, the geographical strip along the coast of California from San Francisco south to San Diego and under the influence of the Pacific Ocean and the Japan Current.

What are the conditions that make it so good? Nice, moist air at all times; never too hot; no sudden and dramatic changes in temperature; a good atmosphere, i.e., no smog; and good water. True, Phalaenopsis can be grown almost anywhere — I've seen them doing superbly in a kitchen window — however, I'm speaking of optimum conditions on a large scale.
— E. Hetherington

(Midlands of England) I consider the watering/feeding regime to be the single most important factor in Phalaenopsis culture. All plants, regardless of pot size are individually watered and by handling each plant I know when it has taken sufficient water. By adopting this tedious and time-consuming method of watering plants, losses due to crown rot and fungal disorders are kept to an absolute minimum.
— P. Hirst

(Arizona Desert US) Enjoying them.
— J&G Johnson

(Florida Caribbean US) Our automatic operation of water-fertilizing-and Physan makes for a good, steady diet and even growth cycles.
— W. Kelly

(Southeastern Australia) Study your environment and actively work to eliminate the weaknesses that arise. Once the conditions have been tailored to suit phals, the rest should be all pleasure.

I think it is important that a grower, in order to be successful with phals, should pay attention not only to the plant, but also the environment the plant is in. Learn what the plant liked in nature and try to duplicate that. Try not to be discouraged by failure because there are going to be failures. I know of many people who have started in with phals and had some luck with them for a while. Then, when problems arise they chuck the whole thing and blame the plants for being finicky. (Does that sound as familiar to the reader as it does to the editor?) Our 'instant gratification' society, accustomed to getting what they want by pushing a button, has to learn patience with these plants. Spend your time finding what the plants want and give it to them. If you're in a hurry, forget Phalaenopsis.

— J. Kilgannon

(Southern California US) When making your own hybrids, use only superior breeding stock.

— T. Koike

(Holland) Temperature. With lower temperatures than 20°C (68°F) day and 18°C (64°F) night in the growing season, the plants are not growing anymore.

— H. Kronenberg

(France) Phalaenopsis grow faster and better with heat and high humidity. However, if you give too much heat and too much humidity, the cells of the leaves may allow the entrance of the diseases found nowadays in some tropical countries. I see that, after a hurricane in a very hot tropical country, how many Phalaenopsis may have been lost. They should be kept out of rain and the injured parts should be cut off every day to avoid the contamination.

— Marcel LeCoufle

(North of England) Good records.

— P. Lindsay

(Central California US) Observation. Learn to recognize when they are not getting the light, heat or feed they need...and when they don't feel good. Practice observing your plants closely.

— B. Livingston and others

(Florida Caribbean US) Two parts: Watering and air movement. Most phals are lost to overwatering which causes rotting of the root system and/or crown rot. Not enough air movement impedes growth and causes bacterial and fungal problems.

— L. Lodyga

(Northeastern US) Air to the roots, while maintaining moisture levels. This is achieved by basket culture or extra drainage holes in the pots.

— B&C Loechel

(Queensland Coast Australia) No one individual culture factor is more important than the others.

— J. Mackinney

(Texas Gulf Coast US) Air movement.

— J. Margolis

(Luzon Philippines) Temperature: 20°C (68°F) nighttime minimum and 29/30°C (84/86°F) daytime high. Temperature determines flowering, transpiration and respiratory activities. We looked for the place we have now in a natural Phalaenopsis environment, i.e. 800 meters above sea level and around a natural forest. That's it.

— D. Mendoza

(Queensland Coast Australia) Water. Overwater and the roots rot. Underwater and leaves collapse and flowers are impaired. Check before each watering with a control plant.
— R. Merritt

(Southern California US) The right light, good air circulation, watering at the right time of day and repotting often. Know your plants. (Harold Moye knows each one of his phals very well. He treats them like good friends. He is one of the quietly competent growers, referred to in the Foreword, who profess to know little about phals...but, he is one of the best phal growers I know. ed.)
— H. Moye

(California Coast US) Sanitation...as for any orchid.
— N. Nash

(California Coast US) Prompt repotting is probably the most important because it is the most neglected. One has to have a good balance on all cultural factors to have show-quality flowers.

The most important part of the plant to monitor is the root tips. If you have nice succulent root tips, half an inch or longer, your plant is doing great! If you can keep it up for a whole year, you're going to see some excellent flowers.
— M&J Nedderman

(Mid-west US) I would say the key word is observation.
— R. Pallister

(Southeastern US) Keep the medium moist and give light to the maximum tolerance. Note: sphagnum, alone or used on the surface of another medium, if allowed to dry out, will resist absorbing water thereafter. (Ernie Campuzano, of Butterfly Orchids, recommends using a wetting agent once each year on the surface of NZ sphagnum moss to correct the problem Dr Pridgen refers to. Physan has a similar effect, but a shorter-lived one. ed.) The same is true for Pro-mix.
— S. Pridgen

(Northcentral US) Automatic watering, fertilizing and humidity control systems. But, to be on the safe side, I periodically hand-water, particularly in the hot weather.
— A. Roberts

(California Coast US) Good air circulation.
— F. Robinson

(Queensland Coast Australia) Repot regularly.
— R. Robinson

(Puerto Rico US) Air circulation...and relative humidity.
— R. Rodriguez

(Mid-Atlantic Coast US) Minimum of three factors — heat, light, moisture.
— E. Rutkowski

(Northcentral US) High humidity. Try suspending plants above water. (Andy Adriaanse has a considerable number of plants grown in this fashion.)
— W. Schumann

(South of England) High relative humidity.
— P. Seaton

(North of England) I cannot accept that there is one single culture factor more important than the others. They're all important.
— D. Shuker

*(Mid-Atlantic Coast US) Under artificial lighting...Good air movement. We employ four fans that go 24 hours a day.
— K&M Smeltz

*(Northeastern US) Under artificial lighting...Proper watering.
— D&D Strack

(Oahu Hawaii US) The control of insects that can infest your plants is most important. Leave them alone and you will have no plants.
— R. Takase

(California Coast US) Balance. You have to keep a balance of light, heat, food and water. Raise any one of them and you'll need to raise the rest. I've seen phals do well in 400-4,000 fc. It's just a matter of balancing the rest of the conditions.
— J. Watkins

(Mid-West US) With all orchids, watering is the most important factor and with phals, I think temperature is extremely important. The phals are really a lot like people: they want comfortable, warm temperatures without a large variation; they like to sleep on cool nights. Excessive heat gives them problems as does excessive cold.
— M. Zimmer

SECTION THIRTEEN
ANYTHING YOU'D LIKE TO ADD?

Anything more you'd like to add to all this?

SECTION 13.1 ANYTHING ELSE?
CONSENSUS AND OPINION

This is a catchall for things that didn't fit anywhere else...and I was surprised to see how good some of the ideas were. I'm grateful that some of the respondents took the time to add ideas that didn't otherwise fit. They probably were as talked out as I am, but pressed on for the good of us all. Super!

Aluminum arbor. Al Rutel, of White Plains, NY, found this use for an old, otherwise-unusable aluminum ladder. Ladder is chained to the roof of the greenhouse. Al is a master of 'make-do'. An elegant solution of a common problem.

SECTION 13.2
SELECTED RESPONSES

QUESTION 13: IS THERE ANYTHING YOU'D LIKE TO ADD TO ALL THIS?

(Southeastern Australia)

LESS WATER NEEDED IN WINTER? I went to England for 5 months during our winter period. The greenhouse was locked against my know-it-all son-in-law, who was keeping tabs on the castle during our absence. No adjustments to the watering frequency was possible, so virtually summer watering was maintained throughout the winter...with no ill effects! Is there a lesson there?

— M. Black

(Central California US)

EXTERIOR SPRAYING I have had few disease or pest problems over the years primarily, I believe, to having removed all growing matter within 3 feet of the exterior of my greenhouse. Whenever I spray inside, I also spray outside.

— R. Buchter

*(Northeastern US) Under artificial lighting...

COLLECTION QUALITY CONTROL Outside of on-going cultural practices, the most important factor is to start with good stock. A mediocre cattleya or oncidium, well-grown, will look half-way decent, but a poor phal looks like a dog, no matter what you do with it. Read the Awards Quarterly, look at winners of shows, read articles in the AOS Bulletin (or other good orchid periodicals) on promising lines. Choose carefully. It is not necessary to spend a fortune on good plants. Buy a promising compot and swap seedlings with friends. Swap keikis of best stock. Give your culls to beginners to practice on.

— I. Cohen

(Indian Coast South Africa)

CULTURE SUMMARY I would just like to tell you we feel three things are important: (1) very good air circulation; not a strong air circulation, but a very gentle air circulation that is continuous; (2) continual moisture; and (3) continual humidity. The last two are important because of the first. Continuous air movement drys things out quickly and therefore the need for moisture and humidity.

— C&I Coll

(Holland)

COMMERCIAL VS HOBBYISTS   We are commercial growers, growing over a million Phalaenopsis a year, so we expect we have a different look on how to grow as compared to people who grow many different plants in the same greenhouse. (Other than activities involving capital equipment and physical plant, not really much different. I trust most of the readers and respondents are dedicated phal growers and their techniques are not all that different, but it is nice to hear how the Big Guys do it. ed.)

— a major commercial grower

(California Coast US)

PHALAENOPSIS BICOLOR?   A lot of years ago we had a plant of cymbidium Rincon 'Clarisse', a very expensive plant, and I wanted to take special care of it while it was in spike (I know, I know, this is a book on Phalaenopsis, but this could affect phals, too), so I put the plant with four spikes in a shady corner and forgot it. As it turned out, two of the spikes wound up in the shade and two in bright light. The spikes in the shade produced green flowers. The spikes in the sun produced whites.

— H. Freed

(Southern California US)

JOURNAL   A practice I believe to be worthwhile is the keeping of a journal or greenhouse log of things I've done to my plants and observations on their progress. I think it is important to keep track of when you did what. . .and then observe the consequences of those actions. It is a running diary of what is going on in the greenhouse and is an attempt to keep a little discipline in how I go about matters over the course of a season. I log the dates I sprayed and with what; when I changed fertilizers, humidity or temperature settings; when I changed shade adjustments and the like.

SCHEDULE   The journal helps me to make cultural decisions that show up on an annual schedule or program that appears on the inside cover. This is a month-by-month schedule of what to do and when to do it. The decisions in this schedule are based on what I learned from the journal. The journal is for short-term activities; the schedule is for long-term.

Barring an extraordinary memory, I don't see how any grower can conduct a systematic program of culture without some such written record and guide. If you have a lousy memory like mine, it may be the only way to go.

— editor

(Northeastern US)

A COMPREHENSIVE VIEW   No one practice can ensure success; it is the combination and balance that counts.

— D. Grove

(Southeastern US)

WATER TEMP/QUALITY   You did not bring up the subject of water quality and water temperature used in watering plants. I use city water. It's good quality water, but complete with chlorine, insecticides and herbicides found in most agricultural communities. Fortunately, last November we installed a water filtration system for our home and the greenhouses. The water is first filtered with a fine mesh fiber to get the particulate matter removed. Next, it passes through an activated charcoal cylinder. The result is pure water with the trace elements intact; no chlorine or other yuck, and all at a pH of 6.2. The plants seem to love it!

I adjust the temperature of the water when watering. There's no cold water on my plants, ever! They don't get it in the wild and they don't get it here, either. By mixing both hot and cold water, the result is a mild water temperature for the tender plants. (You don't say how you do this, Tom, but Ken Smeltz of Wilmington, Delaware, uses a bathroom shower water mixer...and selects the temperature with the same type of valve used in adjusting shower water temperature. Neat. ed.)

MICROFUNGUS   Phal growers may be facing a major newly-discovered (observed?) problem. This is the yellow pitting, necrotic spotting of the leaves, preliminarily diagnosed by John Miller and Rob Griesbach as a micro-fungus. (See Section 7 on plant diseases.)

I have seen it in a number of collections. I have seen it infect ENTIRE collections, resulting in the plants eventual demise or destruction by the growers. It appears to be a problem out of control for some people. Growers who have followed various recommendations on ridding their collections of this problem have largely been unsuccessful. Nothing sprayed, drenched or applied in any manner seems to make any inroads on the disease. (Not surprising; it is systemic and requires a systemic fungicide. ed.) While it may appear to be gone from the collection at certain times of the year, it keeps returning.

I have observed it in my own collection. Suspicious plants are quickly isolated, treated, leaf parts removed, and then watched carefully. Most often these plants are discarded. In every instance, these plants were purchased or traded with other growers who may not have been aware of the problem. How large or serious is it? How widespread? We don't know. But we'd better do something soon.
— T. Harper

(Southern California)

SYSTEMIC MICROFUNGUS   To my knowledge, Ernie Campuzano of Butterfly Orchids in Newbury Park, California, was the first grower to experience the microfungus problem on a large scale. He corrected the problem with the therapy repeated below from Section 7. **He now repeats the treatment every 6 months as a prophylactic measure.** Ernie had all the symptoms Tom Harper talks about above and related the problem to John Miller, who in turn related it to Don Baker of Stoufer Labs. Don identified the problem as a SYSTEMIC MICROFUNGUS and developed the following therapy. (This is a repeat of the formula given in Section 7. ed.)

Day 1:

Ridomil 2E (Subdue), one teaspoon per five gallons
of water and in the same spray mix,

Bayleton 25% WP four teaspoons per five gallons.

Day 2:

Triforine (Funginex), two teaspoons per gallon.

30 days later:

Repeat the process.

Every 6 months thereafter:

Repeat the process.

The reason for the 30-day separation is that Bayleton, if used too strongly or too often, can cause shortening of the flower spikes. Both Ridomil 2E and Triforine are both systemics; that's the reason for separating them.

— editor

(Midlands of England)

LIGHT PROBLEMS   The biggest drawbacks to good Phalaenopsis culture here in South Yorkshire are (1) an imbalance between daylight length in the summer (18 hours max) and daylight in the winter (about 6½ hours max) and; (2) poor quality of daylight, particularly during the winter with a total absence of sunshine for 5 or 6 consecutive days not unusual.

— P. Hirst

(Phil, it is my belief that almost anyone can grow phals where the environmental conditions are favorable...that is how nature does it with no help from man at all. But, folks like you and others with equally hostile growing conditions (like a New York City apartment, for example) are real survival experts and deserve a great deal of credit for just keeping your plants alive, much less blooming well. It's a little off line, but an auto bumper sticker I saw at a sailplane (glider) airfield locally said "Anybody Can Fly With An Engine". My sentiments.

Maybe supplementary light is the answer. Louis Guida has the same problem in Northeastern US)...a bit south of you, Phil, but the problem is the same. See his comments in Section 11. The problem is not unique to the north-latitudes. We all have dark spots in our growing areas that could stand a little touchup of light. ed.)

(Arizona Desert US)

REVERSE OSMOSIS With reverse osmosis treatment of our water, we find we have fewer diseases, better root systems and healthier, better-looking plants all around.
— J&G Johnson

(Florida Caribbean US)

STERILE TOOLS All cutting tools are kept in a super-saturated solution of trisodium phosphate, which seems to help keep virus and bacteria under control.
— W. Kelly

(East Java Indonesia)

THE NATURAL WAY I try to solve problems of how to grow Phalaenopsis in rather a primitive manner...by observing very keenly how they grow in nature. So, I have been able to grow half a million plants now and have been able to find many new species which have never been described; but it is a pity more have not been found. So many beautiful plants are lost forever.
— A. Kolopaking

(Southeastern Australia)

EACH IN HIS OWN WAY I believe that phals are probably the most spectacular raceme of orchid blooms that one could wish to see; however, at the same time they can be the most difficult to grow over a prolonged period. I believe that those poor souls who, after a period of time, 'give the game away' fail because they go in ill-informed as to the needs of these plants **in their own particular glasshouse, in their own particular backyard**. I believe that in order to be a successful grower in the long term, we must 'ask the plant what it needs'. If you ask the question of a plant and don't listen closely to the answer, it may let you know by, in some way, failing to thrive.
— J. Kilgannon

(France)

DO NOT DISTURB Phalaenopsis, if grown in a good location and allowed to remain in place for 3 years, give many spikes. In some hybrids (mostly whites), if the spikes are cut high enough, we get the flowers all the year around. Then these strong plants give also offshoots around and we get clusters with hundreds of magnificent flowers.
— Marcel LeCoufle

(Queensland Coast Australia)

PIECE OF CAKE   With normal conditions as we've detailed above, we find Phalaenopsis no more difficult to grow than other genera of orchids. Brisbane has a subtropical climate with normally warm to hot, moist summers and dry winters...where we can have night temperatures down to as low as 5°C (40°F) with sunny days up to 20°C (68°F). However, Mother Nature does not stick to the rules.
— J. Mackinney

(Luzon Philippines)

ADULTS ONLY   I am surprised at your peculiar interest with only mature phals. I suppose the younger stages would merely be inferred from mature phal requirements with appropriate adjustments in the environmental and cultural requirements.
— D. Mendoza

[Actually, Dr Mendoza, the reason for dealing only with mature plants was to limit the subject and simplify the job of sorting what is already a mountain of information. I hadn't planned another book right away, because my wife won't let me write another one until I clean the garage. (That means my writing career is finished.) Maybe one on seedlings would be useful. I certainly would like to know more about them and writing a book on a subject is a great way to learn. But, I like your reason better; I just wasn't smart enough to think of it. ed.]

(Mid-Atlantic Coast US)

WARM BUNS   *Under artificial lighting...My growing shelves are constructed in such a way that the fluorescent light ballasts warm the water in the tray on the shelf above. This warmth helps the water evaporate quickly, providing good humidity. The warmth also seems to stimulate root growth.
— E. Merkle

(Southern California US)

CONTROLS, NOT CURES   I think it is imperative to stress to growers the importance of control of the variables in phal culture rather than cures. Information is the grower's greatest asset. I would advise, then, to take advantage of all the current information available from such sources as orchid and agricultural publications. Find out what has been learned by others...and reduced to print in a recognized publication... and apply those findings to your own situation rather than blindly following the practices of others. THE THINKING GROWER IS THE MOST IMPORTANT FACET OF PHAL CULTURE.
— J. Miller

(Northeastern US)

ALUMINUM ARBOR   Al Rutel of White Plains, New York found a good use for an old aluminum ladder that was no longer safe to use. He hung the ladder horizontally from his greenhouse ceiling, about 9 or 10 feet off the floor and uses it as an arbor to hang orchids from. It's an extension ladder, so he can adjust it to fit.   An elegant solution to two problems. Slick.
— ed.

(Mid-Atlantic Coast US)

WINTER WETDOWN   I often wet down the plants late at night in winter to raise humidity. No harm to the plants if temp is kept above 60°F.
— E. Rutkowski

(North of England)

SEEDLING SPECIAL   When taking plants from a community pot, I pot up the seedlings in seedling mix in Jiffy Pots (pressed peat) which have been soaked in Natriphene. I insert the Jiffy Pot in a plastic pot large enough to leave a 1-inch space all round and fill that space with used fir bark (sterilized). I leave the Jiffy Pot standing about 1/4 inch above the level of the plastic pot. I've found if the Jiffy Pot is light in colour (dry) it is OK to water/feed. If it is dark (wet), leave well enough alone. (I'm going to try that one. ed.)
— D. Shuker

(Northeastern US)

* CHARCOAL UNDER LIGHTS   Under artificial lighting...Phals in our growing conditions love charcoal in the media. We are convinced that the benefits of charcoal are dependent on the composition of the water.
— D&D Strack

(Oahu Hawaii US)

GET A GOOD START   Start with healthy plants of quality.
— R. Takase

(California Coast US)

VIGILANCE   Good growing requires daily inspections of plants and conditions.
— J. Watkins and others

(Mid-Atlantic Coast US)

EQUESTRIS-LIDENII DIE-BACK   Re: aeration. For the past few years I have been fascinated by equestris and lindenii and their primary hybrids. The equestris has the habit of keiki-ing while the main plant dies off. Lindenii also often dies back, but does not keiki. I was so annoyed with this habit on these two species that I removed all of my clones of them from pots and put them in wooden baskets filled with styrofoam peanuts. They are doing well now and the die-back has stopped.

If my theory of preventing the die-back is correct, I should be able to get the mother plants with all their offsets to produce specimen-sized plants in a single basket.

— M. Werther

IN CLOSING:

I want to thank the hundred and forty or so respondents whose material I've used here. Your ideas will influence worldwide Phalaenopsis cultural practices for years to come. You've influenced mine already.

It is true that no one of us knows as much as all of us together. This assemblage of ideas and opinions allows the reader to see a consensus and decide for himself or herself what best suits, particularly with regard to local growing conditions. I hope the highest level of cultural skill related here will become a baseline from which we all can grow.

The first step in education is to set down in writing what is known on a subject up to that point and this book has been an effort in that direction. Perhaps a survey could be used to do the same for other orchid genera as well.

A lot of people had a lot of useful information to share and most spent a lot of time preparing it well. My editorial work was made easy because of those efforts.

Thank you for reading our book. If you have phal cultural ideas to share with the world and that should be included in revisions of this work, please write to me at the address below. I promise you they will be handled with care.

And now, please excuse me; I have some potting to do.

> — Bob Gordon
> 276 East Shamrock
> Rialto, California 92376 USA
> September 1988

SECTION 14
LIST OF RESPONDENTS

Wanda Adams
919 Palm Ave
South Pasadena, CA 91030 USA

Mr S. Adriaanse
49 Byng Ave
Kings View 4052, Durban, Natal,
REP OF SOUTH AFRICA

Loren & Nancy Batchman
Casa de las Orquideas
170 South Nardo Ave
Solana Beach, CA 92075 USA

Fritz Bieth
Floratech Inc
8315 Excelsior Rd
Sacramento, CA 95829 USA

Maurie Black
13 Boyd St
Doncaster, Victoria 3108
AUSTRALIA

Michael W Bowell
Flora Design Associates
610 Summit House
West Chester, PA 19382 USA

Tim Brown
Martel Orchids (Species phals)
PO Box 9693
College Station, TX 77840 USA

Richard F Buchter
Bear Creek Orchids
2936 Crestwood Ct
Merced, CA 95348 USA

Ernie Campuzano
Butterfly Orchids
821 W Ballina Ct
Newbury Park, CA 91320 USA

Woody Carlson
West Coast Orchids
4905 Cherryvale Ave
Soquel, CA 95073 USA

Walt Cecil
WMC Gallery
310 Corbett Ave #2
San Francisco, CA 94114 USA

Ken Clarke
113 Central Ave
Redcliffe, WA 6104
AUSTRALIA

Larry Clouser
Longwood Gardens
PO Box 501
Kennett Square, PA 19348 USA

Iris Cohen
Aspenwood
58 Bayberry Circle
Liverpool, NY 13088 USA

Carmen and Ivan Coll MD
4 Grosvenor Crescent
Durban, North Natal 4051
REP OF SOUTH AFRICA

Walt Cousineau
W.C. Orchids
1389 Friends Way
Fallbrook, CA 92028 USA

Dan and Ruth Cowden
Dantoria Orchids
3267 Quail Road
Escondido, CA 92026 USA

Bill Crocca
62 East Genesee St
Clyde, NY 14433 USA

Bob Dadd
Greenaway Orchids
Rookery Farm,
Puxton, Weston SM, BS24 6TL
ENGLAND

Diane Davis
The Orchid Plantation
400 N. Fig Tree Lane
Plantation, FL 33317 USA

Pat De Lucia
2705 Scott Place
Bakersfield, CA 93306 USA

Mick Dennis
P.O. Box 566
Whyalla SA 5600
AUSTRALIA

John Dilling
Glasshouse Orchids
P.O. Box 111
Beerwah, QLD 4519 AUSTRALIA

Raymond Drejka
The Greenhouse
200 North Star Rd
Newark, DE 19711 USA

John W Eich
Gulfglade Orchids
7801 N. Airport Rd
Naples, FL 33940 USA

Wade E Eckberg
W.E.E. Orchids
3324 San Luis St
Ventura, CA 93003 USA

Dody Ellenberger
Orchid Eden
6764 Gillis Rd
Victor, NY 14564 USA

Dr Bob Engel
1443 Henrietta
Redlands, CA 92373 USA

Prof Dott Alberto Fanfani
Via Della Storta, 795
00166 Roma, ITALY

(A translation of Prof Fanfani's remarks
was kindly provided by John J Vella of
Bronx, NY.)

Maria Z. Fiorentini
Via di Colleromano 56
00060 Riano Rm ITALY

b.v. Floricultura
Floracultura-Holland
Postbus 19, Croquivsweg 9
2100 A.A. Heemstede, HOLLAND

Jack Fowlie, MD
The Orchid Digest
1793 Foothill Blvd
La Canada, CA 91011 USA

Hugo Freed
Arthur Freed Orchids
29500 Heathercliffe Rd Sp 277
Malibu, CA 90265 USA

Mary Carol Frier
Frier's Orchids
PO Box 8772
Woodcliff Lake, NJ 07675 USA

Roy Fukumura
RT Fukamura Orchids
49 E. Kauai,
Kahului, Maui, HI 96732 USA

Don and Jill Gallagher
Parade Orchids
PO Box 11
Highbury, SA 5089 AUSTRALIA

Eric Goo
2807 West Villa Rita
Phoenix, AZ 85023 USA

Dr Robert J Griesbach
3574 Conchita Dr
Ellicott City, MD 21043 USA

Ken Griffith
Lenette Greenhouses
4345 Rogers Lake Rd
Kannapolis, NC 28081 USA

Jack Grimes
P.O. Box 194
Southaven, MS 38671 USA

Dr David L Grove
5 The Knoll
Armonk, NY 10504 USA

Louis Guida, DVM
87 Clinton Rd
Brookline, MA 02146 USA

Chuck and Lela Hagan
Colee Cove Orchids
Orangedale Rte, Box 803
Green Cove Springs, FL 32043 USA

Tom Harper
Stones River Orchids
Rt 5, Box 262, Clovercroft Rd
Franklin, TN 37064 USA

Mr Arthur Harris
46 Broadway
Westville 4052, Natal,
REP OF SOUTH AFRICA

Steve Hawkins
Rod McLellan Co
1450 El Camino Real
So. San Francisco, CA 94080 USA

Ernest Hetherington
Stewart Orchids
845 Kingsley Drive
Arcadia, CA 91007 USA

Dorothy and Ira Hirsch
The Orchid Carousel
10116 Independence Ave
Chatsworth, CA 91311 USA

Phil Hirst
Woodland, Upper Field Lane,
High Hoyland, Barnsley,
ENGLAND

Bernard M Jesko
333 Crescent Dr
Hewitt, TX 76643 USA

Jim and Georgia Johnson
Jimni Orchids
3738 W. Morten Ave
Phoenix, AZ 85021 USA

Kimberly Kehew
407 Miller Ave
New Cumberland, PA 17070 USA

Warren R Kelly
Orchid World Intl
11295 SW 93rd St
Miami, FL 33176 USA

Jim Kilgannon
Orchidgrove Nursery
3 Mansfield Rd
Galston, NSW AUSTRALIA 2159

Terry Koike
Terry Koike Orchids
8963 Tyler St
Spring Valley, CA 92007 USA

A Kolopaking (Liem Khe Wie)
Simanis Orchids
Djalan Pungkurargo No. 1
Lawang, E. Java, INDONESIA

Dr HG Kronenberg
Holland Beweg 362
Waginen,
NEDERLANDS

Marcel LeCoufle
Marcel LeCoufle Orchids
5, rue de Paris
F-94470 Boissy-St-Leger, FRANCE

Patrick H Lindsay
5 Quatre Bras
Hexham, Nortumberland NE46 3JY
ENGLAND

Bill Livingston
Livingston's Orchids
10321 Reigl Road
Galt, CA 95632 USA

Lou Lodyga
Jones and Scully
18955 SW 168th St
Miami, Fl 33187-1112 USA

Bill and Chris Loechel
80 Church St
Woods Hole, MA 02543 USA

Walter A Loescher
5462 Edgewood Lane
Paradise, CA 95969 USA

Jim Mackinney
Mackinney's Nursery
87 Turton St
Sunnybank, QLD 4109 AUSTRALIA

Marie McCooey
3034 Center St
Arcadia, CA 91006 USA

Judy O Margolis
19 Farnham Park
Houston, TX 77024 USA

Patrick A Meistrell
Glorietta Bay Orchids
1330 Orange Ave, Ste 319
Coronado, CA 92118 USA

Ramon Melendez
Coqui Nurseries
P.O. Box M
Bayamon, PR 00620 USA

Dr Doroteo B Mendoza Jr
Kaligay Orchids and Nursery
89 Lopez Avenue
College, Laguna 372 PHILIPPINES

Edward B Merkle
1916 Columbia #4
Arlington, VA 22202 USA

Alan Merriman
Cecil Park Orchids
89 Levy St
Glenbrook, NSW 2773 AUSTRALIA

Ron Merritt
14 Christina Place
Aitkenvale, Townsville 4814 QLD
AUSTRALIA

John Miller
Miller Flasking Service
2021 Margie Lane
Anaheim, CA 92802 USA

Richard Mizuta
Richella Orchids
2881 Booth Road
Honolulu, HI 96813 USA

Harold Moye
Harold and Ruth's Orchids
1151 North Second St
Colton, CA 92324 USA

Ned Nash
Stewart Orchids
754 Westwood Drive
Santa Barbara, CA 93109 USA

John Niedhamer
1934 Elsinore Rd
Riverside, CA 92506 USA

Martin Nedderman, DDS
5522 Serene
Huntington Beach, CA 92649 USA

Mike Owen
Longwood Gardens, Dept of Hort.
P.O. Box 501
Kennett Square, PA 19348 USA

Ronald E Pallister
4201 Berger
St Louis, MO 63109 USA

Glen Paris
Costa Del Sol Orchids
43 Sherwood Rd
Greenwood Park 4051, Natal, RSA

Doug and Eve Penningh
44 Anzac St
Sarina, QLD 4737
AUSTRALIA

Hugh A Price
14 Cannes Dr
Naples, FL 33962 USA

Steve Pridgen, MD
Green Cote (private)
83 S. Bazemore E.
Cordova, TN 38018 USA

Ken Rex
19 Bradbury Way
Samson, WA 6163
AUSTRALIA

Arden Roberts
Warren Orchids
27704 Haverhill
Warren, MI 48092 USA

James & Mary Roberts
J&M Tropicals
Rt 1, Box 619B
Cantonment, FL 32533 USA

Forrest Robinson, DDS
5120 Soledad
San Diego, CA 92109 USA

Randy J Robinson
8733 Coyle Dr
Pinckney, MI 48169 USA

Ray Robinson
Petra Orchids
P.O. Box 129
Townsville, QLD 4810, AUSTRALIA

Raphael Rodriguez
Sunrise Orchids
P.O. Box 3151
Gurabo, PR 00658-3151 USA

Dr E. Rutkowski
E&E Plant Tissue Laboratory
160 Lawrenceville Rd
Trenton, NJ 08648 USA

Pamela Scholz
1245 Pickett Ave
Baton Rouge, LA 70808 USA

Dr Bill Schumann
Mayfield Village Orchids
6763 Bonnieview
Mayfield, OH 44140 USA

Phillip T Seaton
52 Shrubbery St
Kidderminster, WORC JG10 2QG
ENGLAND

Don Shuker
132 Wetherby Road
Harrogate, North Yorks HG2 7BA
ENGLAND

William Skelly
3612 Kramer St
Harrisburg, PA 17109 USA

Steve Skoien
Rolfe Horticulture
3243 NE 100th St
Seattle, WA 98125 USA

Louise P Slade
15245-105 Ave #114
Surrey, BC V3R 1R9
CANADA

Dr Ken Smeltz
1021 Crestover Rd
Wilmington, DE 19803 USA
(302) 478-7266

Fred W Smith
Rutherglen, 83 Stanwell Way
Wellingborough, Northants NN8 3DD
ENGLAND

Mark Steen
15403 Potter Ct
Mitchellville, MD 20716 USA

Bernice Steiner
178 Sauvc Rd
River Ridge, LA 70123 USA

Walter C Stern
11710 Lindemere
St Louis, MO 63131 USA

Dave and Diane Strack
43 Calumet Ave
Oakland, NJ 07436 USA

Jimmy Stribling
Gallup & Stribling Orchids
3450 North Via Real
Carpinteria, CA 93013 USA

Richard Takase
Leilehua Orchids
166 Kaliko Drive
Wahiawa, HI 96786 USA

Howard Taylor
Southmoor Orchids
Edgehill, Old Skellow
Doncaster, DN6 8JW, ENGLAND

Pat Trumble
3897 N. 57th St
Boulder, CO 80301 USA

Joseph Van Acker
Pleasantville Road
New Vernon, NJ 07976 USA

Doreen Vander Tuin
Orchid Correspondence Club
1230 Plum Avenue
Simi Valley, CA 93065 USA

John J Vella
John and Jeff Orchid Sales
2502 Barnes Ave
Bronx, NY 10467 USA

John Watkins
Sunnybrook Orchids
1533 Playground Way
Modesto, CA 95355 USA

John Webster
220 North Valley Rd
Southern Pines, NC 28387 USA

Lois M Wegner
3533 Cook
Billings, MT 59102 USA

Judith Weinberg
32 Grammercy Park South, Ste 11M
New York City, NY 10003 USA

Mark Werther
1131 Rossiter Lane
Radnor, PA 19087 USA

Charles Williamson
Jungle Gems
300 Edgewood Rd
Edgewood, MD 21040 USA

Charles and Julia Wilson
Orchids by Wilson
1827 Ahrens
Houston, TX 77017 USA

Jack Wilson
Gallup & Stribling Intl
5510 Armitos Ave, Apt 20
Goleta, CA 93117 USA

B Jean Winning
Turkeytown Orchids
535 Salem St
North Andover, MA 01845 USA

Roy Yohiro
2045 9th Ave
Honolulu, HI 96816 USA

Linda Zeeman
3469 Mill Creek Rd, NE
Atlanta, GA 30319 USA

Marilyn Zimmer
MMC Orchids
1330-29th St
Moline, IL 61265 USA

SECTION 15:
INDEX

SECTION 16:
ORCHID OPPORTUNITIES

Since 1970 . . . .

Growers and hybridizers of fine Phalaenopsis.

Seedlings
Mature plants
Select plants
Stem propagations
Species

Phal. amboinensis 'Stones River' AM/AOS

STONES RIVER ORCHIDS
ROUTE 5, BOX 262
CLOVERCROFT ROAD
FRANKLIN, TN 37064
(615) 790-6122

Tom and Laura Harper, Proprietors

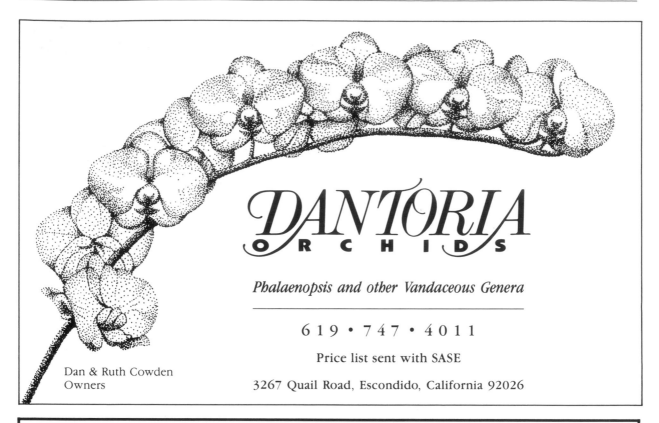

INTERNATIONAL PHALAENOPSIS ALLIANCE:

Carlos Fighetti of the Greater New York Orchid Society suggested the formation of an international phalaenopsis alliance whose purpose would be to act as a communications center for phal growers worldwide.

The centerpiece of the alliance would be a monthly or bimonthly newsletter with current phal-interest items to include such things as:

- Classified ads

- Culture notes

- Feature article — one per issue

- Known dominant/recessive qualities of breeders. (Object here is a register of these qualities for member use.)

- Lab techniques

- Meetings of the Alliance

- Membership roster

- New products — reviews

- New crosses for sale

- New crosses

- Problem solutions

- Recent awards — some photos

- Successful lines of breeding

All these items would be dedicated to phalaenopsis culture alone...no other topics.

An adjunct to the newsletter would be a structure for meetings of members, mostly tied to other major orchid events around the world. The meetings would consist of workshops, papers, discussion groups and some social activity...all intended to further an understanding of the phalaenopsis and its place in the commercial and hobbyist world. Now, we only get to talk to each other once a year at shows...this way once a month. Make sense?

If you arc interested, drop me (or Carlos Fighetti, 325 Piermont Rd, Closter, NJ 07624, USA or Tom Harper, Rte 5 Box 262 Clovercroft Rd, Franklin, TN 37064 USA) a card with your name and address and I'll put it in the Contact File for when we get this thing off the ground. The size of the response will help in determining if this whole effort is worthwhile.

Anyone else interested in launching this enterprise can go to it with our blessing, but put our names on your Contact List, OK?

— Bob Gordon
276 East Shamrock
Rialto, CA 92376 USA

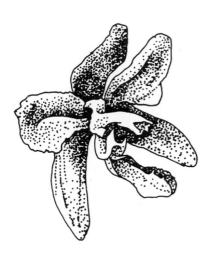